American Social History
Before 1860

GOLDENTREE BIBLIOGRAPHIES

In American History

under the series editorship of

Arthur S. Link

American Social History Before 1860

compiled by

Gerald N. Grob

Rutgers University

APPLETON-CENTURY-CROFTS

Educational Division

New York MEREDITH CORPORATION

230770

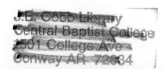

PRINTED IN THE UNITED STATES OF AMERICA
390-39178-6

Editor's Foreword

GOLDENTREE BIBLIOGRAPHIES IN AMERICAN HISTORY are designed to provide students, teachers, and librarians with ready and reliable guides to the literature of American history in all its remarkable scope and variety. Volumes in the series cover comprehensively the major periods in American history, while additional volumes are devoted to all important subjects.

Goldentree Bibliographies attempt to steer a middle course between the brief list of references provided in the average textbook and the long bibliography in which significant items are often lost in the sheer number of titles listed. Each bibliography is, therefore, selective, with the sole criterion for choice being the significance—and not the age—of any particular work. The result is bibliographies of all works, including journal articles and doctoral dissertations, that are still useful, without bias in favor of any particular historiographical school.

Each compiler is a scholar long associated, both in research and teaching, with the period or subject of his volume. All compilers have not only striven to accomplish the objective of this series but have also cheerfully adhered to a general style and format. However, each compiler has been free to define his field, make his own selections, and work out internal organization as the unique demands of his period or subject have seemed to dictate.

The single great objective of *Goldentree Bibliographies in American History* will have been achieved if these volumes help researchers and students to find their way to the significant literature of American history.

Arthur S. Link

Preface

ANY BIBLIOGRAPHY THAT attempts to deal with American social history to 1860 is bound to be highly selective. This bibliography is no exception. Nevertheless, I have attempted to include most of the major contributions on this subject, although I have no doubt that other scholars will dispute (probably justifiably) some of my choices. While this bibliography emphasizes works published within the past fifty years, it does not neglect earlier contributions that still remain important. Because of the breadth of the subject matter, unpublished doctoral dissertations have been omitted entirely.

In compiling this bibliography, I faced the issue of defining social history, a subject that has long eluded any hard and fast definition. In general, I have adopted working categories that define social history in terms of the structure of American society and its peculiar institutions (an approach that puts social history closer to the social and behavioral sciences than to intellectural history). For this reason I have completely excluded any materials dealing with intellectual history, which I regard as quite distinct from social history.

In order to make the coverage more comprehensive, I have refrained from cross-referencing general works on American social history under individual topics. Had this been done, some general works would have then required listing in a dozen or more specialized categories. Any one using this bibliography, therefore, should realize that most of the general works will include material on more specialized topics (i.e., education, immigration, religion, etc.).

Finally, I should like to thank Kenneth P. Moynihan, one of my graduate students, for his help in compiling this bibliography.

G. N. G.

Abbreviations

Ag Hist	Agricultural History
Ala Rev	Alabama Review
Am Eccles Rev	American Ecclesiastical Review
Am Her	American Heritage
Am Hist Rev	American Historical Review
Am J Leg Hist	American Journal of Legal History
Am J Socio	American Journal of Sociology
Am Jew Archiv	American Jewish Archives
Am Jew Hist Q	American Jewish Historical Quarterly
Am Q	American Quarterly
Am Sch	American Scholar
Am Socio Rev	American Sociological Review
Am Swed Hist Found Yrbk	American Swedish Historical Foundation Yearbook
Americana	
Ann Med Hist	Annals of Medical History
Ann Rep Am Hist Assn	Annual Report of the American Historical Association
Ark Hist Q	Arkansas Historical Quarterly
Boston Pub Lib Q	Boston Public Library Quarterly
Bull Frnds Hist Assn	Bulletin of the Friends Historical Association
Bull Hist Med	Bulletin of the History of Medicine
Bull Hist Philos Soc Ohio	Bulletin of the Historical and Philosophical Society of Ohio
Bull N Y Pub Lib	Bulletin of the New York Public Library
Bus Hist Rev	Business History Review
Cath Ed Rev	Catholic Educational Review
Cath Hist Rev	Catholic Historical Review
Chron Okla	Chronicles of Oklahoma
Church Hist	Church History
Civil War Hist	Civil War History
Comp Stud Soc Hist	Comparative Studies in Society and History
Del Hist	Delaware History
E Tenn Hist Soc Pub	East Tennessee Historical Society Publications
Essex Inst Hist Coll	Essex Institute Historical Collections
Explor Entrep Hist	Explorations in Entrepreneurial History
Filson Club Hist Q	Filson Club History Quarterly
Fla Hist Q	Florida Historical Quarterly

French Rev	French Review
Ga Hist Q	Georgia Historical Quarterly
Ga Rev	Georgia Review
Har Ed Rev	Harvard Educational Review
Har Lib Bull	Harvard Library Bulletin
Hist Ed Q	History of Education Quarterly
Hist Mag Prot Epis Church	Historical Magazine of the Protestant Episcopal Church
Historian	The Historian
Hunt Lib Q	Huntington Library Quarterly
Ind Mag Hist	Indiana Magazine of History
Int Rev Soc Hist	International Review of Social History
Iowa J Hist	Iowa Journal of History
Iowa J Hist Pol	Iowa Journal of History and Politics
Isis	
J Am Hist	Journal of American History
J Econ Hist	Journal of Economic History
J Ed Res	Journal of Educational Research
J Hist Ideas	Journal of the History of Ideas
J Hist Med Allied Sci	Journal of the History of Medicine and Allied Sciences
J Ill State Hist Soc	Journal of the Illinois State Historical Society
J Long Island Hist	Journal of Long Island History
J Miss Hist	Journal of Mississippi History
J Neg Hist	Journal of Negro History
J Pol Econ	Journal of Political Economy
J Presby Hist	Journal of Presbyterian History
J Presby Hist Soc	Journal of the Presbyterian Historical Society
J Rel	Journal of Religion
J S Hist	Journal of Southern History
J Soc Hist	Journal of Social History
Labor Hist	Labor History
Lincoln Her	Lincoln Herald
La Hist	Louisiana History
La Hist Q	Louisiana Historical Quarterly
Md Hist Mag	Maryland Historical Magazine
Medical Life	
Mid-America	
Midwest J	Midwest Journal
Minn Hist	Minnesota History
Miss Val Hist Rev	Mississippi Valley Historical Review
Mo Hist Rev	Missouri Historical Review
N C Hist Rev	North Carolina Historical Review
N Eng Q	New England Quarterly
N Y Hist	New York History
N Y Hist Soc Q	New-York Historical Society Quarterly
Neb Hist	Nebraska History
Neg Hist Bull	Negro History Bulletin
New Haven Hist Soc Pap	New Haven Historical Society Papers
Ohio Hist Q	Ohio Historical Quarterly

Ohio State Arch Hist Q	Ohio State Archaeological and Historical Quarterly
Pa Hist	Pennsylvania History
Pa Mag Hist Biog	Pennsylvania Magazine of History and Biography
Pac Hist Rev	Pacific Historical Review
Pac NW Q	Pacific Northwest Quarterly
Phylon	
Pol Sci Q	Political Science Quarterly
Proc Am Ant Soc	Proceedings, American Antiquarian Society
Proc Am Philos Soc	Proceedings, American Philosophical Society
Proc Mass Hist Soc	Proceedings, Massachusetts Historical Society
Proc Miss Val Hist Assn	Proceedings, Mississippi Valley Historical Association
Proc N J Hist Soc	Proceedings, New Jersey Historical Society
Proc N Y Hist Assn	Proceedings, New York Historical Association
Proc Vt Hist Soc	Proceedings, Vermont Historical Society
Pub Am Jew Hist Soc	Publications, American Jewish Historical Society
Pub Am Socio Soc	Publications, American Sociological Society
Pub Col Soc Mass, Trans	Publications, Colonial Society of Massachusetts, Transactions
Pub Opin Q	Public Opinion Quarterly
Q J N Y Hist Assn	Quarterly Journal of the New York Historical Association
Quaker Hist	Quaker History
R I Hist	Rhode Island History
Rec Am Cath Hist Soc Phil	Records, American Catholic Historical Society of Philadelphia
Reg Ky Hist Soc	Register of the Kentucky Historical Society
Rochester Hist	Rochester History
S Atl Q	South Atlantic Quarterly
S C Hist Geneal Mag	South Carolina Historical and Genealogical Magazine
S C Hist Mag	South Carolina Historical Magazine
S Econ J	Southern Economic Journal
Scalpel	
Sch Soc	School and Society
Soc Hist Ger Md Rep	Society for the History of the Germans in Maryland Report
Soc Serv Rev	Social Service Review
Soc Stud	Social Studies
SW Hist Q	Southwestern Historical Quarterly
Tenn Hist Mag	Tennessee Historical Magazine
Tenn Hist Q	Tennessee Historical Quarterly
Trans Am Philos Soc	Transactions of the American Philosophical Society
U S Cath Hist Soc Rec Stud	United States Catholic Historical Society Records and Studies
Va Mag Hist Biog	Virginia Magazine of History and Biography

Va Q Rev	*Virginia Quarterly Review*
Vt Hist	*Vermont History*
Vt Q	*Vermont Quarterly*
W Hum Rev	*Western Humanities Review*
W Pa Hist Mag	*Western Pennsylvania Historical Magazine*
W Va Hist	*West Virginia History*
Wel Rev	*Welfare in Review*
Wis Mag Hist	*Wisconsin Magazine of History*
Worc Hist Soc Pub	*Worcester Historical Society Publications*
Wm Mar Q	*William and Mary Quarterly*
Yale J Biol Med	*Yale Journal of Biology and Medicine*
Yale Rev	*Yale Review*

Note: Cross-references are to page and to item number. Items marked by a dagger (†) are available in paperback edition at the time this bibliography goes to press. The publisher and compiler invite suggestions for additions to future editions of the bibliography.

Contents

Editor's Foreword   v

Preface   vii

Abbreviations   ix

I. Bibliographical Guides and Selected Reference Works   1

II. Travel Accounts and Descriptions   2
   1. Selected Travel Accounts of Foreign and Native Observers   2
   2. Histories of Travel   4

III. American Society and Social History   4
   1. General   4
   2. The Colonial Period (to 1800)   6
   3. The National Period (1800–1860)   8

IV. The Nation and Its Sections   9
   1. The North   9
      A. *GENERAL*   9
      B. *SOCIAL STRUCTURE*   12
   2. The South   14
      A. *GENERAL*   14
      B. *SOCIAL STRUCTURE*   17
   3. The West   19
      A. *GENERAL*   19
      B. *SOCIAL STRUCTURE*   22
   4. Patterns of Internal Migration   22

V. Urban Life in America   23
   1. General   23
   2. Urban Life in Colonial America   24
   3. Urban Life in the Nineteenth Century   25
   4. Rise of the Professions   27

VI. Immigration and Ethnic Groups 28

    1. *General* 28
    2. *United Kingdom* 29
    3. *Irish* 30
    4. *Germans* 31
    5. *French* 32
    6. *Scandinavians* 32
    7. *Dutch* 33
    8. *Italians* 33
    9. *Poles* 34
    10. *Chinese* 34

VII. Negro Americans 34

    1. *General* 34
    2. *The Negro and American Slavery* 36
    3. *The Free Negro, North and South* 42
    4. *The Negro and His Churches* 43
    5. *Negro Education* 44
    6. *White Americans and Negro Americans* 44

VIII. Labor and Laboring Classes 46

    1. *General* 46
    2. *Involuntary Servitude* 47

IX. Domestic Institutions 48

    1. *Women in American Society* 48
    2. *Children and Childhood* 49
    3. *The Family and Marriage* 50

X. Religion and Religious Groups 51

    1. *General* 51
    2. *Protestants and Protestantism* 53
        A. THE CLERGY 53
        B. LOCAL AND DENOMINATIONAL HISTORIES 54
        C. REVIVALISM AND THE GREAT AWAKENINGS 58
        D. PHILANTHROPIC, EDUCATIONAL, AND MISSION-
           ARY ACTIVITIES 60
    3. *Catholics and Catholicism* 61
    4. *Jews and Judaism* 63
    5. *Church and State in America and the Rise of Religious*
        Liberty 64
    6. *Witchcraft* 65

XI. Reform Movements (See also Sections XII, XIII, XIV, XV) 66

    1. General   66
    2. Antislavery and Abolitionism   67
    3. Communitarianism   71
    4. Women's Rights   72
    5. Temperance   73
    6. The Peace Crusade   73
    7. Nativism   74

XII. Education   75

    1. Education and American Society: General Accounts   75
    2. Primary and Secondary Schools and Education   77
    3. Schoolbooks   82
    4. Higher Education   82

XIII. Indigency, Welfare, and Philanthropy   85

    1. General   85
    2. Poverty and the Poor   86

XIV. Medicine and Health   88

    1. General   88
    2. The Medical Profession and Medical Education   89
    3. Medicine and Health in Colonial America (to 1800)   91
    4. Medicine and Health (1800–1860)   93
    5. The Public Health Movement   95
    6. The Mentally Ill   95
    7. Medical Quackery   96

XV. Law Enforcement, Justice, and Crime   97

    1. General   97
    2. Law Enforcement and Punishment   97
    3. Prisons and Prison Reform   99

XVI. Everyday Life   100

    1. Recreation   100
    2. Manners and Customs   100

XVII. Journalism and Libraries   103

    1. Newspapers and the Press   103
    2. Freedom of the Press   104
    3. Magazines   105
    4. Libraries and American Culture   105

XVIII. Culture, Art, and Architecture 106

    1. Cultural Life 106
    2. The Arts and Artists 106
    3. Theatre 108
    4. Architecture 109
    5. Decorative Arts and Interiors 111
    6. Music 112

Notes 115
Index 123

I

I. Bibliographical Guides and Selected Reference Works

1 ADAMS, James T., ed. *Dictionary of American History.* 7 vols. New York, 1940–1963.

2 American Historical Association. *Guide to Historical Literature.* New York, 1961.

3 American Historical Association. *Writings on American History.* 46 vols. Washington, D.C., 1902–1964.

4 BARROW, John G. *A Bibliography of Bibliographies in Religion.* Austin, Tex., 1955.

5 BASSETT, T. D. Seymour. "Bibliography: Descriptive and Critical." Vol. II of *Socialism and American Life.* Ed. by Donald D. Egbert and Stow Persons. 2 vols. Princeton, 1952.

6 BEERS, Henry P., comp. *Bibliographies in American History: Guide to Materials for Research.* Rev. ed. New York, 1942.

7 BOWERS, David F., ed. *Foreign Influences in American Life: Essays and Critical Bibliographies.* Princeton, 1944.†

8 BURR, Nelson R. "A Critical Bibliography of Religion in America." Vols. III and IV of *Religion in American Life.* Ed. by James W. Smith and A. Leland Jamison. 4 vols. in 5 parts. Princeton, 1961.

9 COULTER, Edith M., and Melanie GERSTENFELD, eds. *Historical Bibliographies: A Systematic and Annotated Guide.* Berkeley, Calif., 1935.

10 ELLIS, John T. *A Guide to American Catholic History.* Milwaukee, Wis., 1959.

11 HANDLIN, Oscar, *et al. Harvard Guide to American History.* Cambridge, 1954.†

12 HIGHAM, John, *et al. History.* New York, 1965.†

13 HIGHAM, John, ed. *The Reconstruction of American History.* New York, 1962.†

14 JOHNSON, Allen, ed. *Dictionary of American Biography.* 23 vols. New York, 1928–1958.

15 KRAUS, Michael. *The Writing of American History.* Norman, Okla., 1953.

16 KUEHL, Warren F., ed. *Dissertations in History: An Index to Dissertations Completed in History Departments of United States and Canadian Universities, 1783–1960.* Lexington, Ky., 1965.

17 Library of Congress. *A Guide to the Study of the United States of America: Representative Books Reflecting the Development of American Life and Thought.* Washington, D.C., 1960.

18 MC GIFFERT, Michael. "Selected Writings on American National Character." *Am Q,* XV (1963), 271–288.

19 MC MANIS, Douglas R. *Historical Geography of the United States: A Bibliography.* Ypsilanti, Mich., 1965.†

1   MARCUS, Jacob R. "A Selected Bibliography of American Jewish History." *Am Jew Hist Q*, LI (1961), 97–134.

2   MATTHEWS, William, comp. *American Diaries: An Annotated Bibliography of American Diaries prior to the Year 1861*. Berkeley, 1945.

3   MILLER, Elizabeth W., ed. *The Negro in America: A Bibliography*. Cambridge, 1966.†

4   MORRIS, Richard B., ed. *Encyclopedia of American History*. Rev. ed. New York, 1961.

5   National Research Council, *et al. Doctoral Dissertations Accepted by American Universities*. . . . 22 vols. New York, 1933–1955.

6   NEUFELD, Maurice. *A Representative Bibliography of American Labor History*. Ithaca, N.Y., 1964.

7   U.S. Bureau of the Census. *Historical Statistics of the United States: Colonial Times to 1957*. Washington, D.C., 1960.

II. Travel Accounts and Descriptions

1. Selected Travel Accounts of Foreign and Native Observers

8   CHASTELLUX, Francois Jean, Marquis de. *Travels in North America in the Years 1780, 1781, and 1782*. Trans. and introd. by Howard C. Rice, Jr. 2 vols. Chapel Hill, N.C., 1963.

9   CHEVALIER, Michel. *Society, Manners and Politics in the United States: Being a Series of Letters on North America*. Ed. by John W. Ward. Original ed. 1839. New York, 1961.

10 COBBETT, William. *A Year's Residence in the United States of America*. Original ed. 1818. Carbondale, Ill., 1965.

11 COMMAGER, Henry S., ed. *America in Perspective: The United States Through Foreign Eyes*. New York, 1947.

12 CRÈVECOEUR, Michel G. St. Jean de. *Eighteenth-Century Travels in Pennsylvania & New York*. Trans. and ed. by Percy G. Adams. Lexington, Ky., 1961.

13 CRÈVECOEUR, Michel G. St. Jean de. *Letters from an American Farmer*. Original ed. 1782. New York, 1961.†

14 CRÈVECOEUR, Michel G. St. John de. *Sketches of Eighteenth-Century America: More "Letters from an American Farmer."* Ed. by Henri L. Bourdin, Ralph H. Gabriel, and Stanley T. Williams. New Haven, 1925.

15 D'ARUSMONT, Frances. *Views of Society and Manners in America*. Original ed. 1821. Ed. by Paul Baker. Cambridge, 1963.

16 DICKENS, Charles. *American Notes*. Original ed. 1842. New York, 1957.

17 FOSTER, Sir Augustus John, bart. *Jeffersonian America: Notes on the United States of America, Collected in the Years 1805–6–7 and 11–12*. Ed. by Richard B. Davis. San Marino, Calif., 1954.

1   GRUND, Francis J. *Aristocracy in America.* Original ed. 1839. New York, 1959.

2   HAMILTON, Alexander. *Gentleman's Progress: The Itinerarium of Dr. Alexander Hamilton, 1744.* Ed. by Carl Bridenbaugh. Chapel Hill, N.C., 1948.

3   HANDLIN, Oscar, ed. *This Was America: True Accounts of People and Places, Manners and Customs, as Recorded by European Travelers to the Western Shore in the Eighteenth, Nineteenth and Twentieth Centuries.* Cambridge, 1949.†

4   Indiana Historical Commission. *Indiana as Seen by Early Travelers: A Collection of Reprints from Books of Travel, Letters and Diaries prior to 1830.* Selected and ed. by Harlow Lindley. Indianapolis, Ind., 1916.

5   KEMBLE, Frances A. *Journal of a Residence on a Georgian Plantation in 1838–39.* Ed. by John A. Scott. Original ed. 1863. New York, 1961.

6   MARTINEAU, Harriet. *Society in America.* Ed. and abr. by Seymour M. Lipset. Original ed. 1837. Garden City, N.Y., 1962.

7   MERENESS, Newton D., ed. *Travels in the American Colonies.* New York, 1916.

8   MOREAU DE SAINT-MÉRY, Médéric Louis Elie. *Moreau de St. Méry's American Journey (1793–1798).* Trans. and ed. by Kenneth and Anna M. Roberts. Garden City, N.Y., 1947.

9   MORIZE, André, and Elliott M. GRANT, eds. *Selections from French Travelers in America.* New York, 1929.

10 MUSSEY, June B., ed. *Yankee Life by Those Who Lived It.* Rev. ed. New York, 1947.

11 NEVINS, Allan, ed. *America Through British Eyes.* New ed. New York, 1948.

12 OLMSTED, Frederick L. *The Cotton Kingdom: A Traveller's Observations on Cotton and Slavery in the American Slave States.* Ed. by Arthur M. Schlesinger. New York, 1953.

13 OLMSTED, Frederick L. *The Slave States before the Civil War.* Ed. by Harvey Wish. New York, 1959.†

14 SHERRILL, Charles H. *French Memories of Eighteenth-Century America.* New York, 1915.

15 THWAITES, Reuben G., ed. *Early Western Travels, 1748–1846.* 32 vols. Cleveland, Ohio, 1904–1907.

16 TOCQUEVILLE, Alexis de. *Alexis de Tocqueville: Journey to America.* Trans. by George Lawrence. Ed. by J. P. Mayer. New Haven, 1960.

17 TOCQUEVILLE, Alexis de. *Democracy in America.* Ed. by Phillips Bradley. 2 vols. New York, 1945.†

18 TROLLOPE, Frances M. *Domestic Manners of the Americans.* Ed. by Donald Smalley. Original ed. 1832. New York, 1949.†

19 TRYON, Warren S., ed. *A Mirror for Americans: Life and Manners in the United States, 1790–1870, as Recorded by American Travelers.* 3 vols. Chicago, 1952.

20 WILLIAMS, Samuel C., ed. *Early Travels in the Tennessee Country, 1540–1800.* Johnson City, Tenn., 1928.

2. Histories of Travel

1 BERGER, Max. *The British Traveller in America, 1836–1860.* New York, 1943.

2 BROOKS, John G. *As Others see Us: A Study of Progress in the United States.* New York, 1908.

3 DUNBAR, Seymour. *History of Travel in America.* 4 vols. Indianapolis, Ind., 1915.

4 MESICK, Jane L. *The English Traveller in America, 1785–1835.* New York, 1922.

5 ONIS, José De. *The United States as Seen by Spanish American Writers, 1776–1890.* New York, 1952.

6 PIERSON, George W. *Tocqueville and Beaumont in America.* New York, 1938.

7 RYAN, Lee W. *French Travellers in the Southeastern United States, 1775–1800.* Bloomington, Ind., 1939.

8 SIBLEY, Marilyn M. *Travelers in Texas, 1761–1860.* Austin, Tex., 1967.

9 TUCKERMAN, Henry T. *America and Her Commentators.* New York, 1864.

III. American Society and Social History

1. General

10 BEARD, Charles A., and Mary R. BEARD. *The Rise of American Civilization.* 2 vols. New York, 1927.

11 BERTHOFF, Rowland T. "The American Social Order: A Conservative Hypothesis." *Am Hist Rev*, LXV (1960), 495–514.

12 BOWERS, David F. *Foreign Influences in American Life.* See 1.7.

13 BURLINGAME, Roger. *March of the Iron Men: A Social History of Union through Invention.* New York, 1938.†

14 COCHRAN, Thomas C., and William MILLER. *The Age of Enterprise: A Social History of Industrial America.* New York, 1942.†

15 COCHRAN, Thomas C. "The History of a Business Society." *J Am Hist*, LIV (1967), 5–18.

16 COLE, Arthur C. "The Puritan and Fair Terpsichore." *Miss Val Hist Rev*, XXIX (1942), 3–34.

17 COMMONS, John R., *et al*, eds. *A Documentary History of American Industrial Society.* 10 vols. Cleveland, Ohio, 1910–1911.

18 CURTI, Merle E. *The Growth of American Thought.* 3rd ed. New York, 1964.

1 CURTI, Merle E. *The Roots of American Loyalty*. New York, 1946.†

2 DAVIDSON, Marshall B. *Life in America*. 2 vols. Boston, 1951.

3 DEGLER, Carl N. *Out of our Past: The Forces that Shaped Modern America*. New York, 1959.†

4 DYKSTRA, Robert R. "Town-Country Conflict: A Hidden Dimension in American Social History." *Ag Hist*, XXXVIII (1964), 195–204.

5 EGBERT, Donald D., and Stow PERSONS. *Socialism and American Life*. See 1.5.

6 FOX, Dixon R. *Ideas in Motion*. New York, 1935.

7 GUTTMANN, Allen. *The Conservative Tradition in America*. New York, 1967.

8 HACKER, Louis M. *The Triumph of American Capitalism: The Development of Forces in American History to the End of the Nineteenth Century*. New York, 1946.

9 HARTZ, Louis. *The Liberal Tradition in America: An Interpretation of American Political Thought since the Revolution*. New York, 1955.†

10 HILLQUIT, Morris. *History of Socialism in the United States*. 5th ed. New York, 1910.

11 HOFSTADTER, Richard. *Anti-intellectualism in American Life*. New York, 1963.†

12 LINGELBACH, William E., ed. *Approaches to American Social History*. New York, 1937.

13 LIPSET, Seymour M. *The First New Nation: The United States in Historical and Comparative Perspective*. New York, 1963.*

14 MC KITRICK, Eric L., and Stanley M. ELKINS. "Institutions in Motion." *Am Q*, XII (1960), 188–197.

15 MC MASTER, John B. *The Acquisition of Political, Social, and Industrial Rights of Man in America*. Cleveland, Ohio, 1903.

16 MC MASTER, John B. *A History of the People of the United States from the Revolution to the Civil War*. 8 vols. New York, 1883–1913.

17 MYERS, Gustavus. *History of Bigotry in the United States*. New York, 1943.†

18 OSTRANDER, Gilman M. *The Rights of Man in America, 1606–1861*. Columbia, Mo., 1960.

19 PERSONS, Stow. "The Origins of the Gentry." *Essays on History and Literature*. Ed. by Robert H. Bremner. Columbus, Ohio, 1966, 83–119.

20 PIERSON, George W. "The M-Factor in American History." *Am Q*, XIV (1962), 275–289.

21 PIERSON, George W. "The Moving American." *Yale Rev*, XLIV (1954), 99–112.

22 PIERSON, George W. "A Restless Temper. . . ." *Am Hist Rev*, LXIX (1964), 969–989.

1   PIERSON, George W. "Under a Wandering Star." *Va Q Rev*, XXXIX (1963), 621–638.

2   POTTER, David M. *People of Plenty: Economic Abundance and the American Character*. Chicago, 1954.†

3   SAVETH, Edward N. "The American Patrician Class: A Field for Research." *Am Q*, XV (1963), 232–252.

4   SCHAFER, Joseph. *The Social History of American Agriculture*. New York, 1936.

5   SCHLESINGER, Arthur M. "Biography of a Nation of Joiners." *Am Hist Rev*, L (1944), 1–25.

6   SIZER, Theodore, Andrew C. MC LAUGHLIN, Dixon R. FOX, and Henry S. CANBY. *Aspects of the Social History of America*. Chapel Hill, N.C., 1931.

7   THOMPSON, Warren S., and Pascal K. WHELPTON. *Population Trends in the United States*. New York, 1933.

8   TURNER, Frederick J. *The Significance of Sections in American History*. New York, 1932.

9   WECTER, Dixon. *The Hero in America: A Chronicle of Hero-Worship*. New York, 1941.†

10 WECTER, Dixon. *The Saga of American Society: A Record of Social Aspiration, 1608–1937*. New York, 1937.

11 WISH, Harvey. *Society and Thought in Early America*. New York, 1950.

12 WYLLIE, Irvin G. *The Self-Made Man in America: The Myth of Rags to Riches*. New Brunswick, N.J., 1954.†

2. The Colonial Period (to 1800)

13 ADAMS, James T. *Provincial Society, 1690–1763*. New York, 1927.

14 ANDREWS, Charles M. *Colonial Folkways: A Chronicle of American Life in the Reign of the Georges*. New Haven, 1919.

15 ANDREWS, Charles M. *The Colonial Period of American History*. 4 vols. New Haven, 1934-1938.†

16 BOND, Beverley W. *The Quit-Rent System in the American Colonies*. New Haven, 1919.

17 BOORSTIN, Daniel J. *The Americans: The Colonial Experience*. New York, 1958.†

18 BROWN, Robert E. "Economic Democracy before the Constitution." *Am Q*, VII (1955), 257–274.

19 DIAMOND, Sigmund. "Values as an Obstacle to Economic Growth: The American Colonies." *J Econ Hist*, XXVII (1967), 561–575.

20 EGGLESTON, Edward. *The Transit of Civilization from England to America in the Seventeenth Century*. New York, 1901.†

21 GIPSON, Lawrence H. *The British Empire before the American Revolution*. 13 vols. New York, 1936–1967.

1   GOODMAN, Paul. "Social Status of Party Leadership: The House of Representatives, 1797–1804." *Wm Mar Q*, 3rd ser., XXV (1968), 465–474.

2   GREENE, Evarts B., and Virginia D. HARRINGTON. *American Population before the Federal Census of 1790*. New York, 1932.

3   GREENE, Evarts B. *The Revolutionary Generation, 1763–1790*. New York, 1943.

4   GREVEN, Philip J., Jr. "Historical Demography and Colonial America: A Review Article." *Wm Mar Q*, 3rd ser., XXIV (1967), 438–454.

5   JAMESON, J. Franklin. *The American Revolution Considered as a Social Movement*. Princeton, 1926.†

6   JONES, Howard M. *O Strange New World: American Culture: The Formative Years*. New York, 1964.†

7   KRAUS, Michael. *The Atlantic Civilization: Eighteenth-Century Origins*. Ithaca, N.Y., 1949.†

8   KRAUS, Michael. *Intercolonial Aspects of American Culture on the Eve of the Revolution, with Special Reference to the Northern Towns*. New York, 1928.

9   LABAREE, Leonard W. *Conservatism in Early American History*. New York, 1948.†

10 MAIN, Jackson T. *The Antifederalists: Critics of the Constitution, 1781–1788*. Chapel Hill, N.C., 1961.†

11 MAIN, Jackson T. "Social Origins of a Political Elite: The Upper House in the Revolutionary Era." *Hunt Lib Q*, XXVII (1964), 147–158.

12 MAIN, Jackson T. *The Social Structure of Revolutionary America*. Princeton, 1965.

13 MAIN, Jackson T. *The Upper House in Revolutionary America, 1763–1788*. Madison, Wis., 1967.

14 MOLLER, Herbert. "Sex Composition and Correlated Culture Patterns of Colonial America." *Wm Mar Q*, 3rd ser., II (1945), 113–153.

15 MORRIS, Richard B. *The American Revolution Reconsidered*. New York, 1967.†

16 NELSON, William H. "The Revolutionary Character of the American Revolution." *Am Hist Rev*, LXX (1965), 998–1014.

17 NEVINS, Allan. *The American States during and after the Revolution, 1775–1789*. New York, 1924.

18 OSGOOD, Herbert L. *The American Colonies in the Eighteenth Century*. 4 vols. New York, 1924–1925.

19 OSGOOD, Herbert L. *The American Colonies in the Seventeenth Century*. 3 vols. New York, 1904–1907.

20 POLE, J. R. "Historians and the Problem of Early American Democracy." *Am Hist Rev*, LXVII (1962), 626–646.

21 ROSSITER, Clinton. *Seedtime of the Republic: The Origin of the American Tradition of Political Liberty*. New York, 1953.†

1 RUDOLPH, Lloyd L. "The Eighteenth Century Mob in America and Europe." *Am Q*, XI (1959), 447–469.

2 SACHS, William S., and Ari HOOGENBOOM. *The Enterprising Colonials: Society on the Eve of the Revolution.* Chicago, 1965.

3 SCHLESINGER, Arthur M. "The Aristocracy in Colonial America." *Proc Mass Hist Soc*, LXXIV (1962), 3–21.

4 SCHLESINGER, Arthur M. *The Birth of the Nation: A Portrait of the American People on the Eve of Independence.* New York, 1968.

5 SCHLESINGER, Arthur M. "'What Then is the American, This New Man?'" *Am Hist Rev*, XLVIII (1943), 225–244.

6 SMITH, James M., ed. *Seventeenth-Century America: Essays in Colonial History.* Chapel Hill, N.C., 1959.†

7 SOSIN, Jack M. *The Revolutionary Frontier, 1763–1783.* New York, 1967.†

8 SUTHERLAND, Stella H. *Population Distribution in Colonial America.* New York, 1936.

9 TOLLES, Frederick B. "The American Revolution Considered as a Social Movement: A Re-Evaluation." *Am Hist Rev*, LX (1954), 1–12.

10 VER STEEG, Clarence L. *The Formative Years, 1607–1763.* New York, 1964.

11 WERTENBAKER, Thomas J. *The First Americans, 1607–1690.* New York, 1927.

12 WRIGHT, Louis B. *The Cultural Life of the American Colonies, 1607–1763.* New York, 1957.†

3. *The National Period (1800–1860)*

13 ADAMS, Henry. *History of the United States of America during the Administrations of Jefferson and Madison.* 9 vols. New York, 1888–1891.†

14 ARONSON, Sidney H. *Status and Kinship in the Higher Civil Service: Standards of Selection in the Administrations of John Adams, Thomas Jefferson, and Andrew Jackson.* Cambridge, 1964.

15 BAKER, William D. "The Credulous Age, 1836–1848." *W Hum Rev*, VII (1953), 125–137.

16 BOORSTIN, Daniel J. *The Americans: The National Experience.* New York, 1965.†

17 COLE, Arthur C. *The Irrepressible Conflict, 1850–1865.* New York, 1934.

18 CURTI, Merle E. "Young America." *Am Hist Rev*, XXXII (1926), 34–55.

19 FISH, Carl R. *The Rise of the Common Man, 1830–1850.* New York, 1937.

20 GREENWALD, William I. "The Ante-Bellum Population, 1830–1860." *Mid-America*, XXXVI (1954), 176–189.

1 KROUT, John A., and Dixon R. FOX. *The Completion of Independence, 1790–1830*. New York, 1944.

2 MARTIN, Edgar W. *The Standard of Living in 1860: American Consumption Levels on the Eve of the Civil War*. Chicago, 1942.

3 MINNIGERODE, Meade. *The Fabulous Forties, 1840–1850: A Presentation of Private Life*. New York, 1924.

4 NEVINS, Allan. *The Emergence of Lincoln*. 2 vols. New York, 1950.

5 NEVINS, Allan. *Ordeal of the Union*. 2 vols. New York, 1947.

6 NYE, Russel B. *The Cultural Life of the New Nation, 1776–1830*. New York, 1960.†

7 PATTEE, Fred L. *The Feminine Fifties*. New York, 1940.

8 PESSEN, Edward. *Jacksonian America: Society, Personality, and Politics*. Homewood, Ill., 1969.†

9 REZNECK, Samuel. "The Depression of 1819–1822, A Social History." *Am Hist Rev*, XXXIX (1933), 28–47.

10 REZNECK, Samuel. "The Social History of an American Depression, 1837–1843." *Am Hist Rev*, XL (1935), 662–687.

11 RIEGEL, Robert E. *Young America, 1830–1840*. Norman, Okla., 1949.

12 SCHLESINGER, Arthur M., Jr. *The Age of Jackson*. Boston, 1945.†

13 TAYLOR, George R. *The Transportation Revolution, 1815–1860*. New York, 1951.†

14 THISTLETHWAITE, Frank. *The Anglo-American Connection in the Early Nineteenth Century*. Philadelphia, 1959.

15 TURNER, Frederick J. *The United States 1830–1850: The Nation and Its Sections*. New York, 1935.†

16 VAN DEUSEN, Glyndon G. *The Jacksonian Era, 1828–1848*. New York, 1959.†

17 WHARTON, Anne. *Social Life in the Early Republic*. Philadelphia, 1902.

18 WILLIAMSON, Chilton. *American Suffrage from Property to Democracy, 1760–1860*. Princeton, 1960.

IV. The Nation and Its Sections

1. The North

A. GENERAL

19 ADAMS, James T. *The Founding of New England*. Boston, 1921.

10 THE NATION AND ITS SECTIONS

1 ADAMS, James T. *New England in the Republic, 1776–1850*. Boston, 1926.

2 ADAMS, James T. *Revolutionary New England, 1691–1776*. Boston, 1923.

3 ALBERTSON, Dean. "Puritan Liquor in the Planting of New England." *N Eng Q*, XXIII (1950), 477–490.

4 ALBION, Robert G. *The Rise of New York Port (1815–1860)*. New York, 1939.

5 BASSETT, T. D. Seymour. "A Case Study of Urban Impact on Rural Society: Vermont, 1840–80." *Ag Hist*, XXX (1956), 28–34.

6 BELL, Whitfield J., Jr. "Some Aspects of the Social History of Pennsylvania, 1760–1790." *Pa Mag Hist Biog*, LXII (1938), 281–308.

7 BIRDSALL, Richard D. *Berkshire County: A Cultural History*. New Haven, 1959.

8 BUCK, Solon J., and Elizabeth H. BUCK. *The Planting of Civilization in Western Pennsylvania*. Pittsburgh, Pa., 1939.

9 CRAWFORD, Mary C. *Social Life in Old New England*. Boston, 1914.

10 DEMOS, John. "Notes on Life in Plymouth Colony." *Wm Mar Q*, 3rd ser., XXII (1965), 264–286.

11 DUNAWAY, Wayland F. *A History of Pennsylvania*. 2nd ed. New York, 1948.

12 ELLIS, David M. " 'Upstate Hicks' versus 'City Slickers.' " *N Y Hist Soc Q*, XLIII (1959), 202–220.

13 FISHER, Sydney G. *The Quaker Colonies: A Chronicle of the Proprietors of the Delaware*. New Haven, 1919.

14 FLETCHER, Stevenson W. *Pennsylvania Agriculture and Country Life, 1640–1840*. Harrisburg, Pa., 1950.

15 FLICK, Alexander C., ed. *History of the State of New York*. 10 vols. New York, 1933–1937.

16 FOX, Dixon R. *Yankees and Yorkers*. New York, 1940.

17 GILPIN, Lawrence H. "The Transit of European Civilization to the Middle Colonies of North America." *Pa Hist*, VI (1939), 63–71.

18 HALLER, William, Jr. *The Puritan Frontier: Town-Planting in New England Colonial Development 1630–1660*. New York, 1951.

19 HANDLIN, Oscar, and Mary F. HANDLIN. *Commonwealth: A Study of the Role of Government in the American Economy: Massachusetts, 1774–1861*. Rev. ed. Cambridge, 1969.

20 HART, Albert B., ed. *Commonwealth History of Massachusetts, Colony, Province and State*. 5 vols. New York, 1927–1930.

21 HARTZ, Louis. *Economic Policy and Democratic Thought: Pennsylvania, 1776–1860*. Cambridge, 1948.

22 HEDRICK, Ulysses P. *A History of Agriculture in the State of New York*. Albany, N.Y., 1933.†

1 JONES, Howard M. "The Unity of New England Culture." *Proc Mass Hist Soc*, LXXIX (1967), 74–88.

2 JONES, Mary J. A. *Congregational Commonwealth: Connecticut, 1636–1662*. Middletown, Conn., 1968.

3 JONES, Matt B. *Vermont in the Making, 1750–1777*. Cambridge, 1939.

4 KIRKLAND, Edward C. *Men, Cities and Transportation: A Study in New England History, 1820–1900*. 2 vols. Cambridge, 1948.

5 KITTREDGE, George L. *The Old Farmer and His Almanack: Being Some Observations on Life and Manners in New England a Hundred Years Ago*. Boston, 1904.

6 KLINE, Priscilla C. "New Light on the Yankee Peddler." *N Eng Q*, XII (1939), 80–98.

7 LANGDON, George D. *Pilgrim Colony: A History of New Plymouth, 1620–1691*. New Haven, 1966.

8 MILLER, William D. "The Narragansett Planters." *Proc Am Ant Soc*, N.S. XLIII (1933), 49–115.

9 MORSE, Jarvis M. *A Neglected Period of Connecticut's History, 1818–1850*. New Haven, 1933.

10 NEWCOMER, Lee N. *The Embattled Farmers: A Massachusetts Countryside in the American Revolution*. New York, 1953.

11 NEWTON, Earle. *The Vermont Story: A History of the People of the Green Mountain State, 1749–1949*. Montpelier, Vt., 1949.

12 PARKES, Henry B. "Morals in Colonial New England." *N Eng Q*, V (1932), 431–452.

13 PARKES, Henry B. "New England in the Seventeen-Thirties." *N Eng Q*, III (1930), 397–419.

14 POMFRET, John E. "West New Jersey: a Quaker Society." *Wm Mar Q*, 3rd ser., VIII (1951), 493–519.

15 PRINCE, Walter F. "An Examination of Peter's 'Blue Laws'." *Ann Rep Am Hist Assn*, 1898, 95–138.

16 PURCELL, Richard J. *Connecticut in Transition, 1775–1818*. Washington, D.C., 1918.

17 RAESLY, Ellis L. *Portrait of New Netherland*. New York, 1945.

18 SHIPTON, Clifford K. *New England Life in the 18th Century: Representative Biographies from Sibley's Harvard Graduates*. Cambridge, 1963.

19 SINGLETON, Esther. *Dutch New York*. New York, 1909.

20 SINGLETON, Esther. *Social New York Under the Georges, 1714–1776*. New York, 1902.

21 SPAULDING, E. Wilder. *New York in the Critical Period, 1783–1789*. New York, 1932.

22 UPTON, Richard F. *Revolutionary New Hampshire: An Account of the Social and Political Forces Underlying the Transition from Royal Province to American Commonwealth*. Hanover, N.H., 1936.

23 WEEDEN, William B. *Early Rhode Island: A Social History of the People*. New York, 1910.

1 WEEDEN, William B. *Economic and Social History of New England, 1620–1789.* 2 vols. Boston, 1890.

2 WEISS, Harry B. *Life in Early New Jersey.* Princeton, 1964.

3 WERTENBAKER, Thomas J. *The Founding of American Civilization: The Middle Colonies.* New York, 1938.

4 WERTENBAKER, Thomas J. *The Puritan Oligarchy: The Founding of American Civilization.* New York, 1947.†

5 WILLISON, George F. *Saints and Strangers: Being the Lives of the Pilgrim Fathers & Their Families, with Their Friends and Foes: & an Account of Their Posthumous Wanderings in Limbo, Their Final Resurrection & Rise to Glory, & the Strange Pilgrimages of Plymouth Rock.* New York, 1945.†

6 WILSON, Harold F. *The Hill Country of Northern New England: Its Social and Economic History, 1790–1930.* New York, 1936.

7 WINSLOW, Ola E. *Meetinghouse Hill: 1630–1783.* New York, 1952.

8 WRIGHT, John E., and Doris S. CORBETT. *Pioneer Life in Western Pennsylvania.* Pittsburgh, Pa., 1940.

B. SOCIAL STRUCTURE

9 AKAGI, Roy H. *The Town Proprietors of the New England Colonies.* Philadelphia, 1924.

10 BAILYN, Bernard. *The New England Merchants in the Seventeenth Century.* Cambridge, 1955.†

11 BALTZELL, E. Digby. *Philadelphia Gentlemen: The Making of a National Upper Class.* Glencoe, Ill., 1958.

12 BAXTER, William T. *The House of Hancock: Business in Boston, 1724–1775.* Cambridge, 1945.

13 BEAN, William G. "Puritan versus Celt, 1850–1860." *N Eng Q,* VII (1934), 70–89.

14 BERTHOFF, Rowland T. "The Social Order of the Anthracite Region, 1825–1902." *Pa Mag Hist Biog,* LXXXIX (1965), 261–291.

15 BRIDENBAUGH, Carl. "The New England Town: A Way of Life." *Proc Am Ant Soc,* LVI (1946), 19–48.

16 BROWN, B. Katherine. "Freemanship in Puritan Massachusetts." *Am Hist Rev,* LIX (1954), 865–883.

17 BROWN, B. Katherine. "Puritan Democracy: A Case Study." *Miss Val Hist Rev,* L (1963), 377–396.

18 BROWN, B. Katherine. "Puritan Democracy in Dedham, Massachusetts: Another Case Study." *Wm Mar Q,* 3rd ser., XXIV (1967), 378–396.

19 BROWN, Robert E. *Middle-Class Democracy and the Revolution in Massachusetts, 1691–1780.* Ithaca, N.Y., 1955.

20 BUSHMAN, Richard L. *From Puritan to Yankee: Character and the Social Order in Connecticut, 1690–1765.* Cambridge, 1967.

21 CARY, John. "Statistical Method and the Brown Thesis on Colonial Democracy." *Wm Mar Q,* 3rd ser., XX (1963), 251–276.

1   DAWES, Norman H. "Titles as Symbols of Prestige in Seventeenth-Century New England." *Wm Mar Q*, 3rd ser., VI (1949), 69–83.

2   DUNN, Richard S. *Puritans and Yankees: The Winthrop Dynasty of New England, 1630–1717.* Princeton, 1962.

3   ELLIS, David M. *Landlords and Farmers in the Hudson-Mohawk Region, 1790–1850.* Ithaca, N.Y., 1946.

4   FOX, Dixon R. *The Decline of Aristocracy in the Politics of New York.* New York, 1918.†

5   GOODMAN, Paul. "Ethics and Enterprise: The Values of a Boston Elite, 1800–1860." *Am Q*, XVIII (1966), 437–451.

6   GRANT, Charles S. *Democracy in the Connecticut Frontier Town of Kent.* New York, 1961.

7   HARRINGTON, Virginia D. *The New York Merchant on the Eve of Revolution.* New York, 1935.

8   HENRETTA, James A. "Economic Development and Social Structure in Colonial Boston." *Wm Mar Q*, 3rd ser., XXII (1965), 75–92.

9   KAPLAN, Sidney. "Rank and Status among Massachusetts Continental Officers." *Am Hist Rev*, LVI (1951), 318–326.

10   KENNEY, Alice P. "Dutch Patricians in Colonial Albany." *N Y Hist*, XLIX (1968), 249–283.

11   KLEIN, Milton M. "The Cultural Tyros of Colonial New York." *S Atl Q*, LXVI (1967), 218–232.

12   LABAREE, Benjamin W. *Patriots and Partisans: The Merchants of Newburyport, 1764–1815.* Cambridge, 1962.

13   LEMON, James T., and Gary B. NASH. "The Distribution of Wealth in Eighteenth-Century America: A Century of Change in Chester County, Pennsylvania, 1693–1802." *J Soc Hist*, II (1968), 1–24.

14   LUKE, Myron H. "Some Characteristics of the New York Business Community, 1800–1810." *N Y Hist*, XXXIV (1953), 393–405.

15   MARK, Irving. *Agrarian Conflicts in Colonial New York, 1711–1775.* New York, 1940.

16   MILLER, Douglas T. "Immigration and Social Stratification in Pre-Civil War New York." *N Y Hist*, XLIX (1968), 157–168.

17   MILLER, Douglas T. *Jacksonian Aristocracy: Class and Democracy in New York, 1830–1860.* New York, 1967.

18   MORISON, Samuel E. *Builders of the Bay Colony.* Boston, 1930.†

19   POWELL, Sumner C. *Puritan Village: The Formation of a New England Town.* Middleton, Conn., 1963.†

20   RUTMAN, Darrett B. *Husbandmen of Plymouth: Farms and Villages in the Old Colony, 1620–1692.* Boston, 1967.

21   SIMMONS, Richard C. "Godliness, Property, and the Franchise in Puritan Massachusetts: An Interpretation." *J Am Hist*, LV (1968), 495–511.

22   THERNSTROM, Stephen. *Poverty and Progress: Social Mobility in a Nineteenth Century City.* Cambridge, 1964.

23   TOLLES, Frederick B. *Meeting House and Counting House: The Quaker Merchants of Colonial Philadelphia 1682–1763.* Chapel Hill, N.C., 1948.†

1   WALL, Robert E., Jr. "A New Look at Cambridge." *J Am Hist*, LII (1965), 599–605.

2   ZUCKERMAN, Michael. "The Social Context of Democracy in Massachusetts." *Wm Mar Q*, 3rd ser., XXV (1968), 523–544.

2. The South

A. GENERAL

3   ABERNETHY, Thomas P. "Democracy and the Southern Frontier." *J S Hist*, IV (1938), 3–13.

4   ABERNETHY, Thomas P. *The Formative Period in Alabama, 1815–1828.* Montgomery, Ala., 1922.

5   ABERNETHY, Thomas P. *From Frontier to Plantation in Tennessee: A Study in Frontier Democracy.* Chapel Hill, N.C., 1932.

6   ABERNETHY, Thomas P. "Social Relations and Political Control in the Old Southwest." *Miss Val Hist Rev*, XVI (1930), 529–537.

7   ABERNETHY, Thomas P. *The South in the New Nation, 1789–1819.* Baton Rouge, La., 1961.

8   ABERNETHY, Thomas P. *Three Virginia Frontiers.* University, La., 1940.

9   ALDEN, John R. *The South in the Revolution, 1763–1789.* Baton Rouge, La., 1957.

10 AMES, Susie M. *Studies of the Virginia Eastern Shore in the Seventeenth Century.* Richmond, Va., 1940.

11 ATHERTON, Lewis E. *The Southern Country Store, 1800–1860.* Baton Rouge, La., 1949.

12 BAGOT, D. Huger. "The South Carolina Up Country at the End of the Eighteenth Century." *Am Hist Rev*, XXVIII (1923), 682–698.

13 BONNER, James C. *A History of Georgia Agriculture, 1732–1860.* Athens, Ga., 1964.

14 BOYD, Minnie C. *Alabama in the Fifties: A Social Study.* New York, 1931.

15 BRUCE, Philip A. *The Institutional History of Virginia in the Seventeenth Century: An Inquiry into the Religious, Moral, Educational, Legal, Military, and Political Condition of the People, based on Original and Contemporaneous Records.* 2 vols. New York, 1910.†

16 BRUCE, Philip A. *Social Life of Virginia in the Seventeenth Century.* Richmond, Va., 1907.

17 BRUCE, Philip A. *The Virginia Plutarch.* Chapel Hill, N.C., 1929.

18 CASH, Wilbur J. *The Mind of the South.* New York, 1941.†

19 CLARK, Thomas D. *A History of Kentucky.* New York, 1937.

20 COLEMAN, J. Winston, Jr. *Stage-Coach Days in the Bluegrass: Being an Account of Stagecoach Travel and Tavern Days in Lexington and Central Kentucky, 1800–1900.* Louisville, Ky., 1935.

1 COLEMAN, Kenneth. "Social Life in Georgia in the 1780's." *Ga Rev*, IX (1955), 217–227.

2 COTTERILL, Robert S. *The Old South: The Geographic, Economic, Social, Political, and Cultural Expansion, Institutions, and Nationalism of the Ante-Bellum South.* 2nd ed. Glendale, Calif., 1939.

3 CRANE, Verner W. *The Southern Frontier, 1670–1732.* Durham, N.C., 1928.†

4 CRAVEN, Avery O. *The Growth of Southern Nationalism, 1848–1861.* Baton Rouge, La., 1953.

5 CRAVEN, Wesley F. *The Southern Colonies in the Seventeenth Century, 1607–1689.* Baton Rouge, La., 1949.

6 DAVENPORT, F. Garvin. *Ante-Bellum Kentucky: A Social History, 1800–1860.* Oxford, Ohio, 1943.

7 DAVENPORT, F. Garvin. "Culture versus Frontier in Tennessee, 1825–1850." *J S Hist*, V (1939), 18–33.

8 DAVIS, Charles S. *The Cotton Kingdom of Alabama.* Mongomery, Ala., 1939.

9 DICK, Everett. *The Dixie Frontier: A Social History of the Southern Frontier from the First Transmontane Beginnings to the Civil War.* New York, 1948.†

10 DODD, William E. *The Cotton Kingdom: A Chronicle of the Old South.* New Haven, 1919.

11 DODD, William E. *The Old South.* New York, 1937.

12 EATON, Clement. *The Civilization of the Old South: Writings of Clement Eaton.* Ed. by Albert D. Kirwan. Lexington, Ky., 1968.

13 EATON, Clement. *The Growth of Southern Civilization, 1790–1860.* New York, 1961.†

14 EATON, Clement. *A History of the Old South.* New York, 1949.

15 FAULK, Odie B. *Land of Many Frontiers: A History of the American Southwest.* New York, 1968.

16 FLETCHER, John G. *Arkansas.* Chapel Hill, N.C., 1947.

17 FOREMAN, Grant. *Pioneer Days in the Early Southwest.* Cleveland, Ohio, 1926.

18 FRANKLIN, John Hope. *The Militant South, 1800–1861.* Cambridge, 1956.†

19 GAINES, Francis P. *The Southern Plantation: A Study in the Development and the Accuracy of a Tradition.* New York, 1924.

20 GOVAN, Gilbert E., and James W. LIVINGOOD. *The Chattanooga Country, 1540–1951: From Tomahawks to TVA.* New York, 1952.

21 GOVAN, Thomas P. "Was the Old South Different?" *J S Hist*, XXI (1955), 447–455.

22 GREEN, Fletcher M. "Democracy in the Old South." *J S Hist*, XII (1946), 3–23.

23 HAMILTON, William B. "The Southwestern Frontier, 1795–1817: An Essay in Social History." *J S Hist*, X (1944), 389–403.

1 HANDLIN, Oscar, and Mary F. HANDLIN. "Origins of the Southern Labor System." *Wm Mar Q*, 3rd ser., VII (1950), 199–222.

2 HAYWOOD, C. Robert. "The Influence of Mercantilism on Social Attitudes in the South, 1700–1763." *J Hist Ideas*, XX (1959), 577–586.

3 HEATH, Milton S. *Constructive Liberalism: The Role of the State in Economic Development in Georgia to 1860*. Cambridge, 1954.

4 HOGAN, William R. *The Texas Republic: A Social and Economic History*. Norman, Okla., 1946.

5 HOLLON, William E. *The Southwest: Old and New*. New York, 1961.†

6 HUDSON, Arthur P., ed. *Humor of the Old Deep South*. New York, 1936.

7 JAMES, D. Clayton. *Antebellum Natchez*. Baton Rouge, La., 1968.

8 JOHNSON, Guion G. *Ante-Bellum North Carolina: A Social History*. Chapel Hill, N.C., 1937.

9 JOHNSON, Guion G. *A Social History of the Sea Islands, with Special Reference to St. Helena Island, South Carolina*. Chapel Hill, N.C., 1930.

10 JOHNSTON, James H. *Miscegenation in the Ante-Bellum South*. Chicago, 1939.

11 JORDAN, Weymouth T. *Ante-Bellum Alabama: Town and Country*. Tallahassee, Fla., 1957.

12 KENDRICK, B. B. "The Colonial Status of the South." *J S Hist*, VIII (1942), 3–22.

13 LEFLER, Hugh T., and Albert R. NEWSOME. *North Carolina: The History of a Southern State*. Chapel Hill, N.C., 1954.

14 LYNCH, William O. "The South and Its History." *J S Hist*, VIII (1942), 465–482.

15 MILLER, Perry. "Religion and Society in the Early Literature: The Religious Impulse in the Founding of Virginia." *Wm Mar Q*, 3rd ser., VI (1949), 24–41.

16 MILLER, Perry. "The Religious Impulse in the Founding of Virginia: Religion and Society in the Early Literature." *Wm Mar Q*, 3rd ser., V (1948), 492–522.

17 MITCHELL, Broadus. *Frederick Law Olmsted: A Critic of the Old South*. Baltimore, 1924.

18 MOORE, Albert B. *History of Alabama*. Tuscaloosa, Ala., 1935.

19 MOORE, John H. *Agriculture in Ante-Bellum Mississippi*. New York, 1958.

20 MORTON, Richard L. *Colonial Virginia*. 2 vols. Chapel Hill, N.C., 1960.

21 NOEL-HUME, Ivor. *Here Lies Virginia: An Archaeologist's View of Colonial Life and History*. New York, 1963.

22 OSTERWEIS, Rollin G. *Romanticism and Nationalism in the Old South*. New Haven, 1949.†

23 PATTON, James W. "Facets of the South in the 1850's." *J S Hist*, XXIII (1957), 3–24.

24 PHILLIPS, Ulrich B. *Life and Labor in the Old South*. Boston, 1929.†

1 RICHARDSON, Rupert N., and Carl C. RISTER. *The Greater Southwest: The Economic, Social, and Cultural Development of Kansas, Oklahoma, Texas, Utah, Colorado, Nevada, New Mexico, Arizona, and California, from the Spanish Conquest to the Twentieth Century.* Glendale, Calif., 1934.

2 ROBERT, Joseph C. *The Tobacco Kingdom: Plantation, Market, and Factory in Virginia and North Carolina, 1800–1860.* Durham, N.C., 1938.

3 RUSSEL, Robert R. "The Effects of Slavery upon Nonslaveholders in the Ante Bellum South." *Ag Hist*, XV (1941), 112–126.

4 SAYE, Albert B. "Was Georgia a Debtor Colony?" *Ga Hist Q*, XXIV (1940), 323–341.

5 SCHMIDT, Albert J. "Applying Old World Habits to the New: Life in South Carolina at the Turn of the Eighteenth Century." *Hunt Lib Q*, XXV (1961), 61–68.

6 SHRYOCK, Richard H. "Cultural Factors in the History of the South." *J S Hist*, V (1939), 333–346.

7 SIMKINS, Francis B. *A History of the South.* 2nd ed. New York, 1953.

8 STANARD, Mary N. *Colonial Virginia: Its People and Customs.* Philadelphia, 1917.

9 SYDNOR, Charles S. *The Development of Southern Sectionalism, 1819–1848.* Baton Rouge, La., 1948.

10 SYDNOR, Charles S. *Gentlemen Freeholders: Political Practices in Washington's Virginia.* Chapel Hill, N.C., 1952.†

11 TALPALAR, Morris. *The Sociology of Colonial Virginia.* 2nd ed. New York, 1968.

12 TAYLOR, Rosser H. *Ante-Bellum South Carolina: A Social and Cultural History.* Chapel Hill, N.C., 1942.

13 TAYLOR, William R. *Cavalier and Yankee: The Old South and the American National Character.* New York, 1961.†

14 WALLACE, David D. *South Carolina, A Short History, 1520–1948.* Chapel Hill, N.C., 1951.

15 WERTENBAKER, Thomas J. *The Old South: The Founding of American Civilization.* New York, 1942.

16 YOUNG, Chester R. "The Stress of War upon the Civilian Population of Virginia, 1739–1760." *W Va Hist*, XXVII (1966), 251–277.

B. SOCIAL STRUCTURE

17 APPLEWHITE, Joseph D. "Some Aspects of Society in Rural South Carolina in 1850." *N C Hist Rev*, XXIX (1952), 39–63.

18 BARKER, Charles A. *The Background of the Revolution in Maryland.* New Haven, 1940.

19 BONNER, James C. "Profile of a Late Ante-Bellum Community." *Am Hist Rev*, XLIX (1944), 663–680.

20 BRIDENBAUGH, Carl. *Myths and Realities: Societies of the Colonial South.* Baton Rouge, La., 1952.†

1   BROWN, Robert E., and B. Katherine BROWN. *Virginia, 1705–1786: Democracy or Aristocracy?* East Lansing, Mich., 1964.

2   BUCK, Paul H. "The Poor Whites of the Ante-Bellum South." *Am Hist Rev*, XXX (1925), 41–54.

3   CLARK, Blanche H. *The Tennessee Yeomen, 1840–1860.* Nashville, Tenn., 1942.

4   CRAVEN, Avery O. "Poor Whites and Negroes in the Ante-Bellum South." *J Neg Hist*, XV (1930), 14–25.

5   CROWL, Philip A. *Maryland during and after the Revolution: A Political and Economic Study.* Baltimore, 1943.

6   DIAMOND, Sigmund. "From Organization to Society: Virginia in the Seventeenth Century." *Am J Socio*, LXIII (1958), 457–475.

7   DODD, William E. "The Emergence of the First Social Order in the United States." *Am Hist Rev*, XL (1935), 217–231.

8   EATON, Clement. "Class Differences in the Old South." *Va Q Rev*, XXXIII (1957), 357–370.

9   GENOVESE, Eugene D. *The Political Economy of Slavery: Studies in the Economy and Society of the Slave South.* New York, 1965.†

10 HIGH, James. "The Origins of Maryland's Middle Class in the Colonial Aristocratic Pattern." *Md Hist Mag*, LVII (1962), 334–345.

11 KEIM, C. Ray. "Primogeniture and Entail in Colonial Virginia." *Wm Mar Q*, 3rd ser., XXV (1968), 545–586.

12 LAND, Aubrey C. "Economic Base and Social Structure: The Northern Chesapeake in the Eighteenth Century." *J Econ Hist*, XXV (1965), 639–654.

13 LOW, W. A. "The Farmer in Post-Revolutionary Virginia, 1783–1789." *Ag Hist*, XXV (1951), 122–127.

14 MAIN, Jackson T. "The Distribution of Property in Post-Revolutionary Virginia." *Miss Val Hist Rev*, XLI (1954), 241–258.

15 MENN, Joseph K. *The Large Slaveholders of Louisiana, 1860.* New Orleans, La., 1964.

16 OWSLEY, Frank L., and Harriet C. OWSLEY. "The Economic Basis of Society in the Late Ante-Bellum South." *J S Hist*, VI (1940), 24–45.

17 OWSLEY, Frank L., and Harriet C. OWSLEY. "The Economic Structure of Rural Tennessee, 1850–1860." *J S Hist*, VIII (1942), 161–182.

18 OWSLEY, Frank L. *Plain Folk of the Old South.* Baton Rouge, La., 1949.†

19 PHILLIPS, Ulrich B. *The Slave Economy of the Old South: Selected Essays in Economic and Social History.* Ed. by Eugene D. Genovese. Baton Rouge, La., 1968.†

20 REAVIS, William A. "The Maryland Gentry and Social Mobility, 1737–1776." *Wm Mar Q*, 3rd ser., XIV (1957), 418–428.

21 ROBERSON, Nancy C. "Social Mobility in Ante-Bellum Alabama." *Ala Rev*, XIII (1960), 135–145.

1 SHUGG, Roger W. *Origins of Class Struggle in Louisiana: A Social History of White Farmers and Laborers during Slavery and after, 1840–1875.* Baton Rouge, La., 1939.

2 SKAGGS, David C. "Maryland's Impulse Toward Social Revolution: 1750–1776." *J Am Hist*, LIV (1968), 771–786.

3 SMITH, W. Wayne. "Jacksonian Democracy on the Chesapeake: Class, Kinship and Politics." *Md Hist Mag*, LXIII (1968), 55–67.

4 SUTTON, Robert P. "Nostalgia, Pessimism, and Malaise: The Doomed Aristocrat in Late-Jeffersonian Virginia." *Va Mag Hist Biog*, LXXVI (1968), 41–55.

5 TAYLOR, Rosser H. "The Gentry of Ante-Bellum South Carolina." *N C Hist Rev*, XVII (1940), 114–131.

6 WEAVER, Herbert. *Mississippi Farmers, 1850–1860.* Nashville, Tenn., 1945.

7 WERTENBAKER, Thomas J. *Patrician and Plebian in Virginia, or, The Origin and Development of the Social Classes of the Old Dominion.* Charlottesville, Va., 1910.

8 WERTENBAKER, Thomas J. *The Planters of Colonial Virginia.* Princeton, 1922.

9 WRIGHT, Louis B. *The First Gentlemen of Virginia: Intellectual Qualities of the Early Colonial Ruling Class.* San Marino, Calif., 1940.†

3. The West

A. GENERAL

10 ANDERSON, Hattie M. "The Evolution of a Frontier Society in Missouri, 1818–28." *Mo Hist Rev*, XXXII (1938), 298–326, 458–483; XXXIII (1938), 23–42.

11 ARNOW, Harriette S. *Seedtime on the Cumberland.* New York, 1960.

12 ATHERTON, Lewis E. *The Pioneer Merchant in Mid-America.* Columbia, Mo., 1939.

13 BARNHART, John D. *Valley of Democracy: The Frontier versus the Plantation in the Ohio Valley, 1775–1818.* Bloomington, Ind., 1953.

14 BILLINGTON, Ray A. *America's Frontier Heritage.* New York, 1966.†

15 BILLINGTON, Ray A. *The Far Western Frontier, 1830–1860.* New York, 1956.†

16 BILLINGTON, Ray A. "The Origin of the Land Speculator as a Frontier Type." *Ag Hist*, XIX (1945), 204–212.

17 BILLINGTON, Ray A. *Westward Expansion: History of the American Frontier.* 3rd ed. New York, 1967.

18 BOUGE, Allan G. "Social Theory and the Pioneer." *Ag Hist*, XXXIV (1960), 21–34.

1 BOND, Beverley W. *The Civilization of the Old Northwest: A Study of Political, Social, and Economic Development, 1788–1812*. New York, 1934.

2 BOND, Beverley W. *The Foundations of Ohio*. Columbus, Ohio, 1941.

3 BUCK, Solon J. *Illinois in 1818*. Chicago, 1917.

4 BULEY, R. Carlyle. *The Old Northwest: Pioneer Period, 1815–1840*. 2 vols. Bloomington, Ind., 1951.

5 CARTER, Harvey L. "Rural Indiana in Transition, 1850–1860." *Ag Hist*, XX (1946), 107–121.

6 CARUSO, John A. *The Appalachian Frontier: America's First Surge Westward*. Indianapolis, Ind., 1959.

7 CLARK, Thomas D. *Frontier America: The Story of the Westward Movement*. New York, 1959.

8 COLE, Arthur C. *The Era of the Civil War, 1848–1870*. Springfield, Ill., 1919.

9 DICK, Everett N. *The Sod-House Frontier, 1854–1890: A Social History of the Northern Plains from the Creation of Kansas & Nebraska to the Admission of the Dakotas*. New York, 1937.

10 DICK, Everett N. *Vanguards of the Frontier: A Social History of the Northern Plains and Rocky Mountains from the Earliest White Contacts to the Coming of the Homemaker*. New York, 1941.†

11 DOWNES, Randolph C. *Frontier Ohio, 1788–1803*. Columbus, Ohio, 1935.

12 EIDE, Richard B. "Minnesota Pioneer Life as Reflected in the Press." *Minn Hist*, XII (1931), 391–403.

13 FRENCH, Joseph L., ed. *The Pioneer West: Narratives of the Westward March of Empire*. Boston, 1923.

14 FROST, James A. *Life on the Upper Susquehanna, 1783–1860*. New York, 1951.

15 FULLER, George N. *Economic and Social Beginnings of Michigan: A Study of the Settlement of the Lower Peninsula during the Territorial Period, 1805–1837*. Lansing, Mich., 1916.

16 GREER, Thomas H. "Economic and Social Effects of the Depression of 1819 in the Old Northwest." *Ind Mag Hist*, XLIV (1948), 227–243.

17 HILL, Leslie G. "A Moral Crusade: The Influence of Protestantism on Frontier Society in Missouri." *Mo Hist Rev*, XLV (1950), 16–34.

18 HUBBART, Henry C. *The Older Middle West, 1840–1880: Its Social, Economic and Political Life and Sectional Tendencies before, during and after the Civil War*. New York, 1936.

19 KRUEGER, Lillian. "Social Life in Wisconsin: Pre-Territorial through the Mid-Sixties." *Wis Mag Hist*, XXII (1939), 312–328.

20 LEYBURN, James G. *Frontier Folkways*. New Haven, 1935.

21 LYNCH, William O. "The Mississippi Valley and Its History." *Miss Val Hist Rev*, XXVI (1939), 3–20.

22 MAC BRIDE, Thomas H. *In Cabins and Sod-Houses*. Iowa City, Iowa, 1928.

1   MONAGHAN, Jay. *Australians and the Gold Rush: California and Down Under, 1849–1854.* Berkeley, Calif., 1966.

2   MOORE, Arthur K. *The Frontier Mind: A Cultural Analysis of the Kentucky Frontiersman.* Lexington, Ky., 1957.†

3   NICHOLS, Roy F. "The Territories: Seedbeds of Democracy." *Neb Hist,* XXXV (1954), 159–172.

4   PEASE, Theodore C. *The Frontier State, 1818–1848.* Springfield, Ill., 1918.

.5   POMEROY, Earl. "Toward a Reorientation of Western History: Continuity and Environment." *Miss Val Hist Rev,* XLI (1955), 579–600.

6   POWER, Richard L. *Planting Corn Belt Culture: The Impress of the Upland Southerner and Yankee in the Old Northwest.* Indianapolis, Ind., 1953.

7   PRIMM, James N. *Economic Policy in the Development of a Western State: Missouri, 1820–1860.* Cambridge, 1954.

8   ROLL, Charles. *Indiana: One Hundred and Fifty Years of American Development.* 5 vols. Chicago, 1931.

9   ROSEBOOM, Eugene H. *The Civil War Era, 1850–1873.* Columbus, Ohio, 1944.

10 ROSEBOOM, Eugene H., and Francis P. WEISENBURGER. *A History of Ohio.* New ed. Columbus, Ohio, 1953.

11 SCHAFER, Joseph. "The Yankee and the Teuton in Wisconsin: Characteristic Attitudes Toward the Land." *Wis Mag Hist,* VI (1922), 125–145, 261–279, 386–402; VII (1923), 3–19, 148–171.

12 SCROGGS, William O. "Rural Life in the Lower Mississippi Valley about 1803." *Proc Miss Val Hist Assn,* VIII (1914–1915), 262–277.

13 UTTER, William T. *The Frontier State, 1803–1825.* Columbus, Ohio, 1942.

14 VAIL, Robert W. G. *The Voice of the Old Frontier.* Philadelphia, 1949.

15 VOGEL, William F. "Home Life in Early Indiana." *Ind Mag Hist,* X (1914), 133–161, 284–320.

16 WEISENBURGER, Francis P. *The Passing of the Frontier, 1825–1850.* Columbus, Ohio, 1941.

17 WELTER, Rush. "The Frontier West as Image of American Society, 1776–1860." *Pac NW Q,* LII (1961), 1–7.

18 WELTER, Rush. "The Frontier West as Image of American Society: Conservative Attitudes before the Civil War." *Miss Val Hist Rev,* XLVI (1960), 593–614.

19 WERTENBAKER, Thomas J. "The Molding of the Middle West." *Am Hist Rev,* LIII (1948), 223–234.

20 WILLIAMS, Helen D. "Social Life in St. Louis from 1840 to 1860." *Mo Hist Rev,* XXXI (1936), 10–24.

21 WINTHER, Oscar O. *The Great Northwest: A History.* 2nd ed. New York, 1950.

B. SOCIAL STRUCTURE

1 BARNHART, John D. "Southern Contributions to the Social Order of the Old Northwest." *N C Hist Rev*, XVII (1940), 237–248.

2 CURTI, Merle E. *The Making of an American Community: A Case Study of Democracy in a Frontier County*. Stanford, Calif., 1959.

3 ESAREY, Logan. "The Pioneer Aristocracy." *Ind Mag Hist*, XIII (1917), 270–287.

4 SCHAFER, Joseph. "High Society in Pioneer Wisconsin." *Wis Mag Hist*, XX (1937), 447–461.

4. Patterns of Internal Migration

5 ABBOTT, Richard H. "Yankee Farmers in Northern Virginia, 1840–1860." *Va Mag Hist Biog*, LXXVI (1968), 56–63.

6 ATHEARN, Robert G. *Westward the Briton*. New York, 1953.

7 BARNHART, John D. "Sources of Southern Migration into the Old Northwest." *Miss Val Hist Rev*, XXII (1935), 49–62.

8 CHENAULT, William W., and Robert C. REINDERS. "The Northern-born Community of New Orleans in the 1850s." *J Am Hist*, LI (1964), 232–247.

9 DANHOF, Clarence H. "Economic Validity of the Safety-Valve Doctrine." *J Econ Hist, Supplement*, I (1941), 96–106.

10 DANHOF, Clarence H. "Farm-Making Costs and the 'Safety Valve': 1850–1860." *J Pol Econ*, XLIX (1941), 317–359.

11 DEGLER, Carl N. "The West as a Solution to Urban Unemployment." *N Y Hist*, XXXVI (1955), 63–85.

12 ELLIS, David M. "The Yankee Invasion of New York, 1783–1850." *N Y Hist*, XXXII (1951), 1–17.

13 GATES, Paul W. *The Illinois Central Railroad and its Colonization Work*. Cambridge, 1934.

14 GOODRICH, Carter, and Sol DAVISON. "The Frontier as Safety Valve: A Rejoinder." *Pol Sci Q*, LIII (1938), 268–271.

15 GOODRICH, Carter, and Sol DAVISON. "The Wage-Earner in the Westward Movement." *Pol Sci Q*, L (1935), 161–185; LI (1936), 61–116.

16 HIGGINS, Ruth L. *Expansion in New York, with Especial Reference to the Eighteenth Century*. Columbus, Ohio, 1931.

17 HOLBROOK, Stewart H. *The Yankee Exodus: An Account of Migration from New England*. New York, 1950.†

18 KANE, Murray. "Some Considerations on the Safety Valve Doctrine." *Miss Val Hist Rev*, XXIII (1936), 169–188.

19 LITTLEFIELD, Henry M. "Has the Safety Valve Come Back to Life?" *Ag Hist*, XXXVIII (1964), 47–49.

1   LYNCH, William O. "The Westward Flow of Southern Colonists before 1861." *J S Hist*, IX (1943), 303–327.

2   MATHEWS (ROSENBERRY), Lois K. *The Expansion of New England: The Spread of New England Settlement and Institutions to the Mississippi River, 1620–1865*. Boston, 1909.

3   NORDROFF, Ellen von. "The American Frontier as a Safety Valve—The Life, Death, Reincarnation, and Justification of a Theory." *Ag Hist*, XXXVI (1962), 123–142.

4   OWSLEY, Frank L. "The Pattern of Migration and Settlement on the Southern Frontier." *J S Hist*, XI (1945), 147–176.

5   POWER, Richard L. *Planting Corn Belt Culture*. See 21.6.

6   SCHAFER, Joseph. "Concerning the Frontier as Safety Valve." *Pol Sci Q*, LII (1937), 407–420.

7   SCHAFER, Joseph. "Some Facts Bearing on the Safety Valve Theory." *Wis Mag Hist*, XX (1936), 216–232.

8. SCHAFER, Joseph. "Was the West a Safety Valve for Labor?" *Miss Val Hist Rev*, XXIV (1937), 299–314.

9   SHANNON, Fred A. "A Post Mortem on the Labor-Safety-Valve Theory." *Ag Hist*, XIX (1945), 31–37.

10 SIMLER, Norman J. "The Safety-Valve Doctrine Re-Evaluated." *Ag Hist*, XXXII (1958), 250–257.

11 STILWELL, Lewis D. *Migration from Vermont*. Montpelier, Vt., 1948.

12 TUCKER, Rufus S. "The Frontier as an Outlet for Surplus Labor." *S Econ J*, VII (1940), 158–186.

V. Urban Life in America

1. General

13 BLAKE, John B. *Public Health in the Town of Boston, 1630–1822*. Cambridge, 1959.

14 BLAKE, Nelson M. *Water for the Cities: A History of the Urban Water Supply Problem in the United States*. Syracuse, N.Y., 1956.

15 DUFFY, John. *A History of Public Health in New York City 1625–1866*. New York, 1968.

16 GLAAB, Charles N. *The American City: A Documentary History*. Homewood, Ill., 1963.†

17 GLAAB, Charles N., and A. Theodore BROWN. *A History of Urban America*. New York, 1967.†

18 GREEN, Constance M. *American Cities in the Growth of the Nation*. New York, 1957.†

19 GREEN, Constance M. *The Rise of Urban America*. New York, 1965.†

1 HANDLIN, Oscar, and John BURCHARD, eds. *The Historian and the City.* Cambridge, 1963.†

2 HOOVER, Dwight W. "The Diverging Paths of American Urban History." *Am Q,* XX (1968), 296–317.

3 MC KELVEY, Blake. "American Urban History Today." *Am Hist Rev,* LVII (1952), 919–929.

4 MARSHALL, Leon S. "The English and American Industrial City of the Nineteenth Century." *W Pa Hist Mag,* XX (1937), 169–180.

5 MONTGOMERY, David. "The Working Classes of the Pre-Industrial City, 1780–1830." *Labor Hist,* IX (1968), 3–22.

6 REPS, John W. *The Making of Urban America: A History of City Planning in the United States.* Princeton, 1965.

7 SCHLESINGER, Arthur M. "The City in American History." *Miss Val Hist Rev,* XXVII (1941), 43–66.

8 STILL, Bayrd. "Patterns of Mid-Nineteenth Century Urbanization in the Middle West." *Miss Val Hist Rev,* XXVIII (1941), 187–206.

9 STOKES, I. N. Phelps. *The Iconography of Manhattan Island, 1498–1909.* 6 vols. New York, 1915–1928.

10 TAYLOR, George R. "American Urban Growth Preceding the Railway Age." *J Econ Hist,* XXVII (1967), 309–339.

11 WARNER, Sam B., Jr. "If All the World were Philadelphia: A Scaffolding for Urban History, 1774–1930." *Am Hist Rev,* LXXIV (1968), 26–43.

12 WEBER, Adna F. *The Growth of Cities in the Nineteenth Century: A Study in Statistics.* New York, 1899.

13 WILLIAMSON, Jeffrey G. "Antebellum Urbanization in the American Northeast." *J Econ Hist,* XXV (1965), 592–608.

2. Urban Life in Colonial America

14 BARCK, Oscar T., Jr. *New York City during the War for Independence: With Special Reference to the Period of British Occupation.* New York, 1931.

15 BRIDENBAUGH, Carl. *Cities in Revolt: Urban Life in America, 1743–1776.* New York, 1955.†

16 BRIDENBAUGH, Carl. *Cities in the Wilderness: The First Century of Urban Life in America, 1625–1742.* New York, 1938.†

17 BRIDENBAUGH, Carl, and Jessica BRIDENBAUGH. *Rebels and Gentlemen: Philadelphia in the Age of Franklin.* New York, 1942.†

18 EDWARDS, George W. *New York as an Eighteenth-Century Municipality, 1731–1776.* New York, 1917.

19 LEMON, James T. "Urbanization and Development of Eighteenth-Century Southeastern Pennsylvania and Adjacent Delaware." *Wm Mar Q,* 3rd ser., XXIV (1967), 501–542.

20 LIPPINCOTT, Horace M. *Early Philadelphia, Its People, Life and Progress.* Philadelphia, 1917.

21 MACLEAR, Anne B. *Early New England Towns: A Comparative Study of Their Development.* New York, 1908.

1   NASH, Gary B. "City Planning and Political Tension in the Seventeenth Century: The Case of Philadelphia." *Proc Am Philos Soc*, CXII (1968), 54–73.

2   PETERSON, Arthur E. *New York as an Eighteenth-Century Municipality prior to 1731*. New York, 1917.

3   PETERSON, Charles E. *Colonial St. Louis: Building a Creole Capital*. St. Louis, Mo., 1949.

4   PHILLIPS, James D. *Salem and the Indies: The Story of the Great Commercial Era of the City*. Boston, 1947.

5   PHILLIPS, James D. *Salem in the Eighteenth Century*. Boston, 1937.

6   PHILLIPS, James D. *Salem in the Seventeenth Century*. Boston, 1933.

7   POMERANTZ, Sidney I. *New York: An American City, 1783–1803: A Study of Urban Life*. New York, 1938.

8   REPS, John W. *Town Planning in Frontier America*. Princeton, 1969.

9   ROACH, Hannah B. "The Planting of Philadelphia: A Seventeenth-Century Real Estate Development." *Pa Mag Hist Biog*, XCII (1968), 3–47, 143–194.

10 RUTMAN, Darrett B. *Winthrop's Boston: Portrait of a Puritan Town, 1630–1649*. Chapel Hill, N.C., 1965.

11 WARNER, Sam B., Jr. *The Private City: Philadelphia in Three Periods of Its Growth*. Philadelphia, 1968.

3. Urban Life in the Nineteenth Century

12 ALBION, Robert G. *Rise of New York Port*. See 10.4.

13 ASH, Martha M. "The Social and Domestic Scene in Rochester, 1840–1860." *Rochester Hist*, XVIII (1956), 1–20.

14 BALD, F. Clever. *Detroit's First American Decade, 1796 to 1805*. Ann Arbor, Mich., 1948.

15 BALDWIN, Leland D. *Pittsburgh: The Story of a City*. Pittsburgh, Pa., 1937.

16 BENTON, Elbert J. *Cultural Story of an American City, Cleveland*. Parts I, II, III. Cleveland, Ohio, 1943–1946.

17 BINGHAM, Robert W. *The Cradle of the Queen City: A History of Buffalo to the Incorporation of the City*. Buffalo, N.Y., 1931.

18 BOMAN, Martha. "A City of the Old South: Jackson, Mississippi, 1850–1860." *J Miss Hist*, XV (1953), 1–32.

19 BROWN, A. Theodore. *Frontier Community: Kansas City to 1870*. Columbia, Mo., 1964.

20 CAPERS, Gerald M. *The Biography of a River Town: Memphis: Its Heroic Age*. Chapel Hill, N.C., 1939.

21 COLE, Donald B. *Immigrant City: Lawrence, Massachusetts, 1845–1921*. Chapel Hill, N.C., 1963.

22 DAIN, Floyd R. *Every House a Frontier: Detroit's Economic Progress, 1815–1825*. Detroit, Mich., 1956.

23 ERNST, Robert. *Immigrant Life in New York City, 1825–1863*. New York, 1949.

1 GILCHRIST, David T., ed. *The Growth of the Seaport Cities, 1790–1825.* Charlottesville, Va., 1967.

2 GREEN, Constance M. *History of Naugatuck, Conn.* New Haven, 1948.

3 GREEN, Constance M. *Holyoke, Mass.: A Case History of the Industrial Revolution in America.* New Haven, 1939.

4 GREEN, Constance M. *The Secret City: A History of Race Relations in the Nation's Capital.* Princeton, 1967.

5 GREEN, Constance M. *Washington: Village and Capital, 1800–1878,* Princeton, 1962.

6 HANDLIN, Oscar. *Boston's Immigrants: A Study in Acculturation.* Rev. ed. Cambridge, 1959.†

7 JAMES, D. Clayton. *Antebellum Natchez.* See 16.7.

8 JUDD, Jacob. "Brooklyn's Volunteer Fire Department." *J Long Island Hist,* VI (1966), 29–34.

9 JUDD, Jacob. "Policing the City of Brooklyn in the 1840's and 1850's." *J Long Island Hist,* VI (1966), 13–22.

10 KENNEDY, Charles J. "Commuter Services in the Boston Area, 1835–1860." *Bus Hist Rev,* XXXVI (1962), 153–170.

11 KIRKPATRICK, R. L. "Professional, Religious, and Social Aspects of St. Louis Life, 1804–1816." *Mo Hist Rev,* XLIV (1950), 373–386.

12 LANE, Roger. *Policing the City: Boston 1822–1885.* Cambridge, 1967.

13 MC KELVEY, Blake. *Rochester: The Flower City, 1855–1890.* Cambridge, 1949.

14 MC KELVEY, Blake. *Rochester: The Water-Power City, 1812–1854.* Cambridge, 1945.

15 MOORE, Gay M. *Seaport in Virginia: George Washington's Alexandria.* Richmond, Va., 1949.

16 OSTERWEIS, Rollin G. *Three Centuries of New Haven, 1638–1938.* New Haven, 1953.

17 PIERCE, Bessie L. *A History of Chicago.* 3 vols. New York, 1937–1957.

18 PIERCE, Bessie L., ed. *As Others See Chicago: Impressions of Visitors, 1673–1933.* Chicago, 1933.

19 REINDERS, Robert C. *End of an Era: New Orleans, 1850–1860.* New Orleans, La., 1965.

20 RICHARDSON, James F. "Mayor Fernando Wood and the New York Police Force: 1855–1857." *N Y Hist Soc Q,* L (1966), 5–40.

21 RICHARDSON, James F. "The Struggle to Establish a London-Style Police Force for New York City." *N Y Hist Soc Q,* XLIX (1965), 175–197.

22 ROSENBERG, Charles E. *The Cholera Years: The United States in 1832, 1849, and 1866.* Chicago, 1962.

23 SEMMES, Raphael. *Baltimore as Seen by Visitors, 1783–1860.* Baltimore, 1953.

24 SHLAKMAN, Vera. *Economic History of a Factory Town: A Study of Chicapee, Massachusetts.* Northampton, Mass., 1935.

25 STILL, Bayrd. "Evidences of the 'Higher Life' on the Frontier as Illustrated in the History of Cultural Matters in Chicago, 1830 to 1850." *J Ill State Hist Soc,* XXVIII (1935), 81–99.

26 STILL, Bayrd. *Milwaukee: The History of a City.* Madison, Wis., 1948.

1 STILL, Bayrd. *Mirror for Gotham: New York as Seen by Contemporaries from Dutch Days to the Present.* New York, 1956.

2 SUMMERSELL, Charles G. *Mobile: History of a Seaport Town.* University, Ala., 1949.

3 THERNSTROM, Stephen. *Poverty and Progress.* See 13.22.

4 TREGLE, Joseph G., Jr. "Early New Orleans Society: A Reappraisal." *J S Hist,* XVIII (1952), 20–36.

5 WADE, Richard C. *Slavery in the Cities: The South, 1820–1860.* New York, 1964.†

6 WADE, Richard C. *The Urban Frontier: The Rise of Western Cities, 1790–1830.* Cambridge, 1959.†

7 WARNER, Sam B., Jr. *Private City.* See 25.11.

8 WEISENBURGER, Frances P. "The Urbanization of the Middle West: Town and Village in the Pioneer Period." *Ind Mag Hist,* XLI (1945), 19–30.

9 WELD, Ralph F. *Brooklyn is America.* New York, 1950.

10 WELD, Ralph F. *Brooklyn Village, 1816–1834.* New York, 1938.

11 WERTENBAKER, Thomas J. *Norfolk: Historic Southern Port.* Durham, N.C., 1931.

12 WHEELER, Kenneth W. *To Wear a City's Crown: The Beginnings of Urban Growth in Texas, 1836–1865.* Cambridge, 1968.

13 WHITEHILL, Walter M. *Boston: A Topographical History.* Cambridge, 1959.

14 WILLIAMSON, Jeffrey G., and Joseph A. SWANSON. "The Growth of Cities in the American Northeast, 1820–1870." *Explor Entrep Hist,* 2nd ser., Supplement, IV (1966), 3–101.

15 WILSON, James G., ed. *The Memorial History of the City of New York, from Its First Settlement to the Year 1892.* 4 vols. New York, 1892–1893.

16 WINSOR, Justin, ed. *The Memorial History of Boston, Including Suffolk County, Massachusetts. 1630–1880.* 4 vols. Boston, 1880–1881.

4. Rise of the Professions

17 CALHOUN, Daniel H. *The American Civil Engineer: Origins and Conflict.* Cambridge, 1960.

18 CALHOUN, Daniel H. *Professional Lives in America, Structure and Aspiration, 1750–1850.* Cambridge, 1965.

19 CALVERT, Monte A. *The Mechanical Engineer in America, 1830–1910: Professional Cultures in Conflict.* Baltimore, 1967.

20 CHROUST, Anton-Hermann. *The Rise of the Legal Profession in America.* 2 vols. Norman, Okla., 1965.

21 COCHRAN, Thomas C. *Railroad Leaders, 1845–1890: The Business Mind in Action.* Cambridge, 1953.

22 DANIELS, George H. "The Process of Professionalization in American Science: The Emergent Period, 1820–1860." *Isis,* LVIII (1967), 151–166.

1 KETT, Joseph F. *The Formation of the American Medical Profession: The Role of Institutions, 1780–1860.* New Haven, 1968.

2 ROSENBERG, Charles E. "The American Medical Profession: Mid-Nineteenth Century." *Mid-America,* XLIV (1962), 163–171.

3 SHAFER, Henry B. *The American Medical Profession, 1783–1850.* New York, 1936.

VI. Immigration and Ethnic Groups

1. General

4 ABBOTT, Edith. *Historical Aspects of the Immigration Problem: Select Documents.* Chicago, 1926.

5 ABBOTT, Edith. *Immigration: Select Documents and Case Records.* Chicago, 1924.

6 ANDER, O. Fritiof, ed. *In the Trek of the Immigrants: Essays Presented to Carl Wittke.* Rock Island, Ill., 1964.

7 BLEGEN, Theodore C., ed. *Land of Their Choice: The Immigrants Write Home.* Minneapolis, Minn., 1955.

8 BRIDENBAUGH, Carl. *Vexed and Troubled Englishmen, 1590–1642.* New York, 1968.

9 BUTLER, James D. "British Convicts Shipped to American Colonies." *Am Hist Rev,* II (1896), 12–33.

10 COMMAGER, Henry S., ed. *Immigration and American History: Essays in Honor of Theodore C. Blegen.* Minneapolis, Minn., 1961.

11 CRARY, Catherine S. "The Humble Immigrant and the American Dream: Some Case Histories, 1746–1776." *Miss Val Hist Rev,* XLVI (1959), 46–66.

12 ERNST, Robert. *Immigrant Life in New York City.* See 25.23.

13 GARIS, Roy L. *Immigration Restriction: A Study of the Opposition to and Regulation of Immigration into the United States.* New York, 1927.

14 HANDLIN, Oscar. *Boston's Immigrants.* See 26.6.

15 HANDLIN, Oscar. *Race and Nationality in American Life.* Boston, 1957.†

16 HANDLIN, Oscar. *The Uprooted: The Epic Story of the Great Migrations that Made the American People.* Boston, 1951.

17 HANSEN, Marcus L. *The Atlantic Migration, 1607–1860: A History of the Continuing Settlement of the United States.* Cambridge, 1940.†

18 HANSEN, Marcus. L. *The Immigrant in American History.* Cambridge, 1940.†

19 HANSEN, Marcus L. *The Mingling of the Canadian and American Peoples.* New Haven, 1940.

20 HARDY, James D., Jr. "The Transportation of Convicts to Colonial Louisiana." *La Hist,* VII (1966), 207–220.

1 HEATON, Herbert. "The Industrial Immigrant in the United States, 1783–1812." *Proc Am Philos Soc*, XCV (1951), 519–527.

2 JONES, Maldwyn A. *American Immigration*. Chicago, 1960.†

3 KELLY, Sister Mary G. *Catholic Immigrant Colonization Projects in the United States, 1815–1860*. New York, 1939.

4 KLEBANER, Benjamin J. "The Myth of Foreign Pauper Dumping in the United States." *Soc Serv Rev*, XXXV (1961), 302–309.

5 KLEBANER, Benjamin J. "State and Local Immigration Regulation in the United States before 1882." *Int Rev Soc Hist*, III (1958), 269–295.

6 LEACH, Richard H. "The Impact of Immigration upon New York, 1840–60." *N Y Hist*, XXXI (1950), 15–30.

7 MILLER, Douglas T. "Immigration and Social Stratification in Pre-Civil War New York." See 13.15.

8 RISCH, Erna. "Encouragement of Immigration as Revealed in Colonial Legislation." *Va Mag Hist Biog*, XLV (1937), 1–10.

9 SHAUGHNESSY, Gerald. *Has the Immigrant Kept the Faith? A Study of Immigration and Catholic Growth in the United States, 1790–1920*. New York, 1925.

10 SMITH, Abbot E. "The Transportation of Convicts to the American Colonies in the Seventeenth Century." *Am Hist Rev*, XXXIX (1934), 232–249.

11 SPEAR, Allan H. "Marcus Lee Hansen and the Historiography of Immigration." *Wis Mag Hist*, XLIV (1961), 258–268.

12 STEPHENSON, George M. *A History of American Immigration, 1820–1924*. Boston, 1926.

13 WEAVER, Herbert. "Foreigners in Ante-Bellum Mississippi." *J Miss Hist*, XVI (1954), 151–163.

14 WEAVER, Herbert. "Foreigners in Ante-Bellum Towns in the Lower South." *J S Hist*, XIII (1947), 62–73.

15 WITTKE, Carl F. *We Who Built America: The Saga of the Immigrant*. New York, 1939.

2. *United Kingdom*

16 BERTHOFF, Rowland T. *British Immigrants in Industrial America, 1790–1950*. Cambridge, 1953.

17 BLACK, George F. *Scotland's Mark on America*. New York, 1921.

18 BOLTON, Charles K. *Scotch Irish Pioneers in Ulster and America*. Boston, 1910.

19 BROWNING, Charles H. *Welsh Settlement of Pennsylvania*. Philadelphia, 1912.

20 CONWAY, Alan, ed. *The Welsh in America: Letters from the Immigrants*. Minneapolis, Minn., 1961.

21 COWAN, Helen I. *British Emigration to British North America: The First Hundred Years*. Rev. ed. Toronto, Canada, 1961.

22 DICKSON, R. J. *Ulster Emigration to Colonial America, 1718–1775*. New York, 1966.

23 DUNAWAY, Wayland F. *The Scotch-Irish of Colonial Pennsylvania*. Chapel Hill, N.C., 1944.

1   FORD, Henry J. *The Scotch-Irish in Ameria.* Princeton, 1915.

2   GLASGOW, Maude. *The Scotch-Irish in Northern Ireland and in the American Colonies.* New York, 1936.

3   GOODWIN, Maud W. *Dutch and English on the Hudson: A Chronicle of Colonial New York.* New Haven, 1919.

4   GRAHAM, Ian C. C. *Colonists from Scotland: Emigration to North America, 1707–1783.* Ithaca, N.Y., 1956.

5   GREEN, E. R. R. "The 'Strange Humors' that Drove the Scotch-Irish to America, 1729." *Wm Mar Q*, 3rd ser., XII (1955), 113–123.

6   HANNA, Charles A. *The Scotch-Irish: or, The Scot in North Britain, North Ireland, and North America.* 2 vols. New York, 1902.

7   HARTMANN, Edward G. *Americans from Wales.* Boston, 1967.

8   LEYBURN, James G. *The Scotch-Irish: A Social History.* Chapel Hill, N.C., 1962.

9   MEYER, Duane. *The Highland Scots of North Carolina, 1732–1776.* Chapel Hill, N.C., 1961.

10   PRYDE, George S. "Scottish Colonization in the Province of New York." *N Y Hist*, XVI (1935), 138–157.

11   YEARLEY, Clifton K. *Britons in American Labor: A History of the Influence of the United Kingdom Immigrants on American Labor, 1820–1914.* Baltimore, 1957.

3. Irish

12   ADAMS, William F. *Ireland and Irish Emigration to the New World from 1815 to the Famine.* New Haven, 1932.

13   DONOVAN, George F. *The Pre-Revolutionary Irish in Massachusetts, 1620–1775.* Menasha, Wis., 1932.

14   GITELMAN, Howard M. "The Waltham System and the Coming of the Irish." *Labor Hist*, VIII (1967), 227–253.

15   HANDLIN, Oscar. *Boston's Immigrants.* See 26.6.

16   HANSEN, Marcus L. "The Second Colonization of New England." *N Eng Q*, II (1929), 539–560.

17   MC DONALD, Sister M. Justille. *History of the Irish in Wisconsin in the Nineteenth Century.* Washington, D.C., 1954.

18   MOREHOUSE, Frances. "The Irish Migration of the 'Forties'." *Am Hist Rev*, XXXIII (1928), 579–592.

19   MYERS, Albert C. *Immigration of the Irish Quakers into Pennsylvania, 1682–1750, with Their Early History in Ireland.* Swarthmore, Pa., 1902.

20   NEU, Irene D. "From Kilkenny to Louisiana: Notes on Eighteenth-Century Irish Emigration." *Mid-America*, XLIX (1967), 101–114.

21   NIEHAUS, Earl F. *The Irish in New Orleans, 1800–1860.* Baton Rouge, La., 1965.

22   OLDHAM, Ellen M. "Irish Support of the Abolitionist Movement." *Boston Pub Lib Q*, X (1958), 175–187.

23   PURCELL, Richard J. "Irish Cultural Contribution in Early New York." *Cath Ed Rev*, XXV (1937), 449–460; XXVI (1938), 28–42.

1   WITTKE, Carl F. *The Irish in America*. Baton Rouge, La., 1956.

4. Germans

2   BITTINGER, Lucy F. *The Germans in Colonial Times*. Philadelphia, 1901.

3   CUNZ, Dieter. *The Maryland Germans: A History*. Princeton, 1948.

4   DIFFENDERFFER, Frank R. *The German Immigration into Pennsylvania through the Port of Philadelphia, 1770 to 1775*. Lancaster, Pa., 1900.

5   FAUST, Albert B. *The German Element in the United States, with Special Reference to Its Political, Moral, Social, and Educational Influence*. Rev. ed. 2 vols. in one. New York, 1927.

6   FOGEL, Edwin M. *Beliefs and Superstitions of the Pennsylvania Germans*. Philadelphia, 1915.

7   HAWGOOD, John A. *The Tragedy of German-America: The Germans in the United States of America during the Nineteenth Century—and After*. New York, 1940.

8   KLEES, Fredric. *The Pennsylvania Dutch*. New York, 1950.

9   KNAUSS, James O., Jr. *Social Conditions among the Pennsylvania Germans in the Eighteenth Century, as Revealed in the German Newspapers Published in America*. Lancaster, Pa., 1922.

10   KNITTLE, Walter A. *Early Eighteenth Century Palatine Emigration*. Philadelphia, 1937.

11   KUHNS, Oscar. *The German and Swiss Settlements of Colonial Pennsylvania: A Study of the So-Called Pennsylvania Dutch*. New York, 1901.

12   MYERS, Jacob W. "The Beginning of German Immigration in the Middle West." *J Ill State Hist Soc*, XV (1923), 592–599.

13   REDEKOP, Calvin W. *The Old Colony Mennonites: Dilemmas of Ethnic Minority Life*. Baltimore, 1969.

14   ROTHAN, Emmet H. *The German Catholic Immigrant in the United States (1830–1860)*. Washington, D.C., 1946.

15   ROTHERMUND, Dietmar. *The Layman's Progress: Denominations and Political Behavior in Colonial Pennsylvania*. Philadelphia, 1962.

16   SACHSE, Julius F. *The German Sectarians of Pennsylvania, 1708–1800: A Critical and Legendary History of the Ephrata Cloister and the Dunkers*. 2 vols. Philadelphia, 1899–1900.

17   SCHANTZ, Franklin J. F. *The Domestic Life and Characteristics of the Pennsylvania German Pioneer*. Lancaster, Pa., 1900.

18   SCHROTT, Lambert. *Pioneer German Catholics in the American Colonies (1734–1784)*. New York, 1933.

19   SCHURICHT, Hermann. *History of the German Element in Virginia*. Baltimore, 1900.

20   SESSLER, Jacob J. *Communal Pietism among Early American Moravians*. New York, 1933.

1   SHRYOCK, Richard H. "The Pennsylvania Germans in American History." *Pa Mag Hist Biog*, LXIII (1939), 261–281.

2   SMITH, Charles H. *The Mennonite Immigration to Pennsylvania in the Eighteenth Century*. Norristown, Pa., 1929.

3   VOIGHT, Gilbert P. "Cultural Contributions of German Settlers to South Carolina." *S C Hist Mag*, LIII (1952), 183–189.

4   WITTKE, Carl F. *Refugees of Revolution: The German Forty-Eighters in America*. Philadelphia, 1952.

5   WOOD, Ralph, ed. *The Pennsylvania Germans*. Princeton, 1942.

6   ZUCKER, Adolf E., ed. *The Forty-Eighters, Political Refugees of the German Revolution of 1848*. New York, 1950.

5. French

7   BAIRD, Charles W. *History of the Huguenot Emigration to America*. 2 vols. New York, 1885.

8   CHILDS, Frances S. *French Refugee Life in the United States, 1790–1800: An American Chapter of the French Revolution*. Baltimore, 1940.

9   FOSDICK, Lucian J. *The French Blood in America*. New York, 1906.

10   HIRSCH, Arthur H. *The Huguenots of Colonial South Carolina*. Durham, N.C., 1928.

11   LAUX, James B. *The Huguenot Element in Pennsylvania*. New York, 1896.

12   STRUBLE, George G. "The French in Pennsylvania prior to 1800." *French Rev*, XXVII (1953), 50–58.

6. Scandinavians

13   BABCOCK, Kendric C. *The Scandinavian Element in the United States*. Urbana, Ill., 1914.

14   BENSON, Adolph B., and Naboth HEDIN. *Americans from Sweden*. Philadelphia, 1950.

15   BENSON, Adolph B., and Naboth HEDIN, eds. *Swedes in America, 1638–1938*. New Haven, 1938.

16   BLEGEN, Theodore C. *Norwegian Migration to America*. 2 vols. Northfield, Minn., 1931–1940.

17   DOWIE, J. Iverne, and Ernest M. ESPELIE, eds. *The Swedish Immigrant Community in Transition: Essays in Honor of Conrad Bergendoff*. Rock Island, Ill., 1963.

18   FLOM, George T. *A History of Norwegian Immigration to the United States from the Earliest Beginning down to the Year 1848*. Iowa City, Iowa, 1909.

19   JANSON, Florence E. *The Background of Swedish Immigration, 1840–1930*. Chicago, 1931.

1   JOHNSON, Amandus. *The Swedish Settlements on the Delaware.* 2 vols. Philadelphia, 1911.

2   LEIBY, Adrian C. *The Early Dutch and Swedish Settlers of New Jersey.* Princeton, 1964.

3   LOUHI, Evert A. *The Delaware Finns: or, The First Permanent Settlements in Pennsylvania, Delaware, West New Jersey and Eastern Part of Maryland.* New York, 1925.

4   PAGE, Evelyn. "The First Frontier—The Swedes and the Dutch." *Pa Hist,* XV (1948), 276–304.

5   QUALEY, Carlton C. *Norwegian Settlement in the United States.* Northfield, Minn., 1938.

6   STEPHENSON, George M. *The Religious Aspects of Swedish Immigration: A Study of Immigrant Churches.* Minneapolis, Minn., 1932.

7   WARD, Christopher. *The Dutch & Swedes on the Delaware, 1609–64.* Philadelphia, 1930.

8   WESTIN, Gunnar. "Background of the Swedish Pioneer Immigration, 1840–1850." *Am Swed Hist Found Yrbk,* 1948, 20–31.

9   WUORIN, John H. *The Finns on the Delaware, 1638–1655: An Essay in American Colonial History.* New York, 1938.

7. *Dutch*

10   HULL, William I. *William Penn and the Dutch Quaker Migration to Pennsylvania.* Swarthmore, Pa., 1935.

11   LEIBY, Adrian C. *Early Dutch and Swedish Settlers.* See 33.2.

12   LUCAS, Henry S. *Netherlanders in America: Dutch Immigration to the United States and Canada, 1789–1950.* Ann Arbor, Mich., 1955.

13   MULDER, Arnold. *Americans from Holland.* Philadelphia, 1947.

14   PAGE, Evelyn. "The First Frontier—The Swedes and the Dutch." See 33.4.

15   WARD, Christopher. *Dutch & Swedes on the Delaware.* See 33.7.

16   WABEKE, Bertus H. *Dutch Emigration to North America, 1624–1860.* New York, 1944.

8. *Italians*

17   MARRARO, Howard R. "Italians in New York during the First Half of the Nineteenth Century." *N Y Hist,* XXVI (1945), 278–306.

18   MARRARO, Howard R. "Italians in New York in the Eighteen Fifties." *N Y Hist,* XXX (1949), 181–203, 276–303.

19   MARRARO, Howard R. "Italo-Americans in Eighteenth-Century New York." *N Y Hist,* XXI (1940), 316–323.

20   MARRARO, Howard R. "Italo-Americans in Pennsylvania in the Eighteenth Century." *Pa Hist,* VII (1940), 159–166.

1   SCHIAVO, Giovanni. *The Italians in America before the Civil War.* New York, 1934.

9. Poles

2   LERSKI, Jerzy Jan. *A Polish Chapter in Jacksonian America: The United States and the Polish Exiles of 1831.* Madison, Wis., 1958.

3   WYTRWAL, Joseph A. *America's Polish Heritage: A Social History of the Poles in America.* Detroit, Mich., 1961.

10. Chinese

4   BARTH, Gunther. *Bitter Strength: A History of the Chinese in the United States, 1850–1870.* Cambridge, 1964.

VII. Negro Americans

1. General

5   APTHEKER, Herbert. *The Negro in the Abolitionist Movement.* New York, 1941.

6   APTHEKER, Herbert, ed. *A Documentary History of the Negro People in the United States.* New York, 1951.

7   BARDOLPH, Richard. *The Negro Vanguard.* New York, 1959.†

8   BELL, Howard H. "Expressions of Negro Militancy in the North, 1840–1860." *J Neg Hist*, XLV (1960), 11–20.

9   BELL, Howard H. "The National Negro Convention, 1848." *Ohio Hist Q*, LXVII (1958), 357–368.

10 BELL, Howard H. "The Negro Emigration Movement, 1849–1854: A Phase of Negro Nationalism." *Phylon*, XX (1959), 132–142.

11 BELL, Howard H. "Negro Nationalism: A Factor in Emigration Projects, 1858–1861." *J Neg Hist*, XLVII (1962), 42–53.

12 BELL, Howard H. "Negroes in the Reform Movement, 1847–1853." *Neg Hist Bull*, XXI (1958), 153–155.

13 BOUSFIELD, M. O. "An Account of Physicians of Color in the United States." *Bull Hist Med*, XVII (1945), 61–84.

14 BUTCHER, Margaret J. *The Negro in American Culture, Based on Materials Left by Alain Locke.* New York, 1956.

15 CANTOR, Milton. "The Image of the Negro in Colonial Literature." *N Eng Q*, XXXVI (1963), 452–477.

16 CRUM, Mason. *Gullah: Negro Life in the Carolina Sea Islands.* Durham, N.C., 1940.

1   DU BOIS, W. E. Burghardt. *Black Folk Then and Now: An Essay in the History and Sociology of the Negro Race.* New York, 1939.

2   FARMER, Harold E. "An Account of the Earliest Colored Gentlemen in Medical Science in the United States." *Bull Hist Med*, VIII (1940), 599–618.

3   FOSTER, Charles I. "The Colonization of Free Negroes in Liberia, 1816–1835." *J Neg Hist*, XXXVIII (1953), 41–66.

4   FRANKLIN, John Hope. *From Slavery to Freedom: A History of Negro Americans.* Rev. ed. New York, 1967.†

5   FRAZIER, E. Franklin. *The Negro Family in the United States.* Rev. ed. New York, 1948.†

6   GREENE, Lorenzo J. *The Negro in Colonial New England, 1620–1776.* New York, 1942.†

7   GROSS, Bella. "The First National Negro Convention." *J Neg Hist*, XXXI (1946), 435–443.

8   HERSKOVITS, Melville. *The Myth of the Negro Past.* New York, 1941.†

9   KLINGBERG, Frank J. "The African Immigrant in Colonial Pennsylvania and Delaware." *Hist Mag Prot Epis Church*, XI (1942), 126–153.

10 MEIER, August. "The Emergence of Negro Nationalism: A Study in Ideologies, from the American Revolution to the First World War." *Midwest J*, IV (1951–1952), 96–104.

11 MEIER, August, and Elliott M. RUDWICK. *From Plantation to Ghetto: An Interpretive History of American Negroes.* New York, 1966.

12 MYRDAL, Gunnar. *An American Dilemma: The Negro Problem and Modern Democracy.* New York, 1944.†

13 PORTER, Kenneth W. "Negroes and the Seminole War 1817–1818." *J Neg Hist*, XXXVI (1951), 249–280.

14 QUARLES, Benjamin. *Black Abolitionists.* New York, 1969.

15 QUARLES, Benjamin. *The Negro in the American Revolution.* Chapel Hill, N.C., 1961.†

16 REDDING, J. Saunders. *They Came in Chains: Americans from Africa.* Philadelphia, 1950.

17 SHERWOOD, Henry N. "Early Negro Deportation Projects." *Miss Val Hist Rev*, II (1916), 484–508.

18 STAVISKY, Leonard P. "Negro Craftsmanship in Early America." *Am Hist Rev*, LIV (1949), 315–325.

19 STAVISKY, Leonard P. "The Origins of Negro Craftsmanship in Colonial America." *J Neg Hist*, XXXII (1947), 417–429.

20 STRICKLAND, Arvarh E. "Negro Colonization Movements to 1840." *Lincoln Her*, LXI (1959), 43–56.

21 TATE, Thad W., Jr. *The Negro in Eighteenth-Century Williamsburg.* Charlottesville, Va., 1965.†

22 TAYLOR, Alrutheus A. "Movement of the Negroes from the East to the Gulf States from 1830 to 1850." *J Neg Hist*, VIII (1923), 367–383.

23 U.S. Bureau of the Census. *Negro Population, 1790–1915.* Washington, D.C., 1918.

1 WAX, Darold D. "Georgia and the Negro before the American Revolution." *Ga Hist Q*, LI (1967), 63–77.

2 WESLEY, Charles H. *Negro Labor in the United States, 1850–1925: A Study in American Economic History*. New York, 1927.

3 WESLEY, Charles H. "The Participation of Negroes in Anti-Slavery Political Parties." *J Neg Hist*, XXIX (1944), 32–74.

4 WOODSON, Carter G. *Free Negro Heads of Families in the United States in 1830*. Washington, D.C., 1925.

2. The Negro and American Slavery

5 APTHEKER, Herbert. *American Negro Slave Revolts*. New York, 1943.†

6 BALLAGH, James C. *A History of Slavery in Virginia*. Baltimore, 1902.

7 BANCROFT, Frederic. *Slave-Trading in the Old South*. Baltimore, 1931.

8 BASSETT, John S. *Slavery and Servitude in the Colony of North Carolina*. Baltimore, 1896.

9 BASSETT, John S. *The Southern Plantation Overseer as Revealed in his Letters*. Northampton, Mass., 1925.

10 BAUER, Raymond A., and Alice H. BAUER. "Day to Day Resistance to Slavery." *J Neg Hist*, XXVII 1942), 388–419.

11 BOTKIN, Benjamin A., ed. *Lay My Burden Down: A Folk History of Slavery*. Chicago, 1945.†

12 BRACKETT, Jeffrey R. *The Negro in Maryland: A Study of the Institution of Slavery*. Baltimore, 1889.

13 BRADFORD, S. Sydney. "The Negro Ironworker in Ante Bellum Virginia." *J S Hist*, XXV (1959), 194–206.

14 BRUCE, Kathleen. *Virginia Iron Manufacture in the Slave Era*. New York, 1930.

15 CARROLL, Joseph C. *Slave Insurrections in the United States, 1800–1865*. Boston, 1938.

16 CATTERALL, Helen T., ed. *Judicial Cases Concerning American Slavery and the Negro*. 5 vols. Washington, D.C., 1926–1937.

17 CLARK, Ernest J., Jr. "Aspects of the North Carolina Slave Code, 1715–1860." *N C Hist Rev*, XXXIX (1962), 148–164.

18 CLARK, Thomas D. "The Slave Trade between Kentucky and the Cotton Kingdom." *Miss Val Hist Rev*, XXI (1933), 331–342.

19 COLEMAN, J. Winston, Jr. *Slavery Times in Kentucky*. Chapel Hill, N.C., 1940.

20 COLLINS, Winfred H. *The Domestic Slave Trade of the Southern States*. New York, 1904.

21 COOLEY, Henry S. *A Study of Slavery in New Jersey*. Baltimore, 1896.

22 CONRAD, Alfred H., and John R. MEYER. *The Economics of Slavery and Other Studies in Econometric History*. Chicago, 1964.

23 CONRAD, Alfred H., Douglas DOWD, Stanley ENGERMAN, Eli GINZBERG, Charles KELSO, John R. MEYER, Harry N. SCHEIBER, and Richard SUTCH. "Slavery as an Obstacle to Economic Growth in the United States: A Panel Discussion." *J Econ Hist*, XXVII (1967), 518–560.

24 CRAVEN, Avery O. "Poor Whites and Negroes in the Ante-Bellum South." See 18.4.

1 DAVIS, David B. *The Problem of Slavery in Western Culture.* Ithaca, N.Y., 1966.†

2 DEGLER, Carl N. "Slavery and the Genesis of American Race Prejudice." *Comp Stud Soc Hist*, II (1959), 49–66.

3 DONNAN, Elizabeth, ed. *Documents Illustrative of the History of the Slave Trade to America.* 4 vols. Washington, D.C., 1930–1935.

4 DONNAN, Elizabeth. "The New England Slave Trade after the Revolution." *N Eng Q*, III (1930), 251–278.

5 DONNAN, Elizabeth. "The Slave Trade into South Carolina before the Revolution." *Am Hist Rev*, XXXIII (1928), 804–828.

6 DREWRY, William S. *Slave Insurrections in Virginia (1830–1865).* Washington, D.C., 1900.

7 DU BOIS, W. E. Burghardt. *The Suppression of the African Slave Trade to the United States of America, 1638–1870.* New York, 1896.

8 DUNBAR-NELSON, Alice. "People of Color in Louisiana." *J Neg Hist*, I (1916), 361–376; II (1917), 51–78.

9 EATON, Clement. "Slave-Hiring in the Upper South: A Step Toward Freedom." *Miss Val Hist Rev*, XLVI (1960), 663–678.

10 ELKINS, Stanley M. "Culture Contacts and Negro Slavery." *Proc Am Philos Soc*, CVII (1963), 107–109.

11 ELKINS, Stanley M. *Slavery: A Problem in American Institutional and Intellectual Life.* 2nd ed. Chicago, 1968.†

12 ELKINS, Stanley M., and Eric L. MC KITRICK. "Institutions and the Law of Slavery: The Dynamics of Unopposed Capitalism." *Am Q*, IX (1957), 3–21, 159–179.

13 FISHER, Miles M. *Negro Slave Songs in the United States.* Ithaca, N.Y., 1953.

14 FISHER, Walter. "Physicians and Slavery in the Antebellum Southern Medical Journal." *J Hist Med Allied Sci*, XXIII (1968), 16–35.

15 FLANDERS, Ralph B. *Plantation Slavery in Georgia.* Chapel Hill, N.C., 1933.

16 FRANKLIN, John Hope. "The Enslavement of Free Negroes in North Carolina." *J Neg Hist*, XXIX (1944), 401–428.

17 FRANKLIN, John Hope. "Slaves Virtually Free in Ante-Bellum North Carolina." *J Neg Hist*, XXVIII (1943), 284–310.

18 FREDRICKSON, George M., and Christopher LASCH. "Resistance to Slavery." *Civil War Hist*, XIII (1967), 315–329.

19 GAINES, Francis P. *Southern Plantation.* See 15.19.

20 GEHRKE, William H. "Negro Slavery among the Germans in North Carolina." *N C Hist Rev*, XIV (1937), 307–324.

21 GENOVESE, Eugene D. *Political Economy of Slavery.* See 18.9.

22 GENOVESE, Eugene D. "Rebelliousness and Docility in the Negro Slave: A Critique of the Elkins Thesis." *Civil War Hist*, XIII (1967), 293–314.

23 GRANT, A. Cameron. "George Combe and American Slavery." *J Neg Hist*, XLV (1964), 259–269.

1   HANDLIN, Oscar, and Mary F. HANDLIN. "Origins of the Southern Labor System." See 16.1.

2   HARRIS, N. Dwight. *The History of Negro Servitude in Illinois, and of the Slavery Agitation in that State 1719–1864.* Chicago, 1904.

3   HAYWOOD, C. Robert. "Mercantilism and Colonial Slave Labor 1700–1763." *J S Hist*, XXIII (1957), 454–464.

4   HENRY, Howell M. *The Police Control of the Slave in South Carolina.* Emory, Va., 1914.

5   HOLT, Bryce R. *The Supreme Court of North Carolina and Slavery.* Durham, N.C., 1927.

6   HOWARD, Warren S. *American Slavers and the Federal Law, 1837–1862.* Berkeley, Calif., 1963.

7   HUNTER, Frances L. "Slave Society on the Southern Plantation." *J Neg Hist*, VII (1922), 1–10.

8   IMES, William L. "The Legal Status of Free Negroes and Slaves in Tennessee." *J Neg Hist*, IV (1919), 254–272.

9   IRELAND, Ralph R. "Slavery on Long Island: A Study of Economic Motivation." *J Long Island Hist*, VI (1966), 1–12.

10 JERNEGAN, Marcus W. *Laboring and Dependent Classes in Colonial America, 1607–1783.* Chicago, 1931.

11 JOHNSTON, William D. *Slavery in Rhode Island, 1755–1776.* Providence, R.I., 1894.

12 JORDAN, Winthrop D. *White Over Black: American Attitudes Toward the Negro, 1550–1812.* Chapel Hill, N.C., 1968.†

13 KENDALL, John S. "Shadow over the City." *La Hist Q*, XXII (1939), 819–856.

14 KILSON, Marion D. de B. "Towards Freedom: An Analysis of Slave Revolts in the United States." *Phylon*, XXV (1964), 175–187.

15 KLEBANER, Benjamin J. "American Manumission Laws and the Responsibility for Supporting Slaves." *Va Mag Hist Biog*, LXIII (1955), 443–453.

16 KLEIN, Herbert S. *Slavery in the Americas: A Comparative Study of Cuba and Virginia.* Chicago, 1967.

17 KLINGBERG, Frank J. *An Appraisal of the Negro in Colonial South Carolina: A Study in Americanization.* Washington, D.C., 1941.

18 LANDER, Ernest M., Jr. "Slave Labor in South Carolina Cotton Mills." *J Neg Hist*, XXXVIII (1953), 161–173.

19 LESLIE, William R. "The Pennsylvania Fugitive Slave Act of 1826." *J S Hist*, XVIII (1952), 429–445.

20 LOFTON, John. *Insurrection in South Carolina: The Turbulent World of Denmark Vesey.* Yellow Springs, Ohio, 1964.

21 MC COLLEY, Robert. *Slavery and Jeffersonian Virginia.* Urbana, Ill., 1964.

22 MC CRADY, Edward. "Slavery in the Province of South Carolina, 1670–1770." *Ann Rep Am Hist Assn*, 1895, 631–673.

1 MC DOUGLE, Ivan E. *Slavery in Kentucky, 1792–1865.* Washington, D.C., 1918.

2 MC KIBBEN, Davidson B. "Negro Slave Insurrections in Mississippi, 1800–1865." *J Neg Hist*, XXXIV (1949), 73–90.

3 MC MANUS, Edgar J. *A History of Negro Slavery in New York.* Syracuse, N.Y., 1966.

4 MC PHERSON, Robert G. "Georgia Slave Trials, 1837–1849." *Am J Leg Hist*, IV (1960), 257–284, 364–377.

5 MANNIX, Daniel P., and Malcolm COWLEY. *Black Cargoes: A History of the Atlantic Slave Trade, 1518–1865.* New York, 1962.†

6 MECKLIN, John M. "The Evolution of the Slave Status in the American Democracy." *J Neg Hist*, II (1917), 105–126, 229–251.

7 MILES, Edwin A. "The Mississippi Slave Insurrection Scare of 1835." *J Neg Hist*, XLII (1957), 48–61.

8 MILLER, William M. "Slavery and the Population of the South." *S Econ J*, XXVIII (1961), 46–54.

9 MITCHELL, Mary H. "Slavery in Connecticut and Especially in New Haven." *New Haven Hist Soc Pap*, X (1951), 286–312.

10 MOODY, V. Alton. "Slavery on Louisiana Sugar Plantations." *La Hist Q*, VII (1924), 191–301.

11 MOONEY, Chase C. *Slavery in Tennessee.* Bloomington, Ind., 1957.

12 MOORE, George H. *Notes on the History of Slavery in Massachusetts.* New York, 1866.

13 MOORE, Wilbert E. "Slave Law and the Social Structure." *J Neg Hist*, XXVI (1941), 171–202.

14 MORRIS, Richard B. "The Course of Peonage in a Slave State." *Pol Sci Q*, LXV (1950), 238–263.

15 MORRIS, Richard B. "The Measure of Bondage in the Slave States." *Miss Val Hist Rev*, XLI (1954), 219–240.

16 MOSS, Simeon F. "The Persistence of Slavery and Involuntary Servitude in a Free State (1685–1866)." *J Neg Hist*, XXV (1950), 289–314.

17 MUNFORD, Beverley B. *Virginia's Attitude Toward Slavery and Secession.* New York, 1909.

18 NICHOLS, Charles H., Jr. "Slave Narratives and the Plantation Legend." *Phylon*, X (1949), 201–209.

19 OLSON, Edwin. "Social Aspects of the Slave in New York." *J Neg Hist*, XXVI (1941), 66–77.

20 PALMER, Paul C. "Servant into Slave: The Evolution of the Legal Status of the Negro Laborer in Colonial Virginia." *S Atl Q*, LXV (1966), 355–370.

21 PANKHURST, Jessie W. "The Role of the Black Mammy in the Plantation Household." *J Neg Hist*, XXXIII (1938), 349–369.

22 PHILLIPS, Ulrich B. *American Negro Slavery: A Survey of the Supply, Employment and Control of Negro Labor as Determined by the Plantation Régime.* New York, 1918.†

1 PHILLIPS, Ulrich B. "Plantations with Slave Labor and Free." *Ag Hist*, XII (1938), 77–95.

2 PHILLIPS, Ulrich B. "Slave Crime in Virginia." *Am Hist Rev*, XX (1915), 336–340.

3 POPE-HENNESSY, James. *Sins of the Fathers: A Study of the Atlantic Slave Traders, 1441–1807*. New York, 1968.

4 POSTELL, William D. *The Health of Slaves on Southern Plantations*. Baton Rouge, La., 1951.

5 POTTER, David M., Jr. "Rise of the Plantation System in Georgia." *Ga Hist Q*, XVI (1932), 114–135.

6 PREYER, Norris W. "The Historian, the Slave, and the Ante-Bellum Textile Industry." *J Neg Hist*, XLVI (1961), 67–82.

7 PROCTOR, William G., Jr. "Slavery in Southwest Georgia." *Ga Hist Q*, XLIX (1965), 1–22.

8 REINDERS, Robert C. "Slavery in New Orleans in the Decade before the Civil War." *Mid-America*, XLIV (1962), 211–221.

9 ROTTENBERG, Simon. "The Business of Slave Trading." *S Atl Q*, LXVI (1967), 409–423.

10 RUSSELL, Marion J. "American Slave Discontent in Records of High Courts." *J Neg Hist*, XXXI (1946), 411–434.

11 SCARBOROUGH, Ruth. *The Opposition to Slavery in Georgia prior to 1860*. Nashville, Tenn., 1933.

12 SCARBOROUGH, William K. *The Overseer: Plantation Management in the Old South*. Baton Rouge, La., 1966.

13 SCHNELL, Kempes. "Anti-Slavery Influence on the Status of Slaves in a Free State." *J Neg Hist*, L (1965), 257–273.

14 SCOTT, Kenneth. "The Slave Insurrection in New York in 1712." *N Y Hist Soc Q*, XLV (1961), 43–74.

15 SELLERS, James B. *Slavery in Alabama*. University, Ala., 1950.

16 SETTLE, E. Ophelia. "Social Attitudes during the Slave Regime: Household Servants versus Field Hands." *Pub Am Socio Soc*, XXVIII (1933), 95–98.

17 SIEBERT, Wilbur H. "Slavery and White Servitude in East Florida, 1726–1776." *Fla Hist Q*, X (1931), 3–23.

18 SIO, Arnold A. "Interpretations of Slavery: The Slave Status in the Americas." *Comp Stud Soc Hist*, VII (1965), 289–308.

19 SIRMANS, M. Eugene. "The Legal Status of the Slave in South Carolina, 1670–1740." *J S Hist*, XXVIII (1962), 462–473.

20 SPECTOR, Robert M. "The Quock Walter Cases (1781–83)—Slavery, Its Abolition, and Negro Citizenship in Early Massachusetts." *J Neg Hist*, LIII (1968), 12–32.

21 STAMPP, Kenneth M. *The Peculiar Institution: Slavery in the Ante-Bellum South*. New York, 1956.†

22 STAROBIN, Robert. "Disciplining Industrial Slaves in the Old South." *J Neg Hist*, LIII (1968), 111–128.

23 STEINER, Bernard C. *History of Slavery in Connecticut*. Baltimore, 1893.

1 SWADOES, Felice. "Negro Health on the Ante Bellum Plantations." *Bull Hist Med*, X (1941), 460–472.

2 SYDNOR, Charles S. *Slavery in Mississippi.* New York, 1933.†

3 SZASZ, Ferenc M. "The New York Slave Revolt of 1741: A Re-Examination." *N Y Hist*, XLVIII (1967), 215–231.

4 TAYLOR, Joe G. *Negro Slavery in Louisiana.* Baton Rouge, La., 1963.

5 TAYLOR, Orville W. *Negro Slavery in Arkansas.* Durham, N.C., 1958.

6 TAYLOR, Paul S. "Plantation Laborer before the Civil War." *Ag Hist*, XXVIII (1954), 1–20.

7 TAYLOR, Rosser H. *Slaveholding in North Carolina: An Economic View.* Chapel Hill, N.C., 1926.

8 TREMAIN, Mary. *Slavery in the District of Columbia: The Policy of Congress and the Struggle for Abolition.* New York, 1892.

9 TREXLER, Harrison A. *Slavery in Missouri, 1804–1865.* Baltimore, 1914.

10 TURNER, Edward R. *The Negro in Pennsylvania: Slavery—Servitude— Freedom, 1639–1861.* Washington, D.C., 1911.

11 TURNER, Wallace B. "Kentucky Slavery in the Last Ante Bellum Decade." *Reg Ky Hist Soc*, LVIII (1960), 291–307.

12 WADE, Richard C. *Slavery in the Cities.* See 27.5.

13 WADE, Richard C. "The Vesey Plot: A Reconsideration." *J S Hist*, XXX (1964), 143–161.

14 WAX, Darold D. "The Demand for Slave Labor in Colonial Pennsylvania." *Pa Hist*, XXXIV (1967), 331–345.

15 WAX, Darold D. "Negro Resistance to the Early American Slave Trade." *J Neg Hist*, LI (1966), 1–15.

16 WHITFIELD, Theodore M. *Slavery Agitation in Virginia, 1829–1832.* Baltimore, 1930.

17 WILLIAMS, Edwin L., Jr. "Negro Slavery in Florida." *Fla Hist Q*, XXVIII (1949–1950), 93–110, 182–204.

18 WISH, Harvey. "American Slave Insurrections before 1861." *J Neg Hist*, XXII (1937), 299–320.

19 WISH, Harvey. "The Slave Insurrection Panic of 1856." *J S Hist*, V (1939), 206–222.

20 WOODMAN, Harold D. "The Profitability of Slavery: A Historical Perennial." *J S Hist*, XXIX (1963), 303–325.

21 WOOLFOLK, George R. "Planter Capitalism and Slavery: The Labor Thesis." *J Neg Hist*, XLI (1956), 103–116.

22 YOSHPE, Harry J. "Slave Manumissions in New York." *J Neg Hist*, XXVI (1941), 78–107.

23 YOUNGER, Richard D. "Southern Grand Juries and Slavery." *J Neg Hist*, XL (1955), 166–178.

24 ZILVERSMIT, Arthur. *The First Emancipation: The Abolition of Negro Slavery in the North.* Chicago, 1967.

3. The Free Negro, North and South

1   BLOCH, Herman D. "The New York Negro's Battle for Political Rights, 1775–1865." *Int Rev Soc Hist*, IX (1964), 65–81.

2   BREWER, James H. "Negro Property Owners in Seventeenth-Century Virginia." *Wm Mar Q*, 3rd ser., XII (1955), 575–580.

3   BROWNING, James B. "The Free Negro in Ante-Bellum North Carolina." *N C Hist Rev*, XV (1938), 23–33.

4   CALLIGARO, Lee. "The Negro's Legal Status in Pre-Civil War New Jersey." *N J Hist*, LXXXV (1967), 167–180.

5   ENGLAND, J. Merton. "The Free Negro in Ante-Bellum Tennessee." *J S Hist*, IX (1943), 37–59.

6   EVANS, W. A. "Free Negroes in Monroe County during Slavery." *J Miss Hist*, III (1941), 36–43.

7   EVERETT, Donald E. "Emigres and Militiamen: Free Persons of Color in New Orleans, 1803–1815." *J Neg Hist*, XXXVIII (1953), 377–402.

8   EVERETT, Donald E. "Free Persons of Color in Colonial Louisiana." *La Hist*, VII (1966), 21–50.

9   FLANDERS, Ralph B. "The Free Negro in Ante-Bellum Georgia." *N C Hist Rev*, IX (1932), 250–272.

10 FRANKLIN, John Hope. *The Free Negro in North Carolina, 1790–1860.* Chapel Hill, N.C., 1943.

11 FRAZIER, E. Franklin. *The Free Negro Family: A Study of Family Origins before the Civil War.* Nashville, Tenn., 1932.

12 GARVIN, Russell. "The Free Negro in Florida before the Civil War." *Fla Hist Q*, XLVI (1967), 1–18.

13 JACKSON, Luther P. *Free Negro Labor and Property Holding in Virginia, 1830–1860.* New York, 1942.

14 LITWACK, Leon F. *North of Slavery: The Negro in the Free States, 1790–1860.* Chicago, 1961.†

15 MC CONNELL, Roland C. *Negro Troops of Antebellum Louisiana: A History of the Battalion of Free Men of Color.* Baton Rouge, La., 1968.

16 REINDERS, Robert C. "The Decline of the New Orleans Free Negro in the Decade before the Civil War." *J Miss Hist*, XXIV (1962), 88–98.

17 RUSSELL, John H. *The Free Negro in Virginia, 1619–1865.* Baltimore, 1913.

18 SCHOEN, Harold. "The Free Negro in the Republic of Texas." *SW Hist Q*, XXXIX (1936), 292–308; XL (1936), 26–34.

19 SENESE, Donald J. "The Free Negro and the South Carolina Courts, 1790–1860." *S C Hist Mag*, LXVIII (1967), 140–153.

20 STAHL, Annie L. W. "The Free Negro in Ante-Bellum Louisiana." *La Hist Q*, XXV (1942), 301–396.

1 SYDNOR, Charles S. "The Free Negro in Mississippi before the Civil War." *Am Hist Rev*, XXXII (1927), 769–788.

2 THORNBROUGH, Emma Lou. *The Negro in Indiana: A Study of a Minority.* Indianapolis, Ind., 1957.

3 TURNER, Edward R. *Negro in Pennsylvania.* See 41.10.

4 WADE, Richard C. "The Negro in Cincinnati, 1800–1830." *J Neg Hist*, XXXIX (1954), 43–57.

5 WARNER, Robert A. *New Haven Negroes: A Social History.* New Haven, 1940.

6 WILSON, Charles J. "The Negro in Early Ohio." *Ohio State Arch Hist Q*, XXXIX (1930), 717–768.

7 WOODSON, Carter G. "The Negroes of Cincinnati prior to the Civil War." *J Neg Hist*, I (1916), 1–22.

8 WRIGHT, James M. *The Free Negro in Maryland, 1634–1860.* New York, 1921.

4. The Negro and His Churches

9 DU BOIS, W. E. Burghardt, ed. *The Negro Church.* Atlanta, Ga., 1903.

10 EARNEST, Joseph B. *The Religious Development of the Negro in Virginia.* Charlottesville, Va., 1914.

11 FRANKLIN, John Hope. "Negro Episcopalians in Ante-Bellum North Carolina." *Hist Mag Prot Epis Church*, XIII (1944), 216–234.

12 FRAZIER, E. Franklin. *The Negro Church in America.* Liverpool, England, 1964.

13 GOODWIN, Mary F. "Christianizing and Educating the Negro in Colonial Virginia." *Hist Mag Prot Epis Church*, I (1932), 143–152.

14 HAYNES, Leonard L., Jr. *The Negro Community within American Protestantism, 1619–1844.* Boston, 1954.

15 JACKSON, James C. "The Religious Education of the Negro in South Carolina prior to 1850." *Hist Mag Prot Epis Church*, XXXVI (1967), 35–62.

16 JACKSON, Luther P. "Religious Development of the Negro in Virginia from 1760 to 1860." *J Neg Hist*, XVI (1931), 168–239.

17 JACKSON, Luther P. "Religious Instruction of Negroes, 1830 to 1860, with Special Reference to South Carolina." *J Neg Hist*, XV (1930), 72–114.

18 JOHNSTON, Ruby F. *The Development of Negro Religion.* New York, 1954.

19 KLINGBERG, Frank J. "The S.P.G. Program for Negroes in Colonial New York." *Hist Mag Prot Epis Church*, VIII (1939), 306–371.

20 PERKINS, Haven P. "Religion for Slaves: Difficulties and Methods." *Church Hist*, X (1941), 228–245.

1 SHERER, Robert G., Jr. "Negro Churches in Rhode Island before 1860." *R I Hist*, XXV (1966), 9–24.

2 WILSON, Gold F. "The Religion of the American Negro Slave: His Attitude Toward Life and Death." *J Neg Hist*, VIII (1923), 41–71.

3 WOODSON, Carter G. *The History of the Negro Church.* 2nd ed. Washington, D.C., 1945.

5. Negro Education

4 BRIGHAM, R. I. "Negro Education in Ante-Bellum Missouri." *J Neg Hist*, XXX (1945), 405–420.

5 BULLOCK, Henry A. *A History of Negro Education in the South: From 1619 to the Present.* Cambridge, 1967.

6 MABEE, Carleton. "A Negro Boycott to Integrate Boston Schools." *N Eng Q*, XLI (1968), 341–361.

7 WOODSON, Carter G. *The Education of the Negro prior to 1861: A History of the Education of the Colored People of the United States from the Beginning of Slavery to the Civil War.* New York, 1915.

8 WRIGHT, Marian. *The Education of Negroes in New Jersey.* New York, 1941.

6. White Americans and Negro Americans

9 APTHEKER, Herbert. "The Quakers and Negro Slavery." *J Neg Hist*, XXV (1940), 331–362.

10 BERWANGER, Eugene H. *The Frontier Against Slavery: Western Anti-Negro Prejudice and the Slavery Extension Controversy.* Urbana, Ill., 1967.

11 CARROLL, Kenneth L. "Maryland Quakers and Slavery." *Md Hist Mag*, XLV (1950), 215–242.

12 DEGLER, Carl N. "Slavery and the Genesis of American Race Prejudice." See 37.2.

13 DOYLE, Bertram W. *The Etiquette of Race Relations in the South.* Chicago, 1937.

14 DRAKE, Thomas E. *Quakers and Slavery in America.* New Haven, 1950.

15 FORTENBAUGH, Robert. "American Lutheran Synods and Slavery, 1830–1860." *J Rel*, XIII (1933), 72–92.

16 GOLDSTEIN, Naomi F. *The Roots of Prejudice Against the Negro in the United States.* Boston, 1948.

17 GOSSETT, Thomas F. *Race: The History of an Idea in America.* Dallas, Tex., 1963.†

18 GREEN, Constance M. *Secret City.* See 26.4.

19 GREENE, John C. "The American Debate on the Negro's Place in Nature, 1780–1815." *J Hist Ideas*, XV (1954), 384–396.

1   GRIMSHAW, Allen D. "Lawlessness and Violence in America and Their Special Manifestations in Changing Negro-White Relationships." *J Neg Hist*, XLIV (1959), 52–72.

2   JENKINS, William S. *Pro-Slavery Thought in the Old South*, Chapel Hill, N.C., 1935.

3   JONES, Jerome W. "The Established Virginia Church and the Conversion of Negroes and Indians, 1620–1760." *J Neg Hist*, XLVI (1961), 12–31.

4   JORDAN, Winthrop D. *White over Black*. See 38.12.

5   KORN, Bertram W. "Jews and Negro Slavery in the Old South, 1789–1865." *Pub Am Jew Hist Soc*, L (1961), 151–201.

6   MATHEWS, Donald G. *Slavery and Methodism: A Chapter in American Morality, 1780–1845*. Princeton, 1965.

7   MURRAY, Andrew E. *Presbyterians and the Negro: A History*. Philadelphia, 1966.

8   NORWOOD, John N. *The Schism in the Methodist Episcopal Church, 1844: A Study of Slavery and Ecclesiastical Politics*. Alfred, N.Y., 1923.

9   NUERMBERGER, Ruth K. *The Free Produce Movement: A Quaker Protest Against Slavery*. Durham, N.C., 1942.

10 OSOFSKY, Gilbert, ed. *The Burden of Race: A Documentary History of Negro-White Relations in America*. New York, 1967.

11 POSEY, Walter B. "The Baptists and Slavery in the Lower Mississippi Valley." *J Neg Hist*, XLI (1956), 117–130.

12 POSEY, Walter B. "The Slavery Question in the Presbyterian Church in the Old Southwest." *J S Hist*, XV (1949), 311–324.

13 REDDICK, L. D. "The Negro Policy of the United States Army, 1775–1945." *J Neg Hist*, XXXIV (1949), 9–29.

14 REINDERS, Robert C. "The Churches and the Negro in New Orleans, 1850–1860." *Phylon*, XXII (1961), 241–248.

15 ROBERT, Joseph C. *The Road from Monticello: A Study of the Virginia Slavery Debate of 1832*. Durham, N.C., 1941.

16 RUCHAMES, Louis. "Jim Crow Railroads in Massachusetts." *Am Q*, VIII (1956), 61–75.

17 RUCHAMES, Louis. "The Sources of Racial Thought in Colonial America." *J Neg Hist*, LII (1967), 251–272.

18 RUCHAMES, Louis, ed. *Racial Thought in America: From the Puritans to Abraham Lincoln*. Amherst, Mass., 1969.

19 SMYTHE, Hugh H., and Martin S. PRICE. "The American Jew and Negro Slavery." *Midwest J*, VII (1956), 315–319.

20 STANTON, William R. *The Leopard's Spots: Scientific Attitudes Toward Race in America 1815–59*. Chicago, 1960.†

21 STEELY, Will F. "The Established Churches and Slavery, 1850–1860." *Reg Ky Hist Soc*, LV (1957), 97–104.

1   THEOBALD, Stephen L. "Catholic Missionary Work among the Colored People of the United States (1776–1866)." *Rec Am Cath Hist Soc Phil*, XXXV (1924–1925), 325–356.

2   TODD, Willie G. "North Carolina Baptists and Slavery." *N C Hist Rev*, XXIV (1947), 135–159.

3   WAX, Darold D. "Quaker Merchants and the Slave Trade in Colonial Pennsylvania." *Pa Mag Hist Biog*, LXXXVI (1962), 143–159.

4   WEATHERFORD, Willis D. *American Churches and the Negro: An Historical Study from Early Slave Days to the Present*. Boston, 1957.

5   WEEKS, Stephen B. *Southern Quakers and Slavery: A Study in Institutional History*. Baltimore, 1896.

VIII. Labor and Laboring Classes

1. General

6   ARKY, Louis H. "The Mechanics' Union of Trade Associations and the Formation of the Philadelphia Workingmen's Movement." *Pa Mag Hist Biog*, LXXVI (1952), 142–176.

7   BERNSTEIN, Leonard. "The Working People of Philadelphia from Colonial Times to the General Strike of 1835." *Pa Mag Hist Biog*, LXXIV (1950), 322–339.

8   BRIDENBAUGH, Carl. *The Colonial Craftsman*. New York, 1950.†

9   COMMONS, John R. *et al. History of Labour in the United States*. 4 vols. New York, 1918–1935.

10 DAITSMAN, George. "Labor and the 'Welfare State' in Early New York." *Labor Hist*, IV (1963), 248–256.

11 FONER, Philip. *History of the Labor Movement in the United States*. 4 vols. New York, 1947–1965.

12 FORBES, Allan W. "Apprenticeship in Massachusetts: Its Early Importance and Later Neglect." *Worc Hist Soc Pub*, N.S. II (1936), 5–25.

13 GINGER, Ray. "Labor in a Massachusetts Cotton Mill, 1853–60." *Bus Hist Rev*, XXVIII (1954), 67–91.

14 GITELMAN, Howard M. "The Waltham System and the Coming of the Irish." See 30.14.

15 GRIFFIN, Richard W. "Poor White Laborers in Southern Cotton Factories, 1789–1865." *S C Hist Mag*, LXI (1960), 26–40.

16 HANDLIN, Oscar, and Mary F. HANDLIN. "Origins of the Southern Labor System." See 16.1.

17 JERNEGAN, Marcus W. *Laboring and Dependent Classes*. See 38.10.

18 MC KEE, Samuel, Jr. *Labor in Colonial New York, 1664–1776*. New York, 1935.

1 MIDDLETON, Arthur P. "Colonial Craftsmen." *Am Her*, I, No. 2 (1950), 42–51.

2 MONTGOMERY, David. "The Working Classes of the Pre-Industrial City 1780–1830." See 24.5.

3 MORRIS, Richard B. *Government and Labor in Early America*. New York, 1946.†

4 MORRIS, Richard B. "Labor Controls in Maryland in the Nineteenth Century." *J S Hist*, XIV (1948), 385–400.

5 PELLING, Henry. *American Labor*. Chicago, 1960.†

6 PESSEN, Edward. *Most Uncommon Jacksonians: The Radical Leaders of the Early Labor Movement*. Albany, N.Y., 1968.

7 PESSEN, Edward. "The Workingmen's Movement of the Jacksonian Era." *Miss Val Hist Rev*, XLIII (1956), 428–443.

8 RAYBACK, Joseph G. *A History of American Labor*. New York, 1959.†

9 SULLIVAN, William A. *The Industrial Worker in Pennsylvania, 1800–1840*. Harrisburg, Pa., 1955.

10 WALSH, Richard. *Charleston's Sons of Liberty: A Study of the Artisans, 1763–1789*. Columbia, S.C., 1959.

11 WARE, Norman J. *The Industrial Worker, 1840–1860: The Reaction of American Industrial Society to the Advance of the Industrial Revolution*. Boston, 1924.†

12 WESLEY, Charles H. *Negro Labor in the United States*. See 36.2.

2. Involuntary Servitude

13 BALLAGH, James C. *White Servitude in the Colony of Virginia: A Study of the System of Indentured Labor in the American Colonies*. Baltimore, 1895.

14 BIEHL, Katherine L. "The Indentured Servant in Colonial America." *Soc Stud*, XXXVI (1945), 316–319.

15 HAAR, Charles M. "White Indentured Servants in Colonial New York." *Americana*, XXXIV (1940), 370–392.

16 HERRICK, Cheesman A. *White Servitude in Pennsylvania: Indentured and Redemption Labor in Colony and Commonwealth*, Philadelphia, 1926.

17 JERNEGAN, Marcus W. *Laboring and Dependent Classes*. See 38.10.

18 LAUBER, Almon W. *Indian Slavery in Colonial Times Within the Present Limits of the United States*. New York, 1913.

19 MC CORMAC, Eugene I. *White Servitude in Maryland, 1634–1820*. Baltimore, 1904.

20 MILLER, William. "The Effects of the American Revolution on Indentured Servitude." *Pa Hist*, VII (1940), 131–141.

21 MORRIS, Richard B. "White Bondage in Ante-Bellum South Carolina." *S C Hist Geneal Mag*, LXIX (1948), 191–207.

22 SMITH, Abbot E. *Colonists in Bondage: White Servitude and Convict Labor in America, 1607–1776*. Chapel Hill, N.C., 1947.

1 SMITH, Abbot E. "The Indentured Servant and Land Speculation in Seventeenth Century Maryland." *Am Hist Rev*, XL (1935), 467–472.

2 SMITH, Abbot E. "Indentured Servants: New Light on Some of America's 'First' Families." *J Econ Hist*, II (1942), 40–53.

3 SMITH, Warren B. *White Servitude in Colonial South Carolina*. Columbia, S.C., 1961.

4 TOWNER, Lawrence W. " 'A Fondness for Freedom': Servant Protest in Puritan Society." *Wm Mar Q*, 3rd ser., XIX (1962), 201–219.

IX. Domestic Institutions

1. Women in American Society

5 ABBOTT, Edith. *Women in Industry: A Study in American Economic History*. New York, 1910.

6 ADAMS, Horace. "A Puritan Wife on the Frontier." *Miss Val Hist Rev*, XXVII (1941), 67–84.

7 BEARD, Mary R. *Woman as Force in History: A Study in Traditions and Realities*. New York, 1946.†

8 BENSON, Mary S. *Women in Eighteenth-Century America: A Study of Opinion and Social Usage*. New York, 1935.

9 BLAKE, John B. "Women and Medicine in Ante-Bellum America." *Bull Hist Med*, XXXIX (1965), 99–123.

10 BLUMENTHAL, Walter H. *Women Camp Followers of the American Revolution*. Philadelphia, 1952.

11 COMETTI, Elizabeth. "Women in the American Revolution." *N Eng Q*, XX (1947), 329–346.

12 DEXTER, Elizabeth W. *Colonial Women of Affairs: A Study of Women in Business and the Professions in America before 1776*. Boston, 1924.

13 DITZION, Sidney H. *Marriage, Morals, and Sex in America: A History of Ideas*. New York, 1953.

14 EARLE, Alice M. *Colonial Dames and Good Wives*. Boston, 1895.

15 GRIMES, Alan P. *The Puritan Ethic and Woman Suffrage*. New York, 1967.

16 HOLLIDAY, Carl. *Woman's Life in Colonial Days*. Boston, 1922.

17 KRADITOR, Aileen S., ed. *Up from the Pedestal: Selected Writings in the History of American Feminism*. Chicago, 1968.

18 LUTZ, Alma. *Crusade for Freedom: Women of the Antislavery Movement*. Boston, 1968.

19 MC CLELLAND, Clarence P. "The Education of Females in Early Illinois." *J Ill State Hist Soc*, XXXVI (1943), 378–407.

1   MELDER, Keith. "Ladies Bountiful: Organized Women's Benevolence in Early 19th-Century America." *N Y Hist*, XLVIII (1967), 231–255.

2   MOSES, Mary S. "The Pioneer Woman." *Historian*, II (1939), 5–16.

3   PINCHBECK, Ivy. *Women Workers and the Industrial Revolution, 1750–1850*. New York, 1930.

4   RIEGEL, Robert E. "Women's Clothes and Women's Rights." *Am Q*, XV (1963), 390–401.

5   SINCLAIR, Andrew. *The Emancipation of the American Woman*. New York, 1966.†

6   SMITH, Thelma M. "Feminism in Philadelphia, 1790–1850." *Pa Mag Hist Biog*, LXVIII (1944), 243–268.

7   SPRUILL, Julia C. *Woman's Life and Work in the Southern Colonies*. Chapel Hill, N.C., 1938.

8   STANTON, Elizabeth C., Susan B. ANTHONY, and Matilda J. GAGE, eds. *History of Woman Suffrage*. 6 vols. New York and Rochester, 1881–1922.

9   TAYLOR, James M. *Before Vassar Opened: A Contribution to the History of Higher Education of Women in America*. Boston, 1914.

10 TREUDLEY, Mary B. "The 'Benevolent Fair': A Study of Charitable Organizations among American Women in the First Third of the Nineteenth Century." *Soc Serv Rev*, XIV (1940), 509–522.

11 WELTER, Barbara. "Anti-Intellectualism and the American Woman: 1800–1860." *Mid-America*, XLVIII (1966), 258–270.

12 WELTER, Barbara. "The Cult of True Womanhood: 1820–1860." *Am Q*, XVIII (1966), 151–174.

13 WOODY, Thomas. *A History of Women's Education in the United States*. 2 vols. New York, 1929.

2. Children and Childhood

14 ABBOTT, Grace, ed. *The Child and the State*. 2 vols. Chicago, 1938.

15 CALEY, Percy B. "Child Life in Colonial Western Pennsylvania." *W Pa Hist Mag*, IX (1926), 33–49, 104–121, 188–201, 256–275.

16 EARLE, Alice M. *Child Life in Colonial Days*. New York, 1899.

17 FLEMING, Sandford. *Children & Puritanism: The Place of Children in the Life and Thought of the New England Churches, 1620–1847*. New Haven, 1933.

18 HOMAN, Walter J. *Children & Quakerism: A Study of the Place of Children in the Theory and Practice of the Society of Friends*. Berkeley, Calif., 1939.

19 JACOBY, George P. *Catholic Child Care in Nineteenth Century New York: With a Correlated Summary of Public and Protestant Child Welfare*. Washington, D.C., 1941.

20 KIEFER, Monica M. *American Children Through Their Books, 1700–1835*. Philadelphia, 1948.

1　KUHN, Anne L. *The Mother's Role in Childhood Education: New England Concepts, 1830–1860.* New Haven, 1947.

2　O'BRIEN, Edward J. *Child Welfare Legislation in Maryland 1634–1936.* Washington, D.C., 1937.

3　PICKETT, Robert S. *House of Refuge: Origins of Juvenile Reform in New York State, 1815–1857.* Syracuse, N.Y., 1969.

4　ROSENBACH, Abraham S. W. *Early American Children's Books.* Portland, Me., 1933.

5　SLOANE, William. *Children's Books in England & America in the Seventeenth Century: A History and Checklist: Together with the Young Christian's Library, the First Printed Catalogue of Books for Children.* New York, 1955.

6　WISHY, Bernard. *The Child and the Republic: The Dawn of Modern American Child Nurture.* Philadelphia, 1968.

3. The Family and Marriage

7　ADAMS, Charles F. "Some Phases of Sexual Morality and Church Discipline in Colonial New England." *Proc Mass Hist Soc,* 2nd ser., VI (1891), 477–516.

8　BLAKE, Nelson M. *The Road to Reno: A History of Divorce in the United States.* New York, 1962.

9　BRECKINRIDGE, Sophonisba P., ed. *The Family and the State: Select Documents.* Chicago, 1934.

10　BRIDGES, William E. "Family Patterns and Social Values in America, 1825–1875." *Am Q,* XVII (1965), 3–11.

11　CALHOUN, Arthur W. *A Social History of the American Family from Colonial Times to the Present.* 3 vols. Cleveland, Ohio, 1917–1919.

12　DEMOS, John. "Families in Colonial Bristol, Rhode Island: An Exercise in Historical Demography." *Wm Mar Q,* 3rd ser., XXV (1968), 40–57.

13　DITZION, Sidney H. *Marriage, Morals, and Sex.* See 48.13.

14　EARLE, Alice M. *Home Life in Colonial Days.* New York, 1898.

15　FRAZIER, E. Franklin. *Negro Family.* See 35.5.

16　FRAZIER, E. Franklin. *Free Negro Family.* See 42.11.

17　GOODSELL, Willystine. *A History of the Family as a Social and Educational Institution.* New York, 1915.

18　GOODSELL, Willystine. *A History of Marrige and the Family.* Rev. ed. New York, 1934.

19　GREVEN, Philip J., Jr. "Family Structure in Seventeenth-Century Andover, Massachusetts." *Wm Mar Q,* 3rd ser., XXIII (1966), 234–256.

20　HOWARD, George E. *A History of Matrimonial Institutions, Chiefly in England and the United States, with an Introductory Analysis of the Literature and the Theories of Primitive Marriage and the Family.* 3 vols. Chicago, 1904.

1 JOHNSON, Guion G. "Courtship and Marriage Customs in Ante-Bellum North Carolina." *N C Hist Rev*, VIII (1931), 384–402.

2 LANTZ, Herman R., Margaret BRITTON, Raymond SCHMITT, and Eloise C. SNYDER. "Pre-Industrial Patterns in the Colonial Family in America: A Content Analysis of Colonial Magazines." *Am Socio Rev*, XXXIII (1968), 413–426.

3 MORGAN, Edmund S. *The Puritan Family: Essays on Religion and Domestic Relations in Seventeenth-Century New England.* Boston, 1944.†

4 MORGAN, Edmund S. *Virginians at Home: Family Life in the Eighteenth Century.* Williamsburg, Va., 1952.†

5 POWELL, Chilton L. "Marriage in Early New England." *N Eng Q*, I (1928), 323–334.

6 RIEGEL, Robert E. "Changing American Attitudes toward Prostitution (1800–1920)." *J Hist Ideas*, XXIX (1968), 437–452.

7 ROTHMAN, David J. "A Note on the Study of the Colonial Family." *Wm Mar Q*, 3rd ser., XXIII (1966), 627–634.

8 SPALLETTA, Matteo. "Divorce in Colonial New York." *N Y Hist Soc Q*, XXXIX (1955), 422–440.

9 TAYLOR, Orville W. " 'Jumping the Broomstick': Slave Marriage and Morality in Arkansas." *Ark Hist Q*, XVII (1958), 217–231.

X. Religion and Religious Groups

1. General

10 BRAUER, Jerald C. *Protestantism in America: A Narrative History.* Philadelphia, 1953.

11 BRIDENBAUGH, Carl. *Mitre and Sceptre: Transatlantic Faiths, Ideas, Personalities, and Politics, 1689–1775.* New York, 1962.†

12 CLEBSCH, William A. *From Sacred to Profane America: The Role of Religion in American History.* New York, 1968.

13 CURRAN, Francis X. *The Churches and the Schools: American Protestantism and Popular Elementary Education.* Chicago, 1954.

14 CURRAN, Francis X. *Major Trends in American Church History.* New York, 1946.

15 DALZELL, George W. *Benefit of Clergy in America and Related Matters.* Winston-Salem, N.C., 1955.

16 DRUMMOND, Andrew L. *Story of American Protestantism.* Boston, 1950.

17 EDDY, George S. *The Kingdom of God and the American Dream: The Religious and Secular Ideals of American History.* New York, 1941.

18 GAUSTAD, Edwin S. *Historical Atlas of Religion in America.* New York, 1962.

1 HANLEY, Thomas O. "Colonial Protestantism and the Rise of Democracy." *Am Eccles Rev*, CXLI (1959), 24–32.

2 HARDON, John A. *The Protestant Churches of America*. Westminster, Md., 1957.†

3 HEIMERT, Alan. *Religion and the American Mind: From the Great Awakening to the Revolution*. Cambridge, 1966.

4 HUDSON, Winthrop S. *American Protestantism*. Chicago, 1961.†

5 HUDSON, Winthrop S. *The Great Tradition of the American Churches*. New York, 1953.

6 HUDSON, Winthrop S. *Religion in America*. New York, 1965.†

7 HUMPHREY, Edward F. *Nationalism and Religion in America, 1774–1789*. Boston, 1924.

8 JAMISON, Wallace N. *Religion in New Jersey: A Brief History*. Princeton, 1964.

9 KOCH, G. Adolf. *Republican Religion: The American Revolution and the Cult of Reason*. New York, 1933.

10 LOETSCHER, Lefferts A. "The Problem of Christian Unity in Early Nineteenth-Century America." *Church Hist*, XXXII (1963), 3–16.

11 MEAD, Frank S. *See These Banners Go: The Story of the Protestant Churches in America*. Indianapolis, Ind., 1936.

12 MEAD, Sidney E. "Denominationalism: The Shape of Protestantism in America." *Church Hist*, XXII (1953), 279–297; XXIII (1954), 291–320.

13 MEAD, Sidney E. "From Coercion to Persuasion: Another Look at the Rise of Religious Liberty and the Emergence of Denominationalism." *Church Hist*, XXV (1956), 317–337.

14 MEAD, Sidney E. *The Lively Experiment: The Shaping of Christianity in America*. New York, 1963.

15 MODE, Peter G. *The Frontier Spirit in American Christianity*. New York, 1923.

16 MORAIS, Herbert M. *Deism in Eighteenth Century America*. New York, 1934.

17 NICHOLS, Roy F. *Religion and American Democracy*. Baton Rouge, La., 1959.

18 NIEBUHR, H. Richard. *The Kingdom of God in America*. Chicago, 1937.†

19 NIEBUHR, H. Richard. *The Social Sources of Denominationalism*. New York, 1929.

20 POSEY, Walter B. *Frontier Mission: A History of Religion West of the Southern Appalachians to 1861*. Lexington, Ky., 1966.

21 SMITH, James W., and A. Leland JAMISON, eds. *Religion in American Life*. See 1.8.

22 SMITH, Timothy L. "Congregation, State, and Denomination: The Forming of the American Religious Structure." *Wm Mar Q*, 3rd ser., XXV (1968), 155–176.

1 SWEET, William W. *American Culture and Religion: Six Essays.* Dallas, Tex., 1951.

2 SWEET, William W. *Circuit-Rider Days in Indiana.* Indianapolis, Ind., 1916.

3 SWEET, William W. *Religion in Colonial America.* New York, 1942.

4 SWEET, William W. *Religion in the Development of American Culture, 1765–1840.* New York, 1952.

5 SWEET, William W. *The Story of Religion in America.* 2nd ed. New York, 1950.

2. Protestants and Protestantism

A. THE CLERGY

6 BALDWIN, Alice M. *The New England Clergy and the American Revolution.* Durham, N.C., 1928.

7 BODO, John R. *The Protestant Clergy and Public Issues, 1812–1848.* Princeton, 1954.

8 COLE, Charles C. *The Social Ideas of the Northern Evangelists, 1826–1860.* New York, 1954.

9 CROSS, Arthur L. *The Anglican Episcopate and the American Colonies.* New York, 1902.

10 GAMBRELL, Mary L. *Ministerial Training in Eighteenth-Century New England.* New York, 1937.

11 RIGHTMYER, Nelson W. "The Character of the Anglican Clergy of Colonial Maryland." *Md Hist Mag,* XLIV (1949), 229–250.

12 SHIPTON, Clifford K. "The New England Clergy of the 'Glacial Age'." *Pub Col Soc Mass, Trans,* XXXII (1933–1937), 24–54.

13 VAN TYNE, Claude H. "Influence of the Clergy, and of Religious and Sectarian Forces, on the American Revolution." *Am Hist Rev,* XIX (1913), 44–64.

14 WEIS, Frederick L. *The Colonial Churches and the Colonial Clergy of the Middle and Southern Colonies, 1607–1776.* Lancaster, Mass., 1938.

15 WEIS, Frederick L. *The Colonial Clergy and the Colonial Churches of New England.* Lancaster, Mass., 1936.

16 WEIS, Frederick L. *The Colonial Clergy of Maryland, Delaware, and Georgia.* Lancaster, Mass., 1950.

17 WEIS, Frederick L. "The Colonial Clergy of New York, New Jersey, and Pennsylvania 1628–1776." *Proc Am Ant Soc,* LXVI (1956), 167–351.

18 WEIS, Frederick L. *The Colonial Clergy of Virginia, North Carolina, and South Carolina.* Boston, 1955.

B. LOCAL AND DENOMINATIONAL HISTORIES

1   ADDISON, James T. *The Episcopal Church in the United States, 1789–1931.* New York, 1951.

2   ALBRIGHT, Raymond W. *A History of the Protestant Episcopal Church.* New York, 1964.

3   ANDERSON, Nels. *Desert Saints: The Mormon Frontier in Utah.* Chicago, 1942.†

4   APTHEKER, Herbert. "The Quakers and Negro Slavery." See 44.9.

5   ATKINS, Gaius G., and Frederick L. FAGLEY. *History of American Congregationalism.* Boston, 1942.

6   BOASE, Paul H. "The Methodist Circuit Rider in Southern Ohio." *Bull Hist Philos Soc Ohio,* XII (1954), 27–37.

7   BOASE, Paul H. "Slavery and the Ohio Circuit Rider." *Ohio Hist Q,* LXIV (1955), 195–205.

8   BRINTON, Howard H. *Friends for 300 Years: The History and Beliefs of the Society of Friends Since George Fox Started the Quaker Movement.* New York, 1952.†

9   BROCK, Henry I. *Colonial Churches in Virginia.* Richmond, Va., 1930.

10 BRODIE, Fawn M. *No Man Knows My History: The Life of Joseph Smith, the Mormon Prophet.* New York, 1945.

11 BRONNER, Edwin B. "Intercolonial Relations Among Quakers before 1750." *Quaker Hist,* LVI (1967), 3–17.

12 BROWN, James H. "Presbyterian Social Influence in Early Ohio." *J Presby Hist Soc,* XXX (1952), 209–235.

13 BRYDON, George M. *Virginia's Mother Church and the Conditions Under Which it Grew.* 2 vols. Richmond, Va., 1947–1952.

14 BURR, Nelson R. *The Anglican Church in New Jersey.* Philadelphia, 1954.

15 CABANISS, Frances A., and James A. CABANISS. "Religion in Ante-Bellum Mississippi." *J Miss Hist,* VI (1944), 191–224.

16 CANNON, M. Hamlin. "Migration of English Mormons to America." *Am Hist Rev,* LII (1946), 436–455.

17 CARROLL, Kenneth L. "Maryland Quakers and Slavery." See 44.11.

18 CARROLL, Kenneth L. "Maryland Quakers in the Seventeenth Century." *Md Hist Mag,* XLVII (1952), 297–313.

19 CARROLL, Kenneth L. "Persecution of Quakers in Early Maryland (1658–1661)." *Quaker Hist,* LIII (1964), 67–80.

20 CONKIN, Paul. "The Church Establishment in North Carolina, 1765–1776." *N C Hist Rev,* XXXI (1955), 1–30.

21 COOKE, George W. *Unitarianism in America: A History of its Origin and Development.* Boston, 1902.

22 COX, John, Jr. *Quakerism in the City of New York, 1657–1930.* New York, 1930.

23 DAVIDSON, Elizabeth H. *The Establishment of the English Church in the Continental American Colonies.* Durham, N.C., 1936.

1 DAVIS, David B. "The New England Origins of Mormonism." *N Eng Q*, XXVI (1953), 147–168.

2 DE PILLIS, Mario S. "The Social Sources of Mormonism." *Church Hist*, XXXVII (1968), 50–79.

3 DES CHAMPS, Margaret B. "The Church as a Social Center." *J Presby Hist Soc*, XXXI (1953), 157–165.

4 DOHERTY, Robert W. *The Hicksite Separation: A Sociological Analysis of Religious Schism in Early Nineteenth-Century America.* New Brunswick, N.J., 1967.

5 DOHERTY, Robert W. "Social Bases for the Presbyterian Schism of 1837–1838: The Philadelphia Case." *J Soc Hist*, II (1968), 69–79.

6 DOUGLASS, Harlan P. *Christian Reconstruction in the South.* Boston, 1909.

7 DRAKE, Thomas E. *Quakers and Slavery.* See 44.14.

8 EDDY, Richard. *Universalism in America: A History.* 2 vols. Boston, 1884–1886.

9 ERVIN, Spencer. "The Anglican Church in North Carolina." *Hist Mag Prot Epis Church*, XXV (1956), 102–161.

10 ERVIN, Spencer. "The Established Church of Colonial Maryland." *Hist Mag Prot Epis Church*, XXIV (1955), 232–292.

11 FLANDERS, Robert B. *Nauvoo: Kingdom on the Mississippi.* Urbana, Ill., 1965.

12 FORTENBAUGH, Robert. "American Lutheran Synods and Slavery, 1830–1860." See 44.15.

13 FURNISS, Norman F. *The Mormon Conflict, 1850–1859.* New Haven, 1960.†

14 GAMBRALL, Theodore C. *Church Life in Colonial Maryland.* Baltimore, 1885.

15 GARDINER, John H., Jr. "The Beginnings of the Presbyterian Church in the Southern Colonies." *J Presby Hist Soc*, XXXIV (1956), 36–52.

16 GARRISON, Winfred E., and Alfred T. DE GROOT. *The Disciples of Christ: A History.* St. Louis, Mo., 1948.

17 GOLLIN, Gillian L. *Moravians in Two Worlds: A Study of Changing Communities.* New York, 1967.

18 GOODWIN, Edward L. *The Colonial Church in Virginia.* Milwaukee, Wis., 1927.

19 GREENE, Evarts B. "The Anglican Outlook on the American Colonies in the Early Eighteenth Century." *Am Hist Rev*, XX (1914), 64–85.

20 HANSEN, Klaus J. *Quest for Empire: The Political Kingdom of God and the Council of Fifty in Mormon History.* East Lansing, Mich., 1967.

21 HARRELL, David E., Jr. *Quest for a Christian America: The Disciples of Christ and American Society to 1866.* Nashville, Tenn., 1966.

1 HOMAN, Walter J. *Children & Quakerism.* See 49.18.

2 KLINGBERG, Frank J. "The Expansion of the Anglican Church in the Eighteenth Century." *Hist Mag Prot Epis Church*, XVI (1947), 292–301.

3 JOHNSON, Roy H. "Frontier Religion in Western Pennsylvania." *W Pa Hist Mag*, XVI (1933), 23–37.

4 JONES, Rufus M. *The Quakers in the American Colonies.* London, 1911.

5 KLETT, Guy S. *Presbyterians in Colonial Pennsylvania.* Philadelphia, 1937.

6 LEVY, Babette M. *Preaching in the First Half Century of New England History.* Hartford, Conn., 1945.

7 LINDLEY, Harlow. "The Quakers in the Old Northwest." *Proc Miss Val Hist Assn*, V (1911–1912), 60–72.

8 MC NIFF, William J. *Heaven on Earth: A Planned Mormon Society.* Oxford, Ohio, 1940.

9 MANROSS, William W. *A History of the American Episcopal Church.* 2nd ed. New York, 1950.

10 MATHEWS, Donald G. *Slavery and Methodism.* See 45.6.

11 MILLER, Perry. *Orthodoxy in Massachusetts, 1630–1650: A Genetic Study.* Cambridge, 1933.

12 MIYAKAWA, T. Scott. *Protestants and Pioneers: Individualism and Conformity on the American Frontier.* Chicago, 1964.

13 MOATS, Francis I. "The Rise of Methodism in the Middle West." *Miss Val Hist Rev*, XV (1928), 67–88.

14 MOODY, V. Alton. "Early Religious Efforts in the Lower Mississippi Valley." *Miss Val Hist Rev*, XXII (1935), 161–176.

15 MURRAY, Andrew E. *Presbyterians and the Negro.* See 45.7.

16 MYERS, Albert C. *Immigration of the Irish Quakers into Pennsylvania.* See 30.19.

17 NORWOOD, John N. *Schism in the Methodist Episcopal Church, 1844.* See 45.8.

18 NOTTINGHAM, Elizabeth K. *Methodism and the Frontier: Indiana Proving Ground.* New York, 1941.

19 NUERMBERGER, Ruth K. *Free Produce Movement.* See 45.9.

20 OBERHOLZER, Emil, Jr. *Delinquent Saints: Disciplinary Action in the Early Congregational Churches of Massachusetts.* New York, 1956.

21 O'DEA, Thomas F. *The Mormons.* Chicago, 1957.†

22 PARK, Charles E. "Puritans and Quakers." *N Eng Q*, XXVII (1954), 53–74.

23 PENNINGTON, Edgar L. "Beginnings of the Church of England in Georgia." *Hist Mag Prot Epis Church*, I (1932), 222–234.

24 PENNINGTON, Edgar L. "The Beginnings of the Church of England in South Carolina." *Hist Mag Prot Epis Church*, II (1933), 178–194.

1 PETERS, John L. *Christian Perfection and American Methodism*. New York, 1956.

2 PHILIPS, Edith. *The Good Quaker in French Legend*. Philadelphia, 1932.

3 POSEY, Walter B. "The Baptists and Slavery in the Lower Mississippi Valley." See 45.11.

4 POSEY, Walter B. *The Development of Methodism in the Old Southwest, 1783–1824*. Nashville, Tenn., 1933.

5 POSEY, Walter B. "The Protestant Episcopal Church: An American Adaptation." *J S Hist*, XXV (1959), 3–30.

6 POSEY, Walter B. *Religious Strife on the Southern Frontier*. Baton Rouge, La., 1965.

7 POSEY, Walter B. "The Slavery Question in the Presbyterian Church in the Old Southwest." See 45.12.

8 REINDERS, Robert C. "The Churches and the Negro in New Orleans, 1850–1860." See 45.14.

9 RIGHTMYER, Nelson W. *The Anglican Church in Delaware*. Philadelphia, 1947.

10 RIGHTMYER, Nelson W. *Maryland's Established Church*. Baltimore, 1956.

11 ROLL, Charles. "The Quaker in Anglo-American Cultural Relations." *Ind Mag Hist*, XLV (1949), 135–146.

12 SEARS, Clara. *Days of Delusion: A Strange Bit of History*. Boston, 1924.

13 SEILER, William H. "The Anglican Parish Vestry in Colonial Virginia." *J S Hist*, XXII (1956), 310–337.

14 SLOSSER, Gaius J., ed. *They Seek a Country: The American Presbyterians, Some Aspects*. New York, 1955.

15 SMITH, Elwyn A. "The Role of the South in the Presbyterian Schism of 1837–38." *Church Hist*, XXIX (1960), 44–63.

16 STAIGER, C. Bruce. "Abolitionism and the Presbyterian Schism of 1837–1838." *Miss Val Hist Rev*, XXXVI (1949), 391–414.

17 STEELY, Will F. "The Established Churches and Slavery, 1850–1860." See 45.21.

18 STEPHENSON, George M. *Religious Aspects of Swedish Immigration*. See 33.6.

19 SUAREZ, Raleigh A. "Religion in Rural Louisiana, 1850–1860." *La Hist Q*, XXXVIII (1955), 55–63.

20 SWEET, William W. *Methodism in American History*. Rev. ed. Nashville, Tenn., 1954.

21 SWEET, William W., ed. *Religion on the American Frontier*. 4 vols. New York and Chicago, 1931–1946.

22 THACKER, Joseph A., Jr. "The Concept of Sin in Kentucky during the 1830–1860 Period." *Reg Ky Hist Soc*, LXIV (1966), 121–128.

1 THOMAS, Allen C. *A History of the Friends in America*. 6th ed. Philadelphia, 1930.

2 TODD, Willie G. "North Carolina Baptists and Slavery." See 46.2.

3 TOLLES, Frederick B. *The Atlantic Community of the Early Friends*. London, 1952.

4 TOLLES, Frederick B. *Quakers and the Atlantic Culture*. New York, 1960.

5 TORBET, Robert G. *A History of the Baptists*. Philadelphia, 1950.

6 TRINTERUD, Leonard J. *The Forming of an American Tradition: A Reexamination of Colonial Presbyterianism*. Philadelphia, 1949.

7 VORPHAL, Ben M. "Presbyterianism and the Frontier Hypothesis: Tradition and Modification in the American Garden." *J Presby Hist*, XLV (1967), 180–192.

8 WAX, Darold D. "Quaker Merchants and the Slave Trade in Colonial Pennsylvania." See 46.3.

9 WEATHERFORD, Willis D. *American Churches and the Negro*. See 46.4.

10 WEEKS, Stephen B. *Southern Quakers and Slavery*. See 46.5.

11 WENTZ, Abdel R. *A Basic History of Lutheranism in America*. Philadelphia, 1955.

12 WILBUR, Earl M. *A History of Unitarianism: Socinianism and Its Antecedents*. Cambridge, 1945.

13 WILBUR, Earl M. *A History of Unitarianism, in Transylvania, England, and America*. Cambridge, 1952.

14 WRIGHT, Conrad. *The Beginnings of Unitarianism in America*. Boston, 1955.†

15 ZWIERLEIN, Frederick J. *Religion in New Netherland: A History of the Development of the Religious Conditions in the Province of New Netherland, 1623–1664*. Rochester, N.Y., 1910.

C. REVIVALISM AND THE GREAT AWAKENINGS

16 BROWN, Robert M. "Frontier Revivalism in Kentucky, 1799–1805." *Historian*, IV (1941), 68–83.

17 BRYNESTAD, Lawrence E. "The Great Awakening in the New England and Middle Colonies." *J Presby Hist Soc*, XIV (1930), 80–91, 104–141.

18 CHASE, Wayland J. " 'The Great Awakening' and Its Educational Consequences." *Sch Soc*, XXXV (1932), 443–449.

19 CLEVELAND, Catherine C. *The Great Revival in the West, 1797–1805*. Chicago, 1916.

20 COLE, Charles C. *Social Ideas of the Northern Evangelists*. See 53.8.

21 COWING, Cedric B. "Sex and Preaching in the Great Awakening." *Am Q*, XX (1968), 624–644.

1   CROSS, Whitney R. *The Burned-Over District: The Social and Intellectual History of Enthusiastic Religion in Western New York, 1800–1850.* Ithaca, N.Y., 1950.†

2   EATON, Clement. "The Ebb of the Great Revival." *N C Hist Rev*, XXIII (1946), 1–12.

3   FRANCIS, Russell E. "The Religious Revival of 1858 in Philadelphia." *Pa Mag Hist Biog*, LXX (1946), 52–77.

4   GAUSTAD, Edwin S. *The Great Awakening in New England.* New York, 1957.†

5   GEWEHR, Wesley M. *The Great Awakening in Virginia, 1740–1790.* Durham, N.C., 1930.

6   GOEN, C. C. *Revivalism and Separatism in New England, 1740–1800: Strict Congregationalists and Separate Baptists in the Great Awakening.* New Haven, 1962.

7   JOHNSON, Charles A. *The Frontier Camp Meeting: Religion's Harvest Time.* Dallas, Tex., 1955.

8   JOHNSON, Guion G. "The Camp Meeting in Ante-Bellum North Carolina." *N C Hist Rev*, X (1933), 95–110.

9   JOHNSON, Guion G. "Revival Movements in Ante-Bellum North Carolina." *N C Hist Rev*, X (1933), 1–20.

10   JOHNSTON, James E. "Charles G. Finney and Oberlin Perfectionism." *J Presby Hist*, XLVI (1968), 42–57, 128–138.

11   KELLER, Charles R. *The Second Great Awakening in Connecticut.* New Haven, 1942.

12   LABAREE, Leonard W. "The Conservative Attitude Toward the Great Awakening." *Wm Mar Q*, 3rd ser., I (1944), 331–352.

13   LYNCH, William O. "The Great Awakening." *Ind Mag Hist*, XLI (1945), 107–130.

14   MC LOUGHLIN, William G., Jr. *Modern Revivalism: Charles Grandison Finney to Billy Graham.* New York, 1959.

15   MATHEWS, Donald G. "The Second Great Awakening as an Organizing Process, 1780–1830: An Hypothesis." *Am Q*, XXI (1969), 23–43.

16   MAXSON, Charles H. *The Great Awakening in the Middle Colonies.* Chicago, 1920.

17   MITCHELL, Mary H. *The Great Awakening and Other Revivals in the Religious Life of Connecticut.* New Haven, 1934.

18   MORGAN, David T., Jr. "The Great Awakening in North Carolina, 1740–1775: The Baptist Phase." *N C Hist Rev*, XLV (1968), 264–283.

19   MUNCY, William L. *A History of Evangelism in the United States.* Kansas City, Mo., 1945.

20   ROBERTSON, Archibald T. *That Old-Time Religion.* Boston, 1950.

21   ROTHERMUND, Dietmar. *Layman's Progress.* See 31.15.

22   SHURTER, Robert L. "The Camp Meeting in the Early Life and Literature of the Mid-West." *E Tenn Hist Soc Pub*, V (1933), 142–149.

23   SMITH, Timothy L. *Revivalism and Social Reform in Mid-Nineteenth-Century America.* New York, 1957.†

1 SWEET, William W. *Revivalism in America: Its Origin, Growth and Decline.* New York, 1944.†

2 TOLLES, Frederick B. "Quietism Versus Enthusiasm: The Philadelphia Quakers and the Great Awakening." *Pa Mag Hist Biog*, LXIX (1945), 26–49.

3 WEISBERGER, Bernard A. *They Gathered at the River: The Story of the Great Revivalists and Their Impact Upon Religion in America.* Boston, 1958.†

4 WINDELL, Marie G. "The Camp Meeting in Missouri." *Mo Hist Rev*, XXXVII (1943), 253–270.

D. PHILANTHROPIC, EDUCATIONAL, AND MISSIONARY ACTIVITIES

5 BARCLAY, Wade C. *History of Methodist Missions.* New York, 1949.

6 BEARD, Augustus F. *A Crusade of Brotherhood: A History of the American Missionary Association.* New York, 1909.

7 BEAVER, R. Pierce. "American Missionary Motivation before the Revolution." *Church Hist*, XXXI (1962), 216–226.

8 BERKHOFER, Robert F., Jr. *Salvation and the Savage: An Analysis of Protestant Missions and American Indian Response, 1787–1862.* Lexington, Ky., 1965.

9 BREWER, Clifton H. *A History of Religious Education in the Episcopal Church to 1835.* New Haven, 1924.

10 CLARK, Joseph B. *Leavening the Nation: The Story of American Home Missions.* New York, 1903.

11 DES CHAMPS, Margaret B. "Presbyterians and Southern Education." *J Presby Hist Soc*, XXXI (1953), 113–124.

12 DRURY, Clifford M. *Presbyterian Panorama: One Hundred and Fifty Years of National Missions History.* Philadelphia, 1952.

13 ELSBREE, Oliver W. *The Rise of the Missionary Spirit in America, 1790–1815.* Williamsport, Pa., 1928.

14 FOSTER, Charles I. *An Errand of Mercy: The Evangelical United Front, 1790–1837.* Chapel Hill, N.C., 1960.

15 GEFFEN, Elizabeth M. "Philadelphia Protestantism Reacts to Social Reform Movements before the Civil War." *Pa Hist*, XXX (1963), 192–212.

16 GOODYKOONTZ, Colin B. *Home Missions on the American Frontier.* Caldwell, Idaho, 1939.

17 GREEN, Fletcher M. "Northern Missionary Activities in the South, 1846–1861." *J S Hist*, XXI (1955), 147–172.

18 GRIFFIN, Clifford S. *Their Brothers' Keepers: Moral Stewardship in the United States, 1800–1865.* New Brunswick, N.J., 1960.

19 HOPKINS, Charles H. *History of the Y.M.C.A. in North America.* New York, 1951.

1 JAMES, Sydney V. *A People Among Peoples: Quaker Benevolence in Eighteenth-Century America.* Cambridge, 1963.

2 JONES, Jerome W. "The Established Virginia Church and the Conversion of Negroes and Indians, 1620–1760." See 45.3.

3 KEMP, William W. *The Support of Schools in Colonial New York by the Society for the Propagation of the Gospel in Foreign Parts.* New York, 1913.

4 KLINGBERG, Frank J. *Anglican Humanitarianism in Colonial New York.* Philadelphia, 1940.

5 KLINGBERG, Frank J. "Contributions of the S.P.G. to the American Way of Life." *Hist Mag Prot Epis Church*, XII (1943), 215–244.

6 KLINGBERG, Frank J. "The S.P.G. Program for Negroes in Colonial New York." See 43.19.

7 LANKARD, Frank G. *A History of the American Sunday School Curriculum.* New York, 1927.

8 LEWIT, Robert T. "Indian Missions and Antislavery Sentiment: A Conflict of Evangelical and Humanitarian Ideals." *Miss Val Hist Rev*, L (1963), 39–55.

9 LIVINGOOD, Frederick G. *Eighteenth Century Reformed Church Schools.* Norristown, Pa., 1930.

10 MC CULLOCH, Samuel C. "The Foundation and Early Work of the Society for the Propagation of the Gospel in Foreign Parts." *Hist Mag Prot Epis Church*, XX (1951), 121–135.

11 PASCOE, Charles F. *Two Hundred Years of the S.P.G.: An Historical Account of the Society for the Propagation of the Gospel in Foreign Parts, 1701–1900.* 2 vols. London, 1901.

12 RICE, Edwin W. *The Sunday-School Movement, 1780–1917, and the American Sunday-School Union, 1817–1917.* Philadelphia, 1917.

13 SILVEUS, Marian. "Churches and Social Control on the Western Pennsylvania Frontier." *W Pa Hist Mag*, XIX (1936), 123–164.

14 SMITH, Timothy L. *Revivalism and Social Reform.* See 59.23.

15 STEWART, George. *A History of Religious Education in Connecticut to the Middle of the Nineteenth Century.* New Haven, 1924.

16 WELLS, Guy F. *Parish Education in Colonial Virginia.* New York, 1923.

3. Catholics and Catholicism

17 BAISNÉE, J. A. "The Catholic Church in the United States, 1784–1828." *Rec Am Cath Hist Soc Phil*, LVI (1945), 133–161, 245–292.

18 BARRY, Colman J. *The Catholic Church and German Americans.* Milwaukee, Wis., 1953.

19 BAUMGARTNER, Apollinaris W. *Catholic Journalism: A Study of its Development in the United States, 1789–1930.* New York, 1931.

20 BURNS, James A. *The Catholic School System in the United States: Its Principles, Origin, and Establishment.* New York, 1908.

1   BURNS, James A. *The Growth and Development of the Catholic School System in the United States.* Cincinnati, Ohio, 1912.

2   BURNS, James A., and Bernard J. KOHLBRENNER. *A History of Catholic Education in the United States.* New York, 1937.

3   CASSIDY, Francis P. *Catholic College Foundations and Development in the United States (1677–1850).* Washington, D.C., 1924.

4   ELLIS, John T. *American Catholicism.* 2nd. ed. Chicago, 1969.†

5   ELLIS, John T. *Catholics in Colonial America.* Baltimore, 1965.

6   ERBACHER, Sebastian A. *Catholic Higher Education for Men in the United States, 1850–1866.* Washington, D.C., 1931.

7   GOEBEL, Edmund J. *A Study of Catholic Secondary Education during the Colonial Period up to the First Plenary Council of Baltimore, 1852.* New York, 1937.

8   GUERRIERI, Dora. "Catholic Thought in the Age of Jackson, 1830–1840: Equal Rights and Freedom of Religion." *Rec Am Cath Hist Soc Phil*, LXXIII (1962), 77–91.

9   IVES, Joseph M. "The Catholic Contribution to Religious Liberty in Colonial America." *Cath Hist Rev*, XXI (1935), 283–298.

10 JACOBY, George P. *Catholic Child Care.* See 49.19.

11 KAISER, Laurina. *The Development of the Concept and Function of the Catholic Elementary School in the American Parish.* Washington, D.C., 1955.

12 LANNIE, Vincent P. *Public Money and Parochial Education: Bishop Hughes, Governor Seward, and the New York School Controversy.* Cleveland, Ohio, 1968.

13 MC AVOY, Thomas T. "The Catholic Minority in the United States, 1789–1821." *U S Cath Hist Soc Rec Stud*, XXXIX–XL (1952), 33–50.

14 MC NAMARA, Robert F. "Trusteeism in the Atlantic States, 1785–1863." *Cath Hist Rev*, XXX (1944), 135–154.

15 MAYNARD, Theodore. *The Story of American Catholicism.* New York, 1954.†

16 POWER, Edward J. "The Formative Years of Catholic Colleges Founded before 1850 and Still in Existence as Colleges or Universities." *Rec Am Cath Hist Soc Phil*, LXV (1954), 24–39, 240–250; LXVI (1955), 19–34.

17 RAY, Mary A. *American Opinion of Roman Catholicism in the Eighteenth Century.* New York, 1936.

18 RICE, Madeline H. *American Catholic Opinion in the Slavery Controversy.* New York, 1944.

19 RILEY, Arthur J. *Catholicism in New England to 1788.* Washington, D.C., 1936.

20 ROTHAN, Emmet H. *German-Catholic Immigrant in the United States.* See 31.14.

21 SCHROTT, Lambert. *Pioneer German Catholics in the American Colonies.* See 31.18.

22 SHAUGHNESSY, Gerald. *Has the Immigrant Kept the Faith?* See 29.9.

23 SHEA, John D. G. *A History of the Catholic Church Within the Limits of the United States, from the First Attempted Colonization to the Present Time.* 4 vols. New York, 1886–1892.

24 STRITCH, Alfred G. "Trusteeism in the Old Northwest, 1800–1850." *Cath Hist Rev*, XXX (1944), 155–164.

1 THEOBALD, Stephen L. "Catholic Missionary Work among the Colored People of the United States (1776–1866)." See 46.1.

4. Jews and Judaism

2 ADLER, Selig, and Thomas E. CONNOLLY. *From Ararat to Suburbia: The History of the Jewish Community of Buffalo.* Philadelphia, 1960.

3 American Jewish Archives. *Essays in American Jewish History, to Commemorate the Tenth Anniversary of the Founding of the American Jewish Archives under the Direction of Jacob Rader Marcus.* Cincinnati, Ohio, 1958.

4 BARON, Salo W. *The Jewish Community: Its History and Structure to the American Revolution.* 3 vols. Philadelphia, 1942.

5 BLAU, Joseph L., and Salo W. BARON, eds. *The Jews of the United States, 1790–1840: A Documentary History.* 3 vols. New York, 1963.

6 BUCHLER, Joseph. "The Struggle for Unity: Attempts at Union in American Jewish Life, 1654–1868." *Am Jew Archiv,* II (1949), 21–46.

7 CHYET, Stanley F. "The Political Rights of the Jews in the United States: 1776–1840." *Am Jew Archiv,* X (1958), 14–75.

8 DUKER, Abraham G. "Polish Political Emigrés in the United States and the Jews, 1833–1865." *Pub Am Jew Hist Soc,* XXXIX (1949), 143–168.

9 EMMANUEL, I. S. "New Light on Early American Jewry." *Am Jew Archiv,* VII (1955), 3–64.

10 FONER, Philip S. *The Jews in American History, 1654–1865.* New York, 1946.

11 FRIEDMAN, Lee M. *Early American Jews.* Cambridge, 1934.

12 GLAZER, Nathan. *American Judaism.* Chicago, 1957.†

13 GOODMAN, Abram. *American Overture: Jewish Rights in Colonial Times.* Philadelphia, 1947.

14 GRINSTEIN, Hyman B. *The Rise of the Jewish Community of New York, 1654–1860.* Philadelphia, 1945.

15 HANDLIN, Oscar. *Adventure in Freedom: Three Hundred Years of Jewish Life in America.* New York, 1954.

16 HIGHAM, John. "Social Discrimination Against the Jews in America, 1830–1930." *Pub Am Jew Hist Soc,* XLVII (1957), 1–33.

17 KAGANOFF, Nathan M. "Organized Jewish Welfare Activity in New York City (1848–1860)." *Am Jew Hist Q,* LVI (1966), 27–61.

18 KORN, Bertram W. *Eventful Years and Experiences: Studies in Nineteenth Century American Jewish History.* Cincinnati, Ohio, 1954.

19 KORN, Bertram W. "Factors Bearing Upon the Survival of Judaism in the Ante-Bellum Period." *Am Jew Hist Q,* LIII (1964), 341–351.

20 KORN, Bertram W. "Jewish 48'ers in America." *Am Jew Archiv,* II (1949), 3–20.

21 KORN, Bertram W. "Jews and Negro Slavery in the Old South, 1789–1865." See 45.5.

22 LEBESON, Anite L. *Jewish Pioneers in America, 1492–1848.* New York, 1931.

1   MARCUS, Jacob R. *Early American Jewry.* 2 vols. Philadelphia, 1951–1953.

2   MARCUS, Jacob R., ed. *Memoirs of American Jews, 1775–1865.* 2 vols. Philadelphia, 1955.

3   MORRIS, Richard B. "Civil Liberties and the Jewish Tradition in Early America." *Pub Am Jew Hist Soc*, XLVI (1956), 20–39.

4   POOL, David de Sola. *Portraits Etched in Stone: Early Jewish Settlers, 1682–1831.* New York, 1952.

5   PROCTOR, Samuel. "Jewish Life in New Orleans, 1718–1860." *La Hist Q*, XL (1957), 110–132.

6   ROSENBLOOM, Joseph R. *A Biographical Dictionary of Early American Jews: Colonial Times through 1800.* Lexington, Ky., 1960.

7   RUCHAMES, Louis. "The Abolitionists and the Jews." *Pub Am Jew Hist, Soc*, XLII (1952), 131–156.

8   SANDLER, Philip. "Earliest Jewish Settlers in New York." *N Y Hist*, XXXVI (1955), 39–50.

9   SCHAPPES, Morris U. "Anti-Semitism and Reaction, 1795–1800." *Pub Am Jew Hist Soc*, XXXVIII (1948), 109–138.

10 SCHAPPES, Morris U., ed. *A Documentary History of the Jews in the United States 1654–1875.* New York, 1950.

11 SMYTHE, Hugh H., and Martin S. PRICE. "The American Jew and Negro Slavery." See 45.19.

5. Church and State in America and the Rise of Religious Liberty

12 ANDREWS, Matthew P. "Separation of Church and State in Maryland." *Cath Hist Rev*, XXI (1935), 164–176.

13 BRIDENBAUGH, Carl. "Church and State in America, 1689–1775." *Proc Am Philos Soc*, CV (1961), 521–524.

14 COBB, Sanford H. *The Rise of Religious Liberty in America: A History.* New York, 1902.

15 ECKENRODE, Hamilton J. *Separation of Church and State in Virginia: A Study in the Development of the Revolution.* Richmond, Va., 1910.

16 FORD, David B. *New England's Struggle for Religious Liberty.* Philadelphia, 1896.

17 GOBBEL, Luther L. *Church-State Relationships in Education in North Carolina since 1776.* Durham, N.C., 1938.

18 GRAHAM, John J. "The Development of the Separation of the Church and State in the United States." *Rec Am Cath Hist Soc Phil*, L (1939), 81–87; LI (1940), 1–64, 85–172.

19 GREENE, Evarts B. *Religion and the State: The Making and Testing of an American Tradition.* New York, 1941.†

20 GREENE, M. Louise. *The Development of Religious Liberty in Connecticut.* Boston, 1905.

21 HANLEY, Thomas O. *Their Rights and Liberties: The Beginnings of Religious and Political Freedom in Maryland.* Westminster, Md., 1959.

1 IVES, Joseph M. *The Ark and the Dove: The Beginning of Civil and Religious Liberties in America*. New York, 1936.

2 KINNEY, Charles B., Jr. *Church and State: The Struggle for Separation in New Hampshire, 1630–1900*. New York, 1955.

3 LANNIE, Vincent P. *Public Money and Parochial Education*. See 62.12.

4 MEAD, Nelson P. "Growth of Religious Liberty in New York City." *Proc N Y Hist Assn*, XVII (1919), 141–153.

5 MEAD, Sidney E. "From Coercion to Persuasion: Another Look at the Rise of Religious Liberty and the Emergence of Denominationalism." See 52.13.

6 MEYER, Jacob C. *Church and State in Massachusetts from 1740 to 1833: A Chapter in the History of the Development of Individual Freedom*. Cleveland, Ohio, 1930.

7 NORMAN, E. R. *The Conscience of the State in North America*. New York, 1968.

8 O'NEILL, Charles E. *Church and State in French Colonial Louisiana: Policy and Politics to 1732*. New Haven, 1966.

9 PRATT, John W. *Religion, Politics, and Diversity: The Church-State Theme in New York History*. Ithaca, N.Y., 1967.

10 REED, Susan M. *Church and State in Massachusetts, 1691–1740*. Urbana, Ill., 1914.

11 SEIDMAN, Aaron B. "Church and State in the Early Years of the Massachusetts Bay Colony." *N Eng Q*, XVIII (1945), 211–233.

12 SMITH, Sherman M. *The Relation of the State to Religious Education in Massachusetts*. Syracuse, N.Y., 1926.

13 STOKES, Anson P. *Church and State in the United States*. 3 vols. New York, 1950.

14 STRICKLAND, Reba C. *Religion and the State in Georgia in the Eighteenth Century*. New York, 1939.

15 THOM, William T. *The Struggle for Religious Freedom in Virginia: The Baptists*. Baltimore, 1900.

16 TURNER, Gordon. "Church-State Relationships in Early New Jersey." *Proc N J Hist Soc*, LXIX (1951), 212–222.

6. Witchcraft

17 BURR, George L. "New England's Place in the History of Witchcraft." *Proc Am Antiq Soc*, N.S. XXI (1911), 185–217.

18 BURR, George L., ed. *Narratives of the Witchcraft Cases, 1648–1706*. New York, 1914.

19 DAVIS, Richard B. "The Devil in Virginia in the Seventeenth Century." *Va Mag Hist Biog*, LXV (1957), 131–149.

20 DRAKE, Frederick C. "Witchcraft in the American Colonies, 1647–62." *Am Q*, XX (1968), 694–725.

21 DRAKE, Samuel G. *Annals of Witchcraft in New England, and Elsewhere in the United States, from their First Settlement*. Original ed., 1869. New York, 1967.

1 FOX, Sanford J. *Science and Justice: The Massachusetts Witchcraft Trials.* Baltimore, 1968.

2 HANSEN, Chadwick. *Witchcraft at Salem.* New York, 1969.

3 KITTREDGE, George L. *Witchcraft in Old and New England.* Cambridge, 1929.

4 PARKE, Francis N. *Witchcraft in Maryland.* Baltimore, 1937.

5 PROPER, David R. "Salem Witchcraft, A Brief History." *Essex Inst Hist Coll,* CII (1966), 213–223.

6 STARKEY, Marion L. *The Devil in Massachusetts: A Modern Inquiry into the Salem Witch Trials.* New York, 1949.†

7 TAYLOR, John M. *The Witchcraft Delusion in Colonial Connecticut, 1647–1697.* New York, 1908.

8 UPHAM, Charles W. *Salem Witchcraft: With an Account of Salem Village, and a History of Opinion on Witchcraft and Kindred Subjects.* 2 vols. Boston, 1867.

XI. Reform Movements

1. General

9 BELL, Howard H. "Negroes in the Reform Movement, 1847–1853." See 34.12.

10 BESTOR, Arthur E., Jr. "Patent-Office Models of the Good Society: Some Relationships Between Social Reform and Westward Expansion." *Am Hist Rev,* LVIII (1953), 505–526.

11 BRANCH, E. Douglas. *The Sentimental Years, 1836–1860.* New York, 1934.†

12 BROWN, Ira V. "Watchers for the Second Coming: The Millenarian Tradition in America." *Miss Val Hist Rev,* XXXIX (1952), 441–458.

13 COMMAGER, Henry S., ed. *The Era of Reform, 1830–1860.* Princeton, 1960.†

14 COMMAGER, Henry S. *Theodore Parker.* Boston, 1936.†

15 CRANDALL, John C. "Patriotism and Humanitarian Reform in Children's Literature, 1825–1860." *Am Q,* XXI (1969), 3–22.

16 CROSS, Whitney R. *Burned-Over District.* See 59.1.

17 DAVIES, John D. *Phrenology: Fad and Science: A 19th-Century American Crusade.* New Haven, 1955.

18 GATELL, Frank O. *John Gorham Palfrey and the New England Conscience.* Cambridge, 1963.

19 GRIFFIN, Clifford S. *Their Brothers' Keepers.* See 60.18.

20 GRIFFIN, Clifford S. *The Ferment of Reform, 1830–1860.* New York, 1967.†

21 HALE, William H. *Horace Greeley: Voice of the People.* New York, 1950.†

22 HARLOW, Ralph V. *Gerrit Smith: Philanthropist and Reformer.* New York, 1939.

1 HEALE, M. J. "Humanitarianism in the Early Republic: The Moral Reformers of New York, 1776–1825." *J Am Stud*, II (1968), 161–175.

2 KELLER, Charles R. *Second Great Awakening in Connecticut*. See 59.11.

3 LANGLEY, Harold D. *Social Reform in the United States Navy, 1798–1862*. Urbana, Ill., 1967.

4 LEOPOLD, Richard W. *Robert Dale Owen: A Biography*. Cambridge, 1940.

5 LUDLUM, David M. *Social Ferment in Vermont, 1791–1850*. New York, 1939.

6 POWER, Richard L. "A Crusade to Extend Yankee Culture, 1820–1865." *N Eng Q*, XIII (1940), 638–653.

7 RATNER, Lorman. "Conversion of the Jews and Pre-Civil War Reform." *Am Q*, XIII (1961), 43–54.

8 SCHLESINGER, Arthur M. *The American as Reformer*. Cambridge, 1950.

9 SCHLESINGER, Arthur M., Jr. *Orestes A. Brownson: A Pilgrim's Progress*. Boston, 1939.†

10 SCHWARTZ, Harold. *Samuel Gridley Howe: Social Reformer, 1801–1876*. Cambridge, 1956.

11 SHERWIN, Oscar. *Prophet of Liberty: The Life and Times of Wendell Phillips*. New York, 1958.

12 SEARS, Clara. *Days of Delusion*. See 57.12.

13 SMITH, Timothy L. *Revivalism and Social Reform*. See 59.23.

14 SONNE, Niels H. *Liberal Kentucky, 1780–1828*. New York, 1939.

15 THOMAS, John L. "Romantic Reform in America, 1815–1865." *Am Q*, XVII (1965), 656–681.

16 TURNER, Wallace B. "A Rising Social Consciousness in Kentucky during the 1850's." *Filson Club Hist Q*, XXXVI (1962), 18–31.

17 TYLER, Alice F. *Freedom's Ferment: Phases of American Social History to 1860*. Minneapolis, Minn., 1944.†

18 VAN DEUSEN, Glyndon G. *Horace Greeley, Nineteenth-Century Crusader*. Philadelphia, 1953.†

19 VAN DEUSEN, Glyndon G. *William Henry Seward*. New York, 1967.

20 WINDELL, Marie G. "Reform in the Roaring Forties and Fifties." *Mo Hist Rev*, XXXIX (1945), 291–319.

2. Antislavery and Abolitionism

21 ADAMS, Alice D. *The Neglected Period of Anti-Slavery in America (1808–1831)*. Boston, 1908.

22 APTHEKER, Herbert. *Negro in the Abolitionist Movement*. See 34.5.

23 APTHEKER, Herbert. "The Quakers and Negro Slavery." See 44.9.

24 BARNES, Gilbert H. *The Antislavery Impulse, 1830–1844*. New York, 1933.†

1   BASSETT, John S. *Anti-Slavery Leaders of North Carolina*. Baltimore, 1898.

2   BOASE, Paul H. "Slavery and the Ohio Circuit Rider." See 54.7.

3   BREWSTER, Robert W. "The Rise of the Antislavery Movement in Southwestern Pennsylvania." *W Pa Hist Mag*, XXII (1939), 1–18.

4   BROOKS, Elaine. "Massachusetts Anti-Slavery Society." *J Neg Hist*, XXX (1945), 311–330.

5   CALVERT, Monte A. "The Abolition Society of Delaware, 1801–1807." *Del Hist*, X (1963), 295–320.

6   CARROLL, Kenneth L. "Maryland Quakers and Slavery." See 44.11.

7   CUSHING, John D. "Abolition of Slavery in Massachusetts." *Am J Leg Hist*, V (1961), 118–144.

8   DAVIS, David B. "The Emergence of Immediatism in British and American Antislavery Thought." *Miss Val Hist Rev*, XLIX (1962), 209–230.

9   DEMOS, John. "The Antislavery Movement and the Problem of Violent 'Means'." *N Eng Q*, XXXVII (1964), 501–526.

10 DILLON, Merton L. *Elijah P. Lovejoy: Abolitionist Editor*. Urbana, Ill., 1961.

11 DILLON, Merton L. "The Failure of the American Abolitionists." *J S Hist*, XXV (1959), 159–177.

12 DONALD, David. ["Toward a Reconsideration of Abolitionists."] *Lincoln Reconsidered: Essays on the Civil War Era*. New York, 1956, 19–36.†

13 DRAKE, Thomas E. *Quakers and Slavery*. See 44.14.

14 DUBERMAN, Martin, ed. *The Antislavery Vanguard: New Essays on the Abolitionists*. Princeton, 1965.†

15 DUMOND, Dwight L. *Antislavery: The Crusade for Freedom in America*. Ann Arbor, Mich., 1961.†

16 FILLER, Louis. *The Crusade Against Slavery, 1830–1860*. New York, 1960.†

17 FLADELAND, Betty L. *James Gillespie Birney: Slaveholder to Abolitionist*. Ithaca, N.Y., 1955.

18 FLADELAND, Betty L. "Who Were the Abolitionists?" *J Neg Hist*, XLIX (1964), 99–115.

19 FORTENBAUGH, Robert. "American Lutheran Synods and Slavery, 1830–1860." See 44.15.

20 FOX, Early L. *The American Colonization Society, 1817–1840*. Baltimore, 1919.

21 GARA, Larry. *The Liberty Line: The Legend of the Underground Railroad*. Lexington, Ky., 1961.†

22 GEISER, Karl F. "The Western Reserve in the Anti-Slavery Movement 1840–1860." *Proc Miss Val Hist Assn*, V (1911–1912), 73–98.

23 GRIFFIN, Clifford S. "The Abolitionists and the Benevolent Societies, 1831–1861." *J Neg Hist*, XLIV (1959), 195–216.

1   KATES, Don B. "Abolition, Deportation, Integration: Attitudes Toward Slavery in the Early Republic." *J Neg Hist*, LIII (1968), 33–47.

2   KLEMENT, Frank. "The Abolition Movement in Minnesota." *Minn Hist*, XXXII (1951), 15–33.

3   KORNGOLD, Ralph. *Two Friends of Man: The Story of William Lloyd Garrison and Wendell Phillips, and Their Relationship with Abraham Lincoln.* Boston, 1950.

4   KRADITOR, Aileen S. *Means and Ends in American Abolitionism: Garrison and His Critics on Strategy and Tactics, 1834–1850.* New York, 1969.

5   KRADITOR, Aileen S. "A Note on Elkins and the Abolitionists." *Civil War Hist*, XIII (1967), 330–340.

6   LADER, Lawrence. *The Bold Brahmins: New England's War Against Slavery, 1831–1863.* New York, 1961.

7   LERNER, Gerda. "The Grimké Sisters and the Struggle Against Race Prejudice." *J Neg Hist*, XLVIII (1963), 277–291.

8   LEVY, Leonard W. "The 'Abolition Riot': Boston's First Slave Rescue." *N Eng Q*, XXV (1952), 85–92.

9   LITWACK, Leon F. "The Abolitionist Dilemma: The Antislavery Movement and the Northern Negro." *N Eng Q*, XXXIV (1961), 50–73.

10   LLOYD, Arthur Y. *The Slavery Controversy, 1831–1860.* Chapel Hill, N.C., 1939.

11   LOCKE, Mary S. *Anti-Slavery Sentiment in America from the Introduction of African Slaves to the Prohibition of the Slave Trade (1619–1808).* Boston, 1901.

12   LOFTON, William H. "Abolition and Labor: 1. The Appeal of the Abolitionists to the Northern Working Classes; 2. The Reaction of Northern Labor to the Anti-Slavery Appeal." *J Neg Hist*, XXXIII (1948), 249–283.

13   LOVELAND, Anne C. "Evangelicalism and 'Immediate Emancipation' in American Antislavery Thought." *J S Hist*, XXXII (1966), 172–188.

14   LUTZ, Alma. *Crusade for Freedom.* See 48.18.

15   MANDEL, Bernard. *Labor: Free and Slave: Workingmen and the Anti-Slavery Movement in the United States.* New York, 1955.

16   MARTIN, Asa E. *The Anti-Slavery Movement in Kentucky prior to 1850.* Louisville, Ky., 1918.

17   MATHEWS, Donald G. "The Abolitionists on Slavery: The Critique behind the Social Movement." *J S Hist*, XXIII (1967), 163–182.

18   MATHEWS, Donald G. *Slavery and Methodism.* See 45.6.

19   MAYNARD, Douglas H. "The World's Anti-Slavery Convention of 1840." *Miss Val Hist Rev*, XLVII (1960), 452–471.

20   MERRILL, Walter M. *Against Wind and Tide: A Biography of William Lloyd Garrison.* Cambridge, 1963.

21   MONEY, Charles H. "The Fugitive Slave Law of 1850 in Indiana." *Ind Mag Hist*, XVII (1921), 159–198, 257–297.

1 MUELDER, Herman R. *Fighters for Freedom: The History of Anti-Slavery Activities of Men and Women Associated with Knox College.* New York, 1959.

2 MYERS, John L. "American Antislavery Society Agents and the Free Negro, 1833–1838." *J Neg Hist*, LII (1967), 200–219.

3 MYERS, John L. "The Beginning of Anti-Slavery Agencies in New York State, 1833–1836." *N Y Hist*, XLIII (1962), 149–181.

4 MYERS, John L. "The Early Antislavery Agency System in Pennsylvania, 1833–1837." *Pa Hist*, XXXI (1964), 62–86.

5 NORWOOD, John N. *Schism in the Methodist Episcopal Church, 1844.* See 45.8.

6 NUERMBERGER, Ruth K. *Free Produce Movement.* See 45.9.

7 NYE, Russel B. *Fettered Freedom: Civil Liberties and the Slavery Controversy, 1830–1860.* East Lansing, Mich., 1949.

8 NYE, Russel B. *William Lloyd Garrison and the Humanitarian Reformers.* Boston, 1955.

9 O'BRIEN, William J. "Did the Jennison Case Outlaw Slavery in Massachusetts?" *Wm Mar Q*, 3rd ser., XVII (1960), 219–241.

10 OLDHAM, Ellen M. "Irish Support of the Abolitionist Movement." See 30.22.

11 PEASE, William H., and Jane H. PEASE. "Antislavery Ambivalence: Immediatism, Expediency, Race." *Am Q*, XVII (1965), 682–695.

12 PERRY, Lewis. "Versions of Anarchism in the Antislavery Movement." *Am Q*, XX (1968), 768–782.

13 QUARLES, Benjamin. *Black Abolitionists.* See 35.14.

14 QUARLES, Benjamin. "Sources of Abolitionist Income." *Miss Val Hist Rev*, XXXII (1945), 63–76.

15 RATNER, Lorman. "Northern Concern for Social Order as Cause for Rejecting Anti-Slavery, 1831–1840." *Historian*, XXVIII (1965), 1–18.

16 RATNER, Lorman. *Powder Keg: Northern Opposition to the Antislavery Movement, 1831–1840.* New York, 1968.

17 RAYBACK, Joseph G. "The American Workingman and the Antislavery Crusade." *J Econ Hist*, III (1943), 152–163.

18 RUCHAMES, Louis. "The Abolitionists and the Jews." See 64.7.

19 RUCHAMES, Louis. "Race, Marriage, and Abolition in Massachusetts." *J Neg Hist*, XL (1955), 250–273.

20 SAVAGE, William S. *The Controversy over the Distribution of Abolition Literature, 1830–1860.* Washington, D.C., 1938.

21 SCHWARTZ, Harold. "Fugitive Slave Days in Boston." *N Eng Q*, XXVII (1954), 191–212.

22 SEIFMAN, Eli. "The United Colonization Societies of New-York and Pennsylvania and the Establishment of the African Colony of Bassa Cove." *Pa Hist*, XXXV (1968), 23–44.

23 SEWELL, Richard H. *John P. Hale and the Politics of Abolition.* Cambridge, 1965.

1   SHERWIN, Oscar. *Prophet of Liberty*. See 67.11.

2   SIEBERT, Wilbur H. *The Underground Railroad from Slavery to Freedom*. New York, 1898.

3   SIMMS, Henry H. *Emotion at High Tide: Abolition as a Controversial Factor, 1830–1845*. Richmond, Va., 1960.

4   STAIGER, C. Bruce. "Abolitionism and the Presbyterian Schism of 1837–1838." See 57.16.

5   STAUDENRAUS, Philip J. *The African Colonization Movement, 1816–1865*. New York, 1961.

6   STOPAK, Aaron. "The Maryland State Colonization Society: Independent State Action in the Colonization Movement." *Md Hist Mag*, LXIII (1968), 275–298.

7   THOMAS, Benjamin P. *Theodore Weld: Crusader for Freedom*. New Brunswick, N.J., 1950.

8   THOMAS, John L. *The Liberator: William Lloyd Garrison, A Biography*. Boston, 1963.

9   THORNBROUGH, Emma Lou. "Indiana and Fugitive Slave Legislation." *Ind Mag Hist*, L (1954), 201–228.

10 TURNER, Lorenzo D. *Anti-Slavery Sentiment in American Literature prior to 1865*. Washington, D.C., 1929.

11 WEEKS, Stephen B. *Southern Quakers and Slavery*. See 46.5.

12 WOLF, Hazel C. *On Freedom's Altar: The Martyr Complex in the Abolition Movement*. Madison, Wis., 1952.

13 WOODWARD, C. Vann. "The Antislavery Myth." *Am Sch*, XXI (1962), 312–328.

14 ZILVERSMIT, Arthur. *First Emancipation*. See 41.24.

15 ZORN, Roman J. "The New England Anti-Slavery Society: Pioneer Abolitionist Organization." *J Neg Hist*, XLII (1957), 157–176.

3. Communitarianism

16 ALBERTSON, Ralph. "A Survey of Mutualistic Communities in America." *Iowa J Hist Pol*, XXXIV (1936), 375–444.

17 ANDREWS, Edward D. *The People Called Shakers: A Search for the Perfect Society*. New York, 1953.†

18 ARNDT, Karl J. R. *George Rapp's Harmony Society, 1785–1847*. Philadelphia, 1965.

19 BASSETT, T. D. Seymour. "The Quakers and Communitarianism." *Bull Frnds Hist Assn*, XLIII (1954), 84–99.

20 BESTOR, Arthur E. *Backwoods Utopias: The Sectarian and Owenite Phases of Communitarian Socialism in America, 1663–1829*. Philadelphia, 1950.

21 CALVERTON, Victor F. *Where Angels Dared to Tread*. Indianapolis, Ind., 1941.

22 CARDEN, Maren L. *Oneida: Utopian Community to Modern Corporation*. Baltimore, 1969.

1 COLE, Margaret. *Robert Owen of New Lamark*. New York, 1953.

2 EGBERT, Donald D., and Stow PERSONS, eds. *Socialism and American Life*. See 1.5.

3 HINDS, William A. *American Communities and Co-operative Colonies*. 2nd revision. Chicago, 1908.†

4 HOLLOWAY, Mark. *Heavens on Earth: Utopian Communities in America, 1680–1880*. New York, 1951.

5 LOCKWOOD, George B. *The New Harmony Movement*. New York, 1905.

6 MC BEE, Alice E. *From Utopia to Florence: The Story of a Trancendentalist Community in Northampton, Mass. 1830–1852*. Northampton, Mass., 1947.

7 MELCHER, Marguerite F. *The Shaker Adventure*. Princeton, 1941.

8 NORDHOFF, Charles. *The Communistic Societies of the United States*. New York, 1875.†

9 NOYES, John H. *History of American Socialisms*. Philadelphia, 1870.†

10 PARKER, Robert A. *A Yankee Saint: John Humphrey Noyes and the Oneida Community*. New York, 1935.

11 RUSSELL, C. Allyn. "The Rise and Decline of the Shakers." *N Y Hist*, XLIX (1968), 29–55.

12 WEBBER, Everett. *Escape to Utopia: The Communal Movement in America*. New York, 1959.

13 WILSON, William E. *The Angel and the Serpent: The Story of New Harmony*. Bloomington, Ind., 1964.

4. Women's Rights

14 BLACKWELL, Alice S. *Lucy Stone: Pioneer of Woman's Rights*. Boston, 1930.

15 BROWN, Ira V. "The Woman's Rights Movement in Pennsylvania, 1848–1873." *Pa Hist*, XXXII (1965), 153–165.

16 CROMWELL, Otelia. *Lucretia Mott*. Cambridge, 1958.

17 FLEXNER, Eleanor. *Century of Struggle: The Woman's Rights Movement in the United States*. Cambridge, 1959.†

18 GRIMES, Alan P. *Puritan Ethic and Woman Suffrage*. See 48.15.

19 HAYS, Elinor R. *Morning Star: A Biography of Lucy Stone, 1818–1893*. New York, 1961.

20 KRADITOR, Aileen S., ed. *Up from the Pedestal*. See 48.17.

21 LUTZ, Alma. *Created Equal: A Biography of Elizabeth Cady Stanton 1815–1902*. New York, 1940.

22 LUTZ, Alma. *Susan B. Anthony: Rebel, Crusader, Humanitarian*. Boston, 1959.

23 O'CONNOR, Lillian. *Pioneer Women Orators: Rhetoric in the Ante-Bellum Reform Movement*. New York, 1954.

1 RIEGEL, Robert E. *American Feminists*. Lawrence, Kan., 1963.

2 RIEGEL, Robert E. "Women's Clothes and Women's Rights." See 49.4.

3 SINCLAIR, Andrew. *Emancipation of the American Woman*. See 49.5.

4 SMITH, Thelma M. "Feminism in Philadelphia, 1790–1850." See 49.6.

5 STANTON, Elizabeth C., Susan B. ANTHONY, and Matilda J. GAGE. *History of Woman Suffrage*. See 49.8.

6 STEARNS, Bertha M. "Reform Periodicals and Female Reformers 1830–1860." *Am Hist Rev*, XXXVII (1932), 678–699.

7 VIOLETTE, Augusta G. *Economic Feminism in American Literature prior to 1848*. Orono, Me., 1925.

8 WELTER, Barbara. "The Cult of True Womanhood: 1820–1860." See 49.12.

5. *Temperance*

9 BYRNE, Frank L. *Prophet of Prohibition: Neal Dow and His Crusade*. Madison, Wis., 1961.

10 CHERRINGTON, Ernest H. *The Evolution of Prohibition in the United States of America*. Westerville, Ohio, 1920.

11 GUSFIELD, Joseph R. *Symbolic Crusade: Status Politics and the American Temperance Movement*. Urbana, Ill., 1963.

12 KROUT, John A. *The Origins of Prohibition*. New York, 1925.

13 OSTRANDER, Gilman M. *The Prohibition Movement in California, 1848–1933*. Berkeley, Calif., 1957.

14 SELLERS, James B. *The Prohibition Movement in Alabama, 1702 to 1943*. Chapel Hill, N.C., 1943.†

15 SPRUNGER, Keith L. "Cold Water Congressmen: The Congressional Temperance Society before the Civil War." *Historian*, XXVII (1965), 498–515.

16 WHITENER, Daniel J. *Prohibition in North Carolina, 1715–1945*. Chapel Hill, N.C., 1945.

6. *The Peace Crusade*

17 BROCK, Peter. *Pacifism in the United States: From the Colonial Era to the First World War*. Princeton, 1968.† (Title of paperback edition is *Radical Pacifists in Antebellum America*.)

18 BURRITT, Elihu. *The Learned Blacksmith: The Letters and Journals of Elihu Burritt*. Ed. by Merle E. Curti. New York, 1937.

19 CURTI, Merle E. *Peace or War: The American Struggle 1636–1936*. New York, 1936.

20 GALPIN, W. Freeman. *Pioneering for Peace: A Study of American Peace Efforts to 1846*. Syracuse, N.Y., 1933.

1   PHELPS, Christina. *The Anglo-American Peace Movement in the Mid-Nineteenth Century*. New York, 1930.

7. Nativism

2   BARRY, Colman J. "Some Roots of American Nativism." *Cath Hist Rev*, XLIV (1958), 137–146.

3   BERGER, Max. "The Irish Emigrant and American Nativism as Seen by British Visitors, 1836–1860." *Pa Mag Hist Biog*, LXX (1946), 146–160.

4   BILLINGTON, Ray A. *The Protestant Crusade, 1800–1860: A Study of the Origins of American Nativism*. New York, 1938.†

5   BRAND, Carl F. "History of the Know Nothing Party in Indiana." *Ind Mag Hist*, XVIII (1922), 47–81, 177–206, 266–306.

6   COLE, Arthur C. "Nativism in the Lower Mississippi Valley." *Proc Miss Val Hist Assn*, VI (1912–1913), 258–275.

7   DAVIS, David B. "Some Ideological Functions of Prejudice in Ante-Bellum America." *Am Q*, XV (1963), 115–125.

8   DAVIS, David B. "Some Themes of Counter-Subversion: An Analysis of Anti-Masonic, Anti-Catholic, and Anti-Mormon Literature." *Miss Val Hist Rev*, XLVII (1960), 205–224.

9   ERNST, Robert. "Economic Nativism in New York City during the 1840's." *N Y Hist*, XXIX (1948), 170–186.

10 FELL, Sister Marie Léonore. *The Foundations of Nativism in American Textbooks, 1783–1860*. Washington, D.C., 1941.

11 GOHMANN, Sister Mary de Lourdes. *Political Nativism in Tennessee to 1860*. Washington, D.C., 1938.

12 GRIFFIN, Clifford S. "Converting the Catholics: American Benevolent Societies and the Ante-Bellum Crusade Against the Church." *Cath Hist Rev*, XLVII (1961), 325–341.

13 HIGHAM, John. "Another Look at Nativism." *Cath Hist Rev*, XLIV (1958), 147–158.

14 HINCKLEY, Ted C. "American Anti-Catholicism during the Mexican War." *Pac Hist Rev*, XXXI (1962), 121–138.

15 MC CONVILLE, Sister Mary St. Patrick. *Political Nativism in the State of Maryland, 1830–1860*. Washington, D.C., 1928.

16 MC GANN, Sister Agnes G. *Nativism in Kentucky in 1860*. Washington, D.C., 1944.

17 MC GRATH, Sister Paul of the Cross. *Political Nativism in Texas, 1825–1860*. Washington, D.C., 1930.

18 MORAN, Denis M. "Anti-Catholicism in Early Maryland Politics: The Protestant Revolution." *Rec Am Cath Hist Soc Phil*, LXI (1950), 213–236.

19 MORAN, Denis M. "Anti-Catholicism in Early Maryland Politics: The Puritan Influence." *Rec Am Cath Hist Soc Phil*, LXI (1950), 139–154.

1 NOONAN, Carroll J. *Nativism in Connecticut, 1829–1860*. Washington, D.C. 1938.

2 OVERDYKE, W. Darrell. *The Know-Nothing Party in the South*. Baton Rouge, La., 1950.

3 ST. HENRY, Sister M. "Nativism in Pennsylvania, with Particular Regard to its Effect on Politics and Education 1840–1860." *Rec Am Cath Hist Soc Phil*, XLVII (1936), 5–47.

4 SCHMECKEBIER, Lawrence F. *History of the Know-Nothing Party in Maryland*. Baltimore, 1899.

5 SCISCO, Louis D. *Political Nativism in New York State*. New York, 1901.

6 SENNING, John P. "The Know-Nothing Movement in Illinois 1854–56." *J Ill State Hist Soc*, VII (1914), 9–33.

7 STEPHENSON, George M. "Nativism in the Forties and Fifties, with Special Reference to the Mississippi Valley." *Miss Val Hist Rev*, IX (1922), 185–202.

8 THOMAS, Sister M. Evangeline. *Nativism in the Old Northwest, 1850–1860*. Washington, D.C., 1936.

9 TURNER, Wallace B. "The Know-Nothing Movement in Kentucky." *Filson Club Hist Q*, XXVIII (1954), 266–314.

10 WUST, Klaus G. "German Immigrants and Nativism in Virginia, 1840–1860." *Soc Hist Ger Md Rep*, XXIX (1956), 31–50.

XII. Education

1. Education and American Society: General Accounts

11 BAILYN, Bernard. *Education in the Forming of American Society: Needs and Opportunities for Study*. Chapel Hill, N.C., 1960.†

12 BEALE, Howard K. *A History of Freedom of Teaching in American Schools*. New York, 1941.

13 BENNETT, Charles A. *History of Manual and Industrial Education up to 1870*. Peoria, Ill., 1926.

14 BODE, Carl. *The American Lyceum: Town Meeting of the Mind*. New York, 1956.

15 BROWN, Samuel W. *The Secularization of American Education as Shown by State Legislation, State Constitutional Provisions and State Supreme Court Decisions*. New York, 1912.

16 BULLOCK, Henry A. *History of Negro Education in the South*. See 44.5.

17 BUTLER, Vera M. *Education as Revealed by New England Newspapers prior to 1850*. Philadelphia, 1935.

18 BUTTS, R. Freeman. *The American Tradition in Religion and Education*. Boston, 1950.

1 BUTTS, R. Freeman, and Lawrence A. CREMIN. *A History of Education in American Culture.* New York, 1953.

2 CARLTON, Frank T. *Economic Influences upon Educational Progress in the United States, 1820–1850.* Madison, Wis., 1908.†

3 CLEWS, Elsie W. *Educational Legislation and Administration of the Colonial Governments.* New York, 1899.

4 CUBBERLEY, Ellwood P. *Public Education in the United States: A Study and Interpretation of American Educational History.* Rev. ed. Boston, 1934.

5 CUBBERLEY, Ellwood P., ed. *Readings in Public Education in the United States: A Collection of Sources and Readings to Illustrate the History of Educational Practice and Progress in the United States.* Boston, 1934.

6 CURTI, Merle E. *The Social Ideas of American Educators.* New York, 1935.†

7 EDWARDS, Newton, and Herman G. RICHEY. *The School in the American Social Order: The Dynamics of American Eduction.* Boston, 1947.

8 FISHER, Berenice M. *Industrial Education: American Ideals and Institutions.* Madison, Wis., 1967.

9 GREENE, Evarts B. "Some Educational Values of the American Revolution." *Proc Am Philos Soc,* LXVIII (1929), 185–194.

10 HANSEN, Allen O. *Liberalism and American Education in the Eighteenth Century.* New York, 1926.

11 HAYES, Cecil B. *The American Lyceum: Its History and Contribution to Education.* Washington, D.C., 1932.

12 JERNEGAN, Marcus W. "Factors Influencing the Development of American Education before the Revolution." *Proc Miss Val Hist Assn,* V (1911–1912), 190–206.

13 KNIGHT, Edgar W. *Education in the United States.* 3rd ed. Boston, 1951.

14 KNIGHT, Edgar W., and Clifton L. HALL, eds. *Readings in American Educational History.* New York, 1951.

15 MEAD, David. *Yankee Eloquence in the Middle West: The Ohio Lyceum, 1850–1870.* East Lansing, Mich., 1951.

16 MESSERLI, Jonathan. "The Columbian Complex: The Impulse to National Consolidation." *Hist Ed Q,* VII (1967), 417–431.

17 MONROE, Paul. *Founding of the American Public School System: A History of Education in the United States, from the Early Settlements to the Close of the Civil War Period.* New York, 1940.

18 RUDOLPH, Frederick, ed. *Essays on Education in the Early Republic.* Cambridge, 1965.

19 SHOEMAKER, Ervin C. *Noah Webster: Pioneer of Learning.* New York, 1936.

20 SLOSSON, Edwin E. *The American Spirit in Education: A Chronicle of Great Teachers.* New Haven, 1921.

21 SMITH, Timothy L. "Protestant Schooling and American Nationality, 1800–1850." *J Am Hist,* LIII (1967), 679–695.

1   THWING, Charles F. *American Society: Interpretations of Educational and Other Forces.* New York, 1931.

2   WARFEL, Harry R. *Noah Webster: Schoolmaster to America.* New York, 1936.

3   WELTER, Rush. *Popular Education and Democratic Thought in America.* New York, 1962.†

4   WICKERSHAM, James P. *A History of Education in Pennsylvania, Private and Public, Elementary and Higher.* Lancaster, Pa., 1886.

5   WIEBE, Robert H. "The Social Functions of Public Education." *Am Q,* XXI (1969), 147–164.

6   WOODSON, Carter G. *Education of the Negro prior to 1861.* See 44.7.

2. Primary and Secondary Schools and Education

7   AMBLER, Charles H. *A History of Education in West Virginia from Early Colonial Times to 1949.* Huntington, W. Va., 1951.

8   ANDREWS, Edward D. "The County Grammar Schools and Academies of Vermont." *Proc Vt Hist Soc,* N.S. IV (1936), 117–209.

9   BELL, Sadie. *The Church, the State and Education in Virginia.* Philadelphia, 1930.

10 BIDWELL, Charles E. "The Moral Significance of the Common School: A Sociological Study of Local Patterns of School Control and Moral Education in Massachusetts and New York, 1837–1840." *Hist Ed Q,* VI (1966), 50–91.

11 BONE, Robert G. "Education in Illinois before 1857." *J Ill State Hist Soc,* L (1957), 119–140.

12 BOONE, Richard G. *A History of Education in Indiana.* New York, 1892.

13 BROWN, Elmer E. *The Making of our Middle Schools: An Account of the Development of Secondary Education in the United States.* 3rd ed. New York, 1907.

14 BROWNE, Henry J. "Public Support of Catholic Education in New York, 1825–1842: Some New Aspects." *Cath Hist Rev,* XXXIX (1953), 1–27.

15 BURNS, James A. *Catholic School System in the United States.* See 61.20.

16 BURNS, James A. *Growth and Development of the Catholic School System.* See 62.1.

17 BURNS, James A., and Bernard J. KOHLBRENNER. *History of Catholic Education.* See 62.2.

18 BURR, Nelson R. *Education in New Jersey, 1630–1871.* Princeton, 1942.

19 COON, Charles L. *The Beginnings of Public Education in North Carolina: A Documentary History 1790–1840.* Raleigh, N.C., 1908.

1   CORRY, John P. "Education in Colonial Georgia." *Ga Hist Q*, XVI (1932), 136–145.

2   CREMIN, Lawrence A. *The American Common School: An Historic Conception.* New York, 1951.

3   CULVER, Raymond B. *Horace Mann and Religion in the Massachusetts Public Schools.* New Haven, 1929.

4   CURRAN, Francis X. *Churches and the Schools.* See 51.13.

5   DUNLAP, William C. *Quaker Education in Baltimore and Virginia Yearly Meetings, with an Account of Certain Meetings of Delaware and the Eastern Shore Affiliated with Philadelphia.* Philadelphia, 1936.

6   DUNN, William K. *What Happened to Religious Education? The Decline of Religious Teaching in the Public Elementary School, 1776–1861.* Baltimore, 1958.

7   FUSSELL, Clyde G. "The Emergence of Public Education as a Function of the State in Vermont." *Vt Hist*, XXVIII (1960), 179–196, 268–280; XXIX (1961), 13–47.

8   GOBBEL, Luther L. *Church-State Relationships in Education in North Carolina since 1776.* See 64.17.

9   GOEBEL, Edmund J. *A Study of Catholic Secondary Education.* See 62.7.

10 GORDY, John P. *Rise and Growth of the Normal-School Idea in the United States.* Washington, D.C., 1891.

11 GRIZZELL, Emit D. *Origin and Development of the High School in New England before 1865.* New York, 1923.

12 HANSEN, Allen O. *Early Educational Leadership in the Ohio Valley: A Study of Educational Reconstruction through the Western Library Institute and College of Professional Teachers, 1829–1841.* Bloomington, Ind., 1923.

13 HENDRICK, Irving G. "A Reappraisal of Colonial New Hampshire's Effort in Public Education." *Hist Ed Q*, VI (1966), 43–60.

14 HINSDALE, Burke A. *Horace Mann and the Common School Revival in the United States.* New York, 1898.

15 HOBSON, Elsie G. *Educational Legislation and Administration in the State of New York from 1777 to 1850.* Chicago, 1918.

16 HOLTZ, Adrian A. *A Study of the Moral and Religious Elements in American Secondary Education up to 1800.* Menasha, Wis., 1917.

17 INGLIS, Alexander J. *The Rise of the High School in Massachusetts.* New York, 1911.

18 JACKSON, George L. *The Development of School Support in Colonial Massachusetts.* New York, 1909.

19 JACKSON, Sidney L. *America's Struggle for Free Schools: Social Tensions and Education in New England and New York, 1827–42.* Washington, D.C., 1941.

20 JERNEGAN, Marcus W. *Laboring and Dependent Classes.* See 38.10.

1   JORGENSON, Lloyd P. *The Founding of Public Education in Wisconsin.* Madison, Wis., 1956.

2   KAISER, Laurina. *Development of the Concept and Function of the Catholic Elementary School.* See 62.11.

3   KANDEL, Isaac L. *History of Secondary Education: A Study in the Development of Liberal Education.* Boston, 1930.

4   KATZ, Michael. "The Emergence of Bureaucracy in Urban Education: The Boston Case, 1850–1884." *Hist Ed Q*, VIII (1968), 155–188, 319–357.

5   KATZ, Michael. *The Irony of Early School Reform: Educational Innovation in Mid-Nineteenth Century Massachusetts.* Cambridge, 1968.

6   KILPATRICK, William H. "The Beginnings of the Public School System in Georgia." *Ga Hist Q*, V (1921), 3–19.

7   KILPATRICK, William H. *The Dutch Schools of New Netherland and Colonial New York.* Washington, D.C., 1912.

8   KNIGHT, Edgar W., ed. *A Documentary History of Education in the South before 1860.* 5 vols. Chapel Hill, N.C., 1949–1953.

9   KNIGHT, Edgar W. *Public Education in the South.* Boston, 1922.

10 KLEIN, Milton M. "Church, State, and Education: Testing the Issue in Colonial New York." *N Y Hist*, XLV (1964), 291–303.

11 KOOS, Leonard V. *The American Secondary School.* Boston, 1927.

12 LANNIE, Vincent P. *Public Money and Parochial Education.* See 62.12.

13 LITTLEFIELD, George E. *Early Schools and School-Books of New England.* Boston, 1904.

14 MC CADDEN, Joseph J. *Education in Pennsylvania, 1801–1835, and its Debt to Roberts Vaux.* Philadelphia, 1937.

15 MC CAUL, Robert L. "Education in Georgia during the Period of Royal Control, 1752–1776: Financial Support of Schools and Schoolmasters." *Ga Hist Q*, XL (1956), 103–112.

16 MC CAUL, Robert L. "Education in Georgia during the Period of Royal Government, 1756–1776: Public-School Masters and Private-Venture Teachers." *Ga Hist Q*, XL (1956), 248–259.

17 MAC LEAR, Martha. *The History of the Education of Girls in New York and New England, 1800–1870.* Washington, D.C., 1926.

18 MC CLUSKEY, Neil G. *Public Schools and Moral Education: The Influence of Horace Mann, William Torrey Harris, and John Dewey.* New York, 1958.

19 MANGUM, Vernon L. *The American Normal School: Its Rise and Development in Massachusetts.* Baltimore, 1928.

20 MANN, Mary T. *Life of Horace Mann.* Boston, 1865.

21 MARTIN, George H. *The Evolution of the Massachusetts Public School System: A Historical Sketch.* New York, 1894.

22 MARTIN, William J. "The Old Log School, a Chronicle of Rural Education." *W Pa Mag Hist*, XVI (1933), 163–173.

1 MERIWETHER, Colyer. *Our Colonial Curriculum, 1607–1776.* Washington, D.C., 1907.

2 MESSERLI, Jonathan. "Localism and State Control in Horace Mann's Reform of the Common Schools." *Am Q,* XVII (1965), 104–118.

3 MEYERS, Mary A. "The Children's Crusade: Philadelphia Catholics and the Public Schools, 1840–1844." *Rec Am Cath Hist Soc Phil,* LXXV (1964), 103–127.

4 MIDDLEKAUFF, Robert. *Ancients and Axioms: Secondary Education in Eighteenth-Century New England.* New Haven, 1963.

5 MILLER, Edward A. *The History of Educational Legislation in Ohio from 1803 to 1850.* Chicago, 1920.

6 MILLER, George F. *The Academy System of the State of New York.* Albany, 1922.

7 MONROE, Will S. *The Educational Labors of Henry Barnard: A Study in the History of American Pedagogy.* Syracuse, N.Y., 1893.

8 MONROE, Will S. *A History of the Pestalozzian Movement in the United States.* Syracuse, N.Y., 1907.

9 MULHERN, James. *A History of Secondary Education in Pennsylvania.* Philadelphia, 1933.

10 MURRAY, David. *History of Education in New Jersey.* Washington, D.C., 1899.

11 NOBLE, Stuart G., and Arthur G. NUHRAH. "Education in Colonial Louisiana." *La Hist Q,* XXXII (1949), 759–776.

12 ORR, Dorothy. *A History of Education in Georgia.* Chapel Hill, N.C., 1950.

13 POWELL, Lyman P. *The History of Education in Delaware.* Washington, D.C., 1893.

14 PRATT, John W. "Governor Seward and the New York City School Controversy, 1840–1842: A Milestone in the Advance of Nonsectarian Public Education." *N Y Hist,* XLII (1961), 351–364.

15 PULLIAM, John. "Changing Attitudes Toward Free Public Schools in Illinois 1825–1860." *Hist Ed Q,* VII (1967), 191–208.

16 RILEY, Martin L. "The Development of Education in Louisiana prior to Statehood." *La Hist Q,* XIX (1936), 595–634.

17 ROBERTS, L. E. "Educational Reform in Ante-Bellum Georgia." *Ga Rev,* XVI (1962), 68–82.

18 SACK, Saul. "Student Life in the Nineteenth Century." *Pa Mag Hist Biog,* LXXXV (1961), 255–288.

19 SCHAFER, Joseph. "Public Schools One Hundred Years Ago as Seen through Foreign Eyes." *Wis Mag Hist,* XXII (1939), 435–459.

20 SEYBOLT, Robert F. *Apprenticeship & Apprenticeship Education in Colonial New England & New York.* New York, 1917.

21 SEYBOLT, Robert F. *The Evening School in Colonial America.* Urbana Ill., 1925.

22 SEYBOLT, Robert F. *The Public Schoolmasters of Colonial Boston.* Cambridge, 1939.

1   SEYBOLT, Robert F. *The Public Schools of Colonial Boston, 1635–1775.* Cambridge, 1935.

2   SEYBOLT, Robert F. "The S.P.G. Myth: A Note on Education in Colonial New York." *J Ed Res*, XIII (1926), 129–137.

3   SEYBOLT, Robert F. "Schoolmasters of Colonial Philadelphia." *Pa Mag Hist Biog*, LII (1928), 361–371.

4   SEYBOLT, Robert F. *Source Studies in American Colonial Education: The Private School.* Urbana, Ill., 1925.

5   SHIPTON, Clifford K. "The Puritan Influence in Education." *Pa Hist*, XXV (1958), 223–233.

6   SHIPTON, Clifford K. "Secondary Education in the Puritan Colonies." *N Eng Q*, VII (1934), 646–661.

7   SIDWELL, Robert T. " 'Writers, Thinkers and Fox Hunters'—Educational Theory in the Almanacs of Eighteenth-Century Colonial America." *Hist Ed Q*, VIII (1968), 275–288.

8   SMALL, Walter H. *Early New England Schools.* Boston, 1914.

9   SMITH, Sherman M. *Relation of the State to Religious Education in Massachusetts.* See 65.12.

10 SMITH, William A. *Secondary Education in the United States.* New York, 1932.

11 SMITH, Wilson. "The Teacher in Puritan Culture." *Har Ed Rev*, XXVI (1966), 395–411.

12 STEINER, Bernard C. *History of Education in Connecticut.* Washington, D.C., 1893.

13 STEINER, Bernard C. *History of Education in Maryland.* Washington, D.C., 1894.

14 TAYLOR, William R. "Toward a Definition of Orthodoxy: The Patrician South and the Common Schools." *Har Ed Rev*, XXVI (1966), 412–426.

15 THARP, Louise H. *Until Victory: Horace Mann and Mary Peabody.* Boston, 1953.

16 THURSFIELD, Richard E. *Henry Barnard's American Journal of Education.* Baltimore, 1945.

17 UPDEGRAFF, Harlan. *The Origin of the Moving School in Massachusetts.* New York, 1907.

18 VAN DEUSEN, Glyndon G. "Seward and the School Question Reconsidered." *J Am Hist*, LII (1965), 313–319.

19 WEATHERSBY, William H. *A History of Educational Legislation in Mississippi from 1798 to 1860.* Chicago, 1921.

20 WEBER, Samuel E. *The Charity School Movement in Colonial Pennsylvania.* Philadelphia, 1905.

21 WEEKS, Stephen B. *History of Public School Education in Alabama.* Washington, D.C., 1915.

22 WEEKS, Stephen B. *History of Public School Education in Arkansas.* Washington, D.C., 1912.

23 WEST, Roscoe L. *Elementary Education in New Jersey: A History.* Princeton, 1964.

1 WHITAKER, A. P. "The Public School System of Tennessee, 1834–1860." *Tenn Hist Mag*, II (1916), 1–30.

2 WILLIAMS, Edward I. F. *Horace Mann, Educational Statesman*. New York, 1937.

3 WOODY, Thomas. *Early Quaker Education in Pennsylvania*. New York, 1920.

4 WOODY, Thomas. *History of Women's Education*. See 49.13.

5 WOODY. Thomas. *Quaker Education in the Colony and State of New Jersey: A Source Book*. Philadelphia, 1923.

6 WRIGHT, Marian. *Education of Negroes in New Jersey*. See 44.8.

3. Schoolbooks

7 BELOK, Michael V. "The Courtesy Tradition and Early Schoolbooks." *Hist Ed Q*, VIII (1968), 306–318.

8 CARPENTER, Charles. *History of American Schoolbooks*. Philadelphia, 1963.

9 ELSON, Ruth M. *Guardians of Tradition: American Schoolbooks of the Nineteenth Century*. Lincoln, Neb., 1964.

10 ENGLAND, J. Merton. "The Democratic Faith in American Schoolbooks, 1783–1860." *Am Q*, XV (1963), 191–199.

11 GARFINKLE, Norton. "Conservatism in American Textbooks, 1800–1860." *N Y Hist*, XXXV (1954), 49–63.

12 MINNICH, Harvey C. *William Holmes McGuffey and His Readers*. New York, 1936.

13 MOSIER, Richard D. *Making the American Mind: Social and Moral Ideas in the McGuffey Readers*. New York, 1947.

14 NIETZ, John A. *Old Textbooks: Spelling, Grammar, Reading, Arithmetic, Geography, American History, Civil Government, Physiology, Penmanship, Art, Music—As Taught in the Common Schools from Colonial Days to 1900*. Pittsburgh, Pa., 1961.

15 ROSENBACH, Abraham S. W. *Early American Children's Books*. See 50.4.

16 SLOANE, William. *Children's Books in England & America in the Seventeenth Century*. See 50.5.

17 TOPE, Melancthon. *A Biography of William Holmes McGuffey*. Bowerston, Ohio, 1929.

4. Higher Education

18 AMBROSE, Stephen E. *Duty, Honor, Country: A History of West Point*. Baltimore, 1966.

19 BRINTON, Howard H. "The Quaker Contribution to Higher Education in Colonial America." *Pa Hist*, XXV (1958), 234–250.

1 BRODERICK, Francis L. "Pulpit, Physics, and Politics: The Curriculum of the College of New Jersey, 1746–1794." *Wm Mar Q*, 3rd ser., VI (1949), 42–68.

2 BRONSON, Walter C. *The History of Brown University, 1764–1914.* Providence, R.I., 1914.

3 BRUBACHER, John S., and Willis RUDY. *Higher Education in Transition: An American History.* Rev. ed. New York, 1968.

4 BRUCE, Philip A. *History of the University of Virginia, 1819–1919: The Lengthened Shadow of One Man.* 5 vols. New York, 1920–1922.

5 CARRELL, William D. "American College Professors: 1750–1800." *Hist Ed Q*, VIII (1968), 289–305.

6 CASSIDY, Francis P. *Catholic College Foundations and Development.* See 62.3.

7 CHASE, Wayland J. " 'The Great Awakening' and its Educational Consequences." See 58.18.

8 CHEYNEY, Edward P. *History of the University of Pennsylvania, 1740–1940.* Philadelphia, 1940.

9 COLE, Arthur C. *A Hundred Years of Mount Holyoke College: The Evolution of an Educational Ideal.* New Haven, 1940.

10 COME, Donald R. "The Influence of Princeton on Higher Education in the South before 1825." *Wm Mar Q*, 3rd ser., II (1945), 359–396.

11 COULTER, E. Merton. *College Life in the Old South.* 2nd ed. New York, 1951.

12 COWIE, Alexander. *Educational Problems at Yale College in the Eighteenth Century.* New Haven, 1936.

13 DEMAREST, William H. S. *A History of Rutgers College, 1766–1924.* New Brunswick, N.J., 1924.

14 EARNEST, Ernest P. *Academic Procession: An Informal History of the American College, 1636 to 1953.* Indianapolis, Ind., 1953.

15 ERBACHER, Sebastian A. *Catholic Higher Education.* See 62.6.

16 FLETCHER, Robert S. *A History of Oberlin College from the Foundation through the Civil War.* Oberlin, Ohio, 1943.

17 FOSTER, Margery S. *"Out of Smalle Beginnings . . .": An Economic History of Harvard College in the Puritan Period (1636 to 1712).* Cambridge, 1962.

18 GABRIEL, Ralph H. *Religion and Learning at Yale: The Church of Christ in the College and University, 1757–1957.* New Haven, 1958.

19 GODBOLD, Albea. *The Church College of the Old South.* Durham, N.C., 1944.

20 HADDOW, Anna. *Political Science in American Colleges and Universities, 1636–1900.* New York, 1939.

21 HALLER, Mabel. "Moravian Influence on Higher Education in Colonial America." *Pa Hist*, XXV (1958), 205–222.

1   HOFSTADTER, Richard, and Wilson SMITH, eds. *American Higher Education: A Documentary History.* 2 vols. Chicago, 1961.†

2   HOFSTADTER, Richard, and Walter P. METZGER. *The Development of Academic Freedom in the United States.* New York, 1955.†

3   HOFSTADTER, Richard, and C. De Witt HARDY. *The Development and Scope of Higher Education in the United States.* New York, 1952.

4   HOOVER, Thomas N. "The Beginnings of Higher Education in the Northwest Territory." *Ohio State Arch Hist Q*, L (1941), 244–260.

5   HORNBERGER, Theodore. *Scientific Thought in American Colleges 1638–1800.* Austin, Tex., 1945.

6   KELLY, Robert L. *The American Colleges and the Social Order.* New York, 1940.

7   LOCKARD, E. Kidd. "The Influence of New England in Denominational Colleges in the Northwest, 1830–1860." *Ohio State Arch Hist Q*, LIII (1944), 1–13.

8   MC ANEAR, Beverly. "College Founding in the American Colonies, 1745–1775." *Miss Val Hist Rev*, XLII (1955), 24–44.

9   MC ANEAR, Beverly. "The Raising of Funds by the Colonial Colleges." *Miss Val Hist Rev*, XXXVIII (1952), 591–612.

10   MC ANEAR, Beverly. "The Selection of an Alma Mater by Pre-Revolutionary Students." *Pa Mag Hist Biog*, LXXIII (1949), 429–440.

11   MC KEEHAN, Louis W. *Yale Science: The First Hundred Years, 1701–1801.* New York, 1947.

12   MADSEN, David. *The National University: Enduring Dream of the USA.* Detroit, Mich., 1966.

13   MIDDLETON, Arthur P. "Anglican Contributions to Higher Education in Colonial America." *Pa Hist*, XXV (1958), 251–268.

14   MORISON, Samuel E. *Harvard College in the Seventeenth Century.* 2 vols. Cambridge, 1936.

15   MORISON, Samuel E. *Three Centuries of Harvard, 1636–1936.* Cambridge, 1936.

16   OVIATT, Edwin. *The Beginnings of Yale (1701–1726).* New Haven, 1916.

17   POTTER, David. *Debating in the Colonial Chartered Colleges: An Historical Survey, 1642 to 1900.* New York, 1944.

18   POWER, Edward J. "The Formative Years of Catholic Colleges Founded before 1850 and Still in Existence as Colleges or Universities." See 62.16.

19   RICHARDSON, Leon B. *History of Dartmouth College.* 2 vols. Hanover, N.H., 1932.

20   RUDOLPH, Frederick. *The American College and University: A History.* New York, 1962.†

21   RUDOLPH, Frederick. *Mark Hopkins and the Log: Williams College, 1836–1872.* New Haven, 1956.

1 SACK, Saul. *History of Higher Education in Pennsylvania.* 2 vols. Harrisburg, Pa., 1963.

2 SCHMIDT, George P. *The Liberal Arts College: A Chapter in American Cultural History.* New Brunswick, N.J., 1957.

3 SCHMIDT, George P. *The Old Time College President.* New York, 1930.

4 SCHMIDT, George P. *Princeton and Rutgers: The Two Colonial Colleges of New Jersey.* Princeton, 1964.

5 STEVENS, Raymond B. *The Social and Religious Influences of the Small Denominational College of the Middle West.* New York, 1929.

6 STORR, Richard J. *The Beginnings of Graduate Education in America.* Chicago, 1953.

7 TAYLOR, James M. *Before Vassar Opened.* See 49.9.

8 TEWKSBURY, Donald G. *The Founding of American Colleges and Universities before the Civil War, with Particular Reference to the Religious Influences Bearing upon the College Movement.* New York, 1932.

9 THWING, Charles F. *A History of Higher Education in America.* New York, 1906.

10 TILGHMAN, Tench F. "An Early Victorian College, St. John's, 1830–1860." *Md Hist Mag*, XLIV (1949), 251–268.

11 TOLMAN, William H. *The History of Higher Education in Rhode Island.* Washington, D.C., 1894.

12 WALSH, James J. *Education of the Founding Fathers of the Republic: Scholasticism in Colonial Colleges: A Neglected Chapter in the History of American Education.* New York, 1935.

13 WERTENBAKER, Thomas J. *Princeton 1746–1896.* Princeton, 1946.

14 YAKELEY, Leon. "The Development of Higher Education in the Jacksonian Period, 1825–1840." *Historian*, III (1940), 37–51.

XIII. Indigency, Welfare, and Philanthropy

1. General

15 ABBOTT, Edith, ed. *Some American Pioneers in Social Welfare: Selected Documents with Editorial Notes.* Chicago, 1937.

16 BEST, Harry. *Blindness and the Blind in the United States.* New York, 1934.

17 BEST, Harry. *Deafness and the Deaf in the United States, Considered Primarily in Relation to Those Sometime More or Less Erroneously Known as "Deaf-Mutes."* New York, 1943.

18 BREMNER, Robert H. *American Philanthropy.* Chicago, 1960.†

1 BREMNER, Robert H. *From the Depths: The Discovery of Poverty in the United States.* New York, 1956.†

2 COLEMAN, Sydney H. *Humane Society Leaders in America: With a Sketch of the Early History of the Humane Movement in England.* Albany, N.Y., 1924.

3 COLL, Blanche D. "The Baltimore Society for the Prevention of Pauperism, 1820–1822." *Am Hist Rev*, LXI (1955), 77–87.

4 COLL, Blanche D. "Perspectives in Public Welfare: Colonial Times to 1860." *Wel Rev*, V (1967), 1–9; VI (1968), 12–22.

5 CURTI, Merle E. "American Philanthropy and the National Character." *Am Q*, X (1958), 420–437.

6 CURTI, Merle E. "The History of American Philanthropy as a Field of Research." *Am Hist Rev*, LXII (1957), 352–363.

7 CURTI, Merle E. "Tradition and Innovation in American Philanthropy." *Proc Am Philos Soc*, CV (1961), 146–156.

8 JACOBY, George P. *Catholic Child Care.* See 49.19.

9 JAMES, Sydney V. *A People Among Peoples.* See 61.1.

10 LEIBY, James. *Charity and Correction in New Jersey: A History of State Welfare Institutions.* New Brunswick, N.J., 1967.

11 LUBOVE, Roy. "The New York Association for Improving the Condition of the Poor: The Formative Years." *N Y Hist Soc Q*, XLIII (1959), 307–328.

12 MELDER, Keith. "Ladies Bountiful: Organized Women's Benevolence in Early 19th-Century America." See 49.1.

13 MILLER, Howard S. *The Legal Foundations of American Philanthropy, 1776–1844.* Madison, Wis., 1961.

14 O'BRIEN, Edward J. *Child Welfare Legislation in Maryland.* See 50.2.

15 PICKETT, Robert S. *House of Refuge.* See 50.3.

16 PUMPHREY, Ralph E., and Muriel W. PUMPHREY. *The Heritage of American Social Work: Readings in its Philosophical and Institutional Development.* New York, 1961.

17 ROSS, Ishbel. *Journey into Light: The Story of the Education of the Blind.* New York, 1951.

18 TREUDLEY, Mary B. "The 'Benevolent Fair': A Study of Charitable Organizations among American Women in the First Third of the Nineteenth Century." See 49.10.

19 WATSON, Frank D. *The Charity Organization Movement in the United States: A Study in American Philanthropy.* New York, 1922.

20 WYLLIE, Irvin G. "The Search for an American Law of Charity, 1776–1844." *Miss Val Hist Rev*, XLVI (1959), 203–221.

2. Poverty and the Poor

21 AMBLER, Charles H. "Poor Relief Education: Kanawha County, Virginia, 1819–1847." *W Va Hist*, III (1942), 285–304.

22 BECKER, Dorothy G. "The Visitor to the New York City Poor, 1843–1920." *Soc Serv Rev*, XXXV (1961), 382–396.

1 BENTON, Josiah H. *Warning Out in New England, 1656–1817*. Boston, 1911.

2 BROWN, Roy M. *Public Poor Relief in North Carolina*. Chapel Hill, N.C., 1928.

3 BRUCE, Isabel C., Edith EICKHOFF, and Sophonisba P. BRECKINRIDGE. *The Michigan Poor Law: Its Development and Administration with Special Reference to State Provision for Medical Care of the Indigent*. Chicago, 1936.

4 CAPEN, Edward W. *The Historical Development of the Poor Law of Connecticut*. New York, 1905.

5 CREECH, Margaret. "Six Colonial 'Case Histories.' " *Soc Serv Rev*, XIII (1939), 246–262.

6 CREECH, Margaret. "Some Colonial Case Histories." *Soc Serv Rev*, IX (1935), 699–730.

7 CREECH, Margaret. *Three Centuries of Poor Law Administration: A Study of Legislation in Rhode Island*. Chicago, 1936.

8 D'AGOSTINO, Lorenzo. *The History of Public Welfare in Vermont*. Winooski, Vt., 1948.

9 DEUTSCH, Albert. "The Sick Poor in Colonial Times." *Am Hist Rev*, XLVI (1941), 560–579.

10 DREWS, Robert S. "A History of the Care of the Sick Poor of the City of Detroit (1703–1855)." *Bull Hist Med*, VII (1939), 759–782.

11 FOLKS, Homer. "Some Historical Aspects of Relief Work in New York State." *Q J N Y Hist Assn*, XIX (1921), 3–46.

12 GILLIN, John L. *History of Poor Relief Legislation in Iowa*. Iowa City, Iowa, 1914.

13 HEFFNER, William C. *History of Poor Relief Legislation in Pennsylvania 1682–1913*. Cleona, Pa., 1913.

14 JERNEGAN, Marcus W. *Laboring and Dependent Classes*. See 38.10.

15 KELSO, Robert W. *The History of Public Poor Relief in Massachusetts, 1620–1920*. Boston, 1922.

16 KENNEDY, Aileen E. *The Ohio Poor Law and Its Administration*. Chicago, 1934.

17 KLEBANER, Benjamin J. "Employment of Paupers at Philadelphia's Almshouse before 1861." *Pa Hist*, XXIV (1957), 137–148.

18 KLEBANER, Benjamin J. "The Home Relief Controversy in Philadelphia, 1782–1861." *Pa Mag Hist Biog*, LXXVIII (1954), 413–423.

19 KLEBANER, Benjamin J. "Pauper Auctions: The 'New England Method' of Public Poor Relief." *Essex Inst Hist Coll*, XCI (1955), 195–210.

20 KLEBANER, Benjamin J. "Poor Relief and Public Works during the Depression of 1857." *Historian*, XXII (1960), 264–279.

21 KLEBANER, Benjamin J. "Poverty and Its Relief in American Thought, 1815–61." *Soc Serv Rev*, XXXVIII (1964), 382–399.

1 KLEBANER, Benjamin J. "Public Poor Relief in Charleston, 1800–1860." *S C Hist Mag*, LV (1954), 210–220.

2 KLEBANER, Benjamin J. "Some Aspects of North Carolina Public Poor Relief, 1700–1860." *N C Hist Rev*, XXXI (1954), 479–493.

3 MC CAMIC, Charles. "Administration of Poor Relief in the Virginias." *W Va Hist*, I (1940), 171–191.

4 MACKEY, Howard. "The Operation of the English Old Poor Law in Colonial Virginia." *Va Mag Hist Biog*, LXXIII (1965), 29–40.

5 MACKEY, Howard. "Social Welfare in Colonial Virginia: The Importance of the English Old Poor Law." *Hist Mag Prot Epis Church*, XXXVI (1967), 357–382.

6 PARKHURST, Eleanor. "Poor Relief in a Massachusetts Village in the Eighteenth Century." *Soc Serv Rev*, XI (1937), 446–464.

7 PENDLETON, O. A. "Poor Relief in Philadelphia, 1790–1840." *Pa Mag Hist Biog*, LXX (1946), 161–172.

8 SCHNEIDER, David M. *The History of Public Welfare in New York State 1609–1866.* Chicago, 1938.

9 SHAFFER, Alice, Mary W. KEEFER, and Sophonisba P. BRECKINRIDGE. *The Indiana Poor Law: Its Development and Administration with Special Reference to the Provision of State Care for the Sick Poor.* Chicago, 1932.

10 TEETERS, Negley K. "The Early Days of the Philadelphia House of Refuge." *Pa Hist*, XXVII (1960), 165–187.

11 WALLS, Otto F. "A History of Social Welfare in Indiana." *Ind Mag Hist*, XLV (1949), 383–400.

12 WISNER, Elizabeth. "The Puritan Background of the New England Poor Laws." *Soc Serv Rev*, XIX (1945), 381–390.

XIV. Medicine and Health

1. General

13 ALLEN, Phyllis. "Etiological Theory in America prior to the Civil War." *J Hist Med Allied Sci*, II (1947), 489–520.

14 ASHBURN, Percy M. *The Ranks of Death: A Medical History of the Conquest of America.* New York, 1947.

15 BEALL, Otho T., Jr. "*Aristotle's Master Piece* in America: A Landmark in the Folklore of Medicine." *Wm Mar Q*, 3rd ser., XX (1963), 207–222.

16 BLAKE, John B. "Women and Medicine in Ante-Bellum America." See 48.9.

17 BOUSFIELD, M. O. "An Account of Physicians of Color in the United States." See 34.13.

18 CHAMBERS, John S. *The Conquest of Cholera, America's Greatest Scourge.* New York, 1938.

19 FARMER, Harold E. "An Account of the Earliest Colored Gentlemen in Medical Science in the United States." See 35.2.

1   FLEXNER, James T. *Doctors on Horseback: Pioneers of American Medicine.*
New York, 1937.†

2   HEATON, Oliver S. "Three Hundred Years of Medicine in New York City."
Bull Hist Med, XXXII (1958), 517–530.

3   LONG, Esmond R. *A History of American Pathology.* Springfield, Ill., 1962.

4   MARTI-IBANEZ, Felix, ed. *History of American Medicine: A Symposium.*
New York, 1959.

5   MATAS, Rudolph. *The Rudolph Matas History of Medicine in Louisiana.* Ed.
by John Duffy. 2 vols. Baton Rouge, La., 1958–1962.

6   PACKARD, Francis R. *History of Medicine in the United States.* New ed.
2 vols. New York, 1931.

7   RANSOM, John E. "The Beginnings of Hospitals in the United States."
Bull Hist Med, XIII (1943), 514–539.

8   RODABAUGH, James H., and Mary J. RODABAUGH. *Nursing in Ohio:
A History.* Columbus, Ohio, 1951.

9   SHRYOCK, Richard H. *American Medical Research, Past and Present.* New
York, 1947.

10 SHRYOCK, Richard H. *The Development of Modern Medicine: An Interpretation of the Social and Scientific Factors Involved.* Rev. ed. New York,
1947.

11 SHRYOCK, Richard H. *The History of Nursing.* Philadelphia, 1959.

12 SHRYOCK, Richard H. *Medicine in America: Historical Essays.* Baltimore,
1966.

13 SHRYOCK, Richard H. *Medicine and Society in America, 1660–1860.* New
York, 1960.†

14 STEARN, E. Wagner, and Allen E. STEARN. *The Effect of Smallpox on the
Destiny of the Amerindian.* Boston, 1945.

15 TOP, Franklin H., ed. *The History of American Epidemiology.* St. Louis,
Mo., 1952.

16 VIETS, Henry R. *A Brief History of Medicine in Massachusetts.* Boston, 1930.

17 WALSH, James J. *History of Medicine in New York: Three Centuries of
Medical Progress.* 5 vols. New York, 1919.

2. The Medical Profession and Medical Education

18 ABRAHAMS, Harold J. *Extinct Medical Schools of Nineteenth-Century
Philadelphia.* Philadelphia, 1966.

19 BURRAGE, Walter L. *A History of the Massachusetts Medical Society, with
Brief Biographies of the Founders and Chief Officers, 1781–1922.* Norwood,
Mass., 1923.

20 COWEN, David L. *Medical Education: The Queen's-Rutgers Experience
1792–1830.* New Brunswick, N.J., 1966.

1   DUFFY, John. "Sectional Conflict and Medical Education in Louisiana." *J S Hist*, XXIII (1957), 53–72.

2   FISHBEIN, Morris. *A History of the American Medical Association, 1847 to 1947*. Philadelphia, 1947.

3   HAMER, Philip M. *The Centennial History of the Tennessee State Medical Association, 1830–1930*. Nashville, Tenn., 1930.

4   KETT, Joseph F. *Formation of the American Medical Profession*. See 28.1.

5   KONOLD, Donald E. *A History of American Medical Ethics, 1847–1912*. Madison, Wis., 1962.

6   MOORE, Thomas E., Jr. "The Early Years of the Harvard Medical School: Its Founding and Curriculum, 1782–1810." *Bull Hist Med*, XXVII (1953), 530–561.

7   NORWOOD, William F. *Medical Education in the United States before the Civil War*. Philadelphia, 1944.

8   POSTELL, William D. "The Doctor in the Old South." *S Atl Q*, LI (1952), 393–400.

9   RICHMAN, Irwin. *The Brightest Ornament: A Biography of Nathaniel Chapman, M.D.* Bellefonte, Pa., 1967.

10   RIZNIK, Barnes. "The Professional Lives of Early Nineteenth-Century New England Doctors." *J Hist Med Allied Sci*, XIX (1964), 1–16.

11   ROGERS, Fred B., and A. Reasoner SAYRE. *The Healing Art: A History of the Medical Society of New Jersey*. Trenton, N.J., 1966.

12   ROSEN, George. *Fees and Fee Bills: Some Economic Aspects of Medical Practice in Nineteenth Century America*. Baltimore, 1946.

13   ROSENBERG, Charles E. "The American Medical Profession: Mid-Nineteenth Century." See 28.2.

14   SHAFER, Henry B. *The American Medical Profession*. See 28.3.

15   SHIRA, Donald D. "The Legal Requirements for Medical Practice—An Attempt to Regulate by Law and the Purpose Behind the Movement." *Ohio State Arch Hist Q*, XLVIII (1939), 181–188.

16   SHRYOCK, Richard H. *Medical Licensing in America, 1650–1965*. Baltimore, 1967.

17   SHRYOCK, Richard H. "Public Relations of the Medical Profession in Great Britain and the United States, 1600–1870: A Chapter in the Social History of Medicine." *Ann Med Hist*, N.S. II (1930), 308–339.

18   STOOKEY, Byron. *A History of Colonial Medical Education: In the Province of New York, with its Subsequent Development (1767–1830)*. Springfield, Ill., 1962.

19   THOMS, Herbert. *The Doctors of Yale College 1702–1815 and the Founding of the Medical Institution*. Hamden, Conn., 1960.

20   WAITE, Frederick C. "American Sectarian Medical Colleges before the Civil War." *Bull Hist Med*, XIX (1946), 148–166.

1 WAITE, Frederick C. *The First Medical College in Vermont: Castleton 1818–1862.* Montpelier, Vt., 1949.

2 WAITE, Frederick C. "The First Medical Diploma Mill in the United States." *Bull Hist Med*, XX (1946), 495–504.

3 WAITE, Frederick C. *History of the New England Female Medical College, 1848–1874.* Boston, 1950.

4 WAITE, Frederick C. "The Professional Education of Pioneer Ohio Physicians." *Ohio State Arch Hist Q*, XLVIII (1939), 189–197.

5 WAITE, Frederick C. *The Story of a Country Medical College: A History of the Clinical School of Medicine and the Vermont Medical College, Woodstock, Vermont, 1827–1856.* Montpelier, Vt., 1945.

3. *Medicine and Health in Colonial America (to 1800)*

6 BARRETT, John T. "The Innoculation Controversy in Puritan New England." *Bull Hist Med*, XII (1942), 169–190.

7 BEALL, Otho T., Jr., and Richard H. SHRYOCK. *Cotton Mather, First Significant Figure in American Medicine.* Baltimore, 1954.

8 BEEKMAN, Fenwick. "The Origin of 'Bellevue' Hospital as Shown in the New York Health Committee Minutes during the Yellow Fever Epidemics of 1793–1795." *N Y Hist Soc Q*, XXXVII (1953), 205–227.

9 BEHNKE, Helen D. "Colonies Theories Concerning the Cause of Disease." *Medical Life*, XLI (1934), 59–74.

10 BEINFIELD, Malcolm S. "The Early New England Doctor: An Adaptation to a Provincial Environment." *Yale J Biol Med*, XV (1942), 99–132.

11 BELL, Whitfield J., Jr. "The American Philosophical Society and Medicine." *Bull Hist Med*, XL (1966), 112–123.

12 BELL, Whitfield J., Jr. "Medical Practice in Colonial America." *Bull Hist Med*, XXXI (1957), 442–453.

13 BINGER, Carl. *Revolutionary Doctor: Benjamin Rush, 1746–1813.* New York, 1966.

14 BLAKE, John B. *Benjamin Waterhouse and the Introduction of Vaccination: A Reappraisal.* Philadelphia, 1957.

15 BLAKE, John B. "The Innoculation Controversy in Boston: 1721–1722." *N Eng Q*, XXV (1952), 489–506.

16 BLAKE, John B. "Smallpox Innoculation in Colonial Boston." *J Hist Med Allied Sci*, VIII (1953), 284–300.

17 BLANTON, Wyndham B. *Medicine in Virginia in the Eighteenth Century.* Richmond, Va., 1931.

18 BLANTON, Wyndham B. *Medicine in Virginia in the Seventeenth Century.* Richmond, Va., 1930.

19 CAULFIELD, Ernest. "Some Common Diseases of Colonial Children." *Pub Col Soc Mass, Trans*, XXXV (1942–1946), 4–65.

1 CAULFIELD, Ernest. *A True History of the Terrible Epidemic Vulgarly Called the Throat Distemper, Which Occurred in His Majesty's New England Colonies Between the Years 1735 and 1740.* New Haven, 1939.

2 CHILDS, St. Julian R. *Malaria and Colonization in the Carolina Low Country, 1526–1696.* Baltimore, 1940.

3 DEUTSCH, Albert. "The Sick Poor in Colonial Times." See 87.9.

4 DUFFY, John. "Eighteenth-Century Carolina Health Conditions." *J S Hist*, XVIII (1952), 289–302.

5 DUFFY, John. *Epidemics in Colonial America.* Baton Rouge, La., 1953.

6 DUFFY, John. "The Passage to the Colonies." *Miss Val Hist Rev*, XXXVIII (1951), 21–38.

7 EGGLESTON, Edward. "Some Curious Colonial Remedies." *Am Hist Rev*, V (1899), 199–206.

8 GOODMAN, Nathan G. *Benjamin Rush: Physician and Citizen, 1746–1813.* Philadelphia, 1934.

9 GORDON, Maurice B. *Aesculapius Comes to the Colonies: The Story of the Early Days of Medicine in the Thirteen Original Colonies.* Ventnor, N.J., 1949.

10 HEATON, Claude E. "Medicine in New Amsterdam." *Bull Hist Med*, IX (1941), 125–143.

11 HEATON, Claude E. "Medicine in New York during the English Colonial Period, 1664–1775." *Bull Hist Med*, XVII (1945), 9–37.

12 HOLMES, Chris. "Benjamin Rush and the Yellow Fever." *Bull Hist Med*, XL (1966), 246–263.

13 HUNTER, Robert J. "Benjamin Franklin and the Rise of Free Treatment of the Poor by the Medical Profession of Philadelphia." *Bull Hist Med*, XXI (1957), 137–146.

14 JONES, Gordon W. "The First Epidemic in English America." *Va Mag Hist Biog*, LXXI (1963), 3–10.

15 KRAFKA, Joseph, Jr. "Notes on Medical Practice in Colonial Georgia." *Ga Hist Q*, XXIII (1939), 351–361.

16 MILLER, Genevieve. "Smallpox Innoculation in England and America: A Reappraisal." *Wm Mar Q*, 3rd ser., XIII (1956), 476–492.

17 POWELL, John H. *Bring Out Your Dead: The Great Plague of Yellow Fever in Philadelphia in 1793.* Philadelphia, 1949.

18 ROSEN, George. "Political Order and Human Health in Jeffersonian Thought." *Bull Hist Med*, XXVI (1952), 32–44.

19 SCRIVEN, George R. "Maryland Medicine in the Seventeenth Century." *Md Hist Mag*, LVII (1962), 29–46.

20 SHRYOCK, Richard H. "Eighteenth Century Medicine in America." *Proc Am Ant Soc*, LIX (1949), 275–292.

21 WARING, Joseph I. *A History of Medicine in South Carolina, 1670–1825.* Charleston, S.C., 1964.

4. Medicine and Health (1800–1860)

1 ACKERKNECHT, Erwin H. *Malaria in the Upper Mississippi Valley 1760–1900*. Baltimore, 1945.

2 ANDERSON, Fannie. *Doctors Under Three Flags*. Detroit, Mich., 1951.

3 AYER, Hugh M. "Nineteenth Century Medicine." *Ind Mag Hist*, XLVIII (1952), 233–254.

4 BAUR, John E. "The Health Seeker in the Westward Movement, 1830–1900." *Miss Val Hist Rev*, XLVI (1959), 91–110.

5 BERMAN, Alex. "Neo-Thomsonianism in the United States." *J Hist Med Allied Sci*, XI (1956), 133–155.

6 BERMAN, Alex. "The Thomsonian Movement and Its Relation to American Pharmacy and Medicine." *Bull Hist Med*, XXV (1951), 519–538.

7 BLAKE, John B. "The Early History of Vital Statistics in Massachusetts." *Bull Hist Med*, XXIX (1955), 46–68.

8 BLANTON, Wyndham B. *Medicine in Virginia in the Nineteenth Century*. Richmond, Va., 1933.

9 CARRIGAN, Jo Ann. "Impact of Epidemic Yellow Fever on Life in Louisiana." *La Hist*, IV (1963), 5–34.

10 CARRIGAN, Jo Ann. "Some Medical Remedies of the Early Nineteenth Century." *Historian*, XXII (1959), 64–88.

11 CARRIGAN, Jo Ann. "Yellow Fever in New Orleans, 1853: Abstractions and Realities." *J S Hist*, XXV (1959), 339–355.

12 CROCKETT, Bernice N. "Health Conditions in Indian Territory, 1830 to the Civil War." *Chron Okla*, XXXV (1957), 80–90.

13 DALE, Edward E. "Medical Practices on the Frontier." *Ind Mag Hist*, XLIII (1947), 307–328.

14 DREWS, Robert S. "A History of the Care of the Sick Poor of the City of Detroit (1703–1855)." See 87.10.

15 DUFFY, John. "An Account of the Epidemic Fevers that Prevailed in the City of New York from 1791 to 1822." *N Y Hist Soc Q*, L (1966), 333–364.

16 DUFFY, John. "The Impact of Asiatic Cholera on Pittsburgh, Wheeling, and Charleston." *W Pa Hist Mag*, XLVII (1964), 199–212.

17 DUFFY, John. "Medical Practice in the Ante-Bellum South." *J S Hist*, XXV (1959), 53–72.

18 DUFFY, John. "Medicine and Medical Practice in Early Pittsburgh." *W Pa Hist Mag*, XLV (1962), 333–344.

19 DUFFY, John. "Smoke, Smog, and Health in Early Pittsburgh." *W Pa Hist Mag*, XLV (1962), 93–106.

20 DUFFY, John. *Sword of Pestilence: The New Orleans Yellow Fever Epidemic of 1853*. Baton Rouge, La., 1966.

21 EATON, Leonard K. *New England Hospitals 1790–1833*. Ann Arbor, Mich., 1957.

22 EVERETT, Donald E. "The New Orleans Yellow Fever Epidemic of 1853." *La Hist Q*, XXXIII (1950), 380–405.

1 FISHER, Walter. "Physicians and Slavery in the Antebellum Southern Medical Journal." See 37.14.

2 FOSSIER, A. E. "History of Yellow Fever in New Orleans." *La Hist Q*, XXXIV (1951), 205–216.

3 HAGGARD, J. Villasana. "Epidemic Cholera in Texas, 1833–1834." *SW Hist Q*, XL (1937), 216–230.

4 HARSTAD, Peter T. "Disease and Sickness on the Wisconsin Frontier: Smallpox and Other Diseases." *Wis Mag Hist*, XLIII (1960), 253–263.

5 HARSTAD, Peter T. "Sickness and Disease on the Wisconsin Frontier: Malaria, 1820–1850." *Wis Mag Hist*, XLIII (1959–1960), 83–96.

6 HORINE, Emmet F. *Daniel Drake (1785–1852): Pioneer Physician of the Midwest*. Philadelphia, 1961.

7 JONES, Billy M. *Health-Seekers in the Southwest, 1817–1900*. Norman, Okla., 1967.

8 MERRITT, Webster. *A Century of Medicine in Jacksonville and Duval County*. Gainesville, Fla., 1949.

9 MITCHELL, Martha C. "Health and the Medical Profession in the Lower South, 1845–1860." *J S Hist*, X (1944), 424–446.

10 MYER, Jesse S. *Life and Letters of Dr. William Beaumont*. St. Louis, Mo., 1912.

11 O'CONNER, Stella. "The Charity Hospital at New Orleans: An Administration and Financial History, 1736–1941." *La Hist Q*, XXI (1948), 1–109.

12 PETERSEN, William J. "Diseases and Doctors in Pioneer Iowa." *Iowa J Hist*, XLIX (1951), 97–116.

13 PICKARD, Madge E., and R. Carlyle BULEY. *The Midwest Pioneer: His Ills, Cures, & Doctors*. Crawfordsville, Ind., 1945.

14 POSTELL, William D. *Health of Slaves*. See 40.4.

15 ROBINSON, G. Canby. "Malaria in Virginia in the Early Nineteenth Century." *Bull Hist Med*, XXXII (1958), 531–536.

16 ROSEN, George. "The Medical Aspects of the Controversy Over Factory Conditions in New England, 1840–1850." *Bull Hist Med*, XV (1944), 483–497.

17 ROSENBERG, Charles E. *Cholera Years*. See 26.22.

18 SHRYOCK, Richard H. "Medical Practice in the Old South." *S Atl Q*, XXIX (1930), 160–178.

19 SHRYOCK, Richard H. "The Relations of Medicine to Society in the 1840's." In *Social Medicine: Its Derivations and Objectives*. Ed. by Iago Galdston. New York, 1949, 30–43.

20 SHRYOCK, Richard H. "The Yellow Fever Epidemics, 1793–1905." In *America in Crisis: Fourteen Crucial Episodes in American History*. Ed. by Daniel Aaron. New York, 1952, 51–70.

21 SIGERIST, Henry E. "The Cost of Illness to the City of New Orleans in 1850." *Bull Hist Med*, XV (1944), 498–507.

1 SMILLIE, Wilson G. "An Early Prepayment Plan for Medical Care: The Thomsonian System of Botanical Medicine." *J Hist Med Allied Sci*, VI (1951), 253–257.

2 SWADOES, Felice. "Negro Health on the Ante Bellum Plantations." See 41.1.

3 WARING, Joseph I. *A History of Medicine in South Carolina, 1825–1900.* Charleston, S.C., 1967.

5. *The Public Health Movement*

4 BLAKE, John B. "Lemuel Shattuck and the Boston Water Supply." *Bull Hist Med*, XXIX (1955), 554–562.

5 BLAKE, John B. *Public Health in the Town of Boston.* See 23.13.

6 CAVINS, Harold M. "The National Quarantine and Sanitary Conventions of 1857 to 1860 and the Beginnings of the American Public Health Association." *Bull Hist Med*, XIII (1943), 404–426.

7 DUFFY, John. *History of Public Health in New York City.* See 23.15.

8 HOWARD, William T. *Public Health Administration and the Natural History of Disease in Baltimore, Maryland, 1797–1920.* Washington, D.C., 1924.

9 JUDD, Jacob. "Brooklyn's Health and Sanitation, 1834–1855." *J Long Island Hist*, VII (1967), 40–52.

10 KRAMER, Howard D. "The Beginnings of the Public Health Movement in the United States." *Bull Hist Med*, XXI (1947), 352–376.

11 ROSEN, George. "Politics and Public Health in New York City (1838–1842)." *Bull Hist Med*, XXIV (1950), 441–461.

12 ROSENBERG, Charles E., and Carroll S. ROSENBERG. "Pietism and the Origins of the American Public Health Movement: A Note on John H. Griscom and Robert H. Hartley." *J Hist Med Allied Sci*, XXIII (1968), 16–35.

13 SHRYOCK, Richard H. "The Origins and Significance of the Public Health Movement in the United States." *Ann Med Hist*, N.S. I (1929), 645–665.

14 SMILLIE, Wilson G. *Public Health: Its Promise for the Future. A Chronicle of the Development of Public Health in the United States, 1607–1914.* New York, 1955.

15 WILLIAMS, Ralph C. *The United States Public Health Service, 1798–1950.* Washington, D.C., 1951.

6. *The Mentally Ill*

16 ADAMS, Evelyn C. "The Growing Concept of Social Responsibility Illustrated by a Study of the State's Care of the Insane in Indiana." *Ind Mag Hist*, XXXII (1936), 1–22.

1   American Psychiatric Association. *One Hundred Years of American Psychiatry* Ed. by J. K. Hall *et al.* New York, 1944.

2   BOND, Earl D. *Dr. Kirkbride and His Mental Hospital.* Philadelphia, 1947.

3   COCHRANE, Hortense S. "Early Treatment of the Mentally Ill in Georgia." *Ga Hist Q*, XXXII (1948), 105–118.

4   DAIN, Norman. *Concepts of Insanity in the United States, 1789–1865.* New Brunswick, N.J., 1964.

5   DAIN, Norman, and Eric T. CARLSON. "Social Class and Psychological Medicine in the United States, 1789–1824." *Bull Hist Med*, XXXIII (1959), 454–465.

6   DEUTSCH, Albert. "The First U.S. Census of the Insane (1840) and its Use as Pro-Slavery Propaganda." *Bull Hist Med*, XV (1944), 469–482.

7   DEUTSCH, Albert. *The Mentally Ill in America: A History of Their Care and Treatment from Colonial Times.* 2nd ed. New York, 1949.

8   GROB, Gerald N. *The State and the Mentally Ill: A History of Worcester State Hospital in Massachusetts, 1830–1920.* Chapel Hill, N.C., 1966.

9   HATHWAY, Marion. "Dorothea Dix and Social Reform in Western Pennsylvania 1845–1875." *W Pa Hist Mag*, XVII (1934), 247–258.

10 HURD, Henry M., ed. *The Institutional Care of the Insane in the United States and Canada.* 4 vols. Baltimore, 1916–1917.

11 MC CULLOCH, Margaret C. "Founding the North Carolina Asylum for the Insane." *N C Hist Rev*, XIII (1936), 185–201.

12 MARSHALL, Helen E. *Dorothea L. Dix: Forgotten Samaritan.* Chapel Hill, N.C., 1937.

13 RUSSELL, William L. *The New York Hospital: A History of the Psychiatric Service, 1771–1936.* New York, 1945.

14 THOMPSON, E. Bruce. "Reforms in the Care of the Insane in Tennessee, 1830–1850." *Tenn Hist Q*, III (1944), 319–334.

7. *Medical Quackery*

15 FISHBEIN, Morris. *Fads and Quackery in Healing: An Analysis of the Foibles of the Healing Cults, with Essays on Various Other Peculiar Notions in the Health Field.* New York, 1932.

16 REEVES, Dorothea D. "Come All for the Cure-all: Patent Medicines, Nineteenth Century Bonanza." *Har Lib Bull*, XV (1967), 253–272.

17 SHRYOCK, Richard H. "Quakery and Sectarianism in American Medicine." *Scalpel*, XIX (1949), 91–96.

18 SHRYOCK, Richard H. "Sylvester Graham and the Health Reform Movement, 1830–1870." *Miss Val Hist Rev*, XVIII (1931), 172–183.

19 YOUNG, James H. *The Toadstool Millionaires: A Social History of Patent Medicines in America before Federal Regulation.* Princeton, 1961.

XV. Law Enforcement, Justice, and Crime

1. General

1 BILLIAS, George A., ed. *Law and Authority in Colonial America: Selected Essays.* Barre, Mass., 1965.

2 CHROUST, Anton-Hermann. *Rise of the Legal Profession.* See 27.20.

3 ENGLISH, William F. *The Pioneer Lawyer and Jurist in Missouri.* Columbia, Mo., 1947.

4 FLAHERTY, David H., ed. *Essays in the History of Early American Law.* Chapel Hill, N.C., 1969.

5 HASKINS, George L. *Law and Authority in Early Massachusetts: A Study in Tradition and Design.* New York, 1960.

6 HASKINS, George L. "Law and Colonial Society." *Am Q*, IX (1957), 355–364.

7 HURST, James W. *The Growth of American Law: The Law Makers.* Boston, 1950.

8 HURST, James W. *Law and the Conditions of Freedom in the Nineteenth-Century United States.* Madison, Wis., 1956.

9 HURST, James W. *Law and Social Process in United States History.* Ann Arbor, Mich., 1960.

10 KOMMERS, Donald P. "The Emergence of Law and Justice in Pre-Territorial Wisconsin." *Am J Leg Hist*, VIII (1964), 20–33.

11 MORRIS, Richard B. *Studies in the History of American Law, with Special Reference to the Seventeenth and Eighteenth Centuries.* New York, 1930.

12 REINSCH, Paul S. *English Common Law in the Early American Colonies.* Madison, Wis., 1899.

13 WARREN, Charles. *A History of the American Bar.* Boston, 1911.

2. Law Enforcement and Punishment

14 CHITWOOD, Oliver P. *Justice in Colonial Virginia.* Baltimore, 1905.

15 CHUMBLEY, George L. *Colonial Justice in Virginia: The Development of a Judicial System: Typical Laws and Cases of the Period.* Richmond, Va., 1938.

16 COLEMAN, Peter J. "The Insolvent Debtor in Rhode Island: 1745–1828." *Wm Mar Q*, 3rd ser., XXII (1965), 413–434.

17 CONANT, H. J. "Imprisonment for Debt in Vermont: A History." *Vt Q*, N.S. XIX (1951), 67–81.

1 CUTLER, James E. *Lynch-Law: An Investigation into the History of Lynching in the United States.* New York, 1905.

2 DAVIS, David B. "The Movement to Abolish Capital Punishment in America, 1787–1861." *Am Hist Rev*, LXIII (1957), 23–46.

3 EARLE, Alice M. *Curious Punishments of Bygone Days.* Chicago, 1896.

4 ERIKSON, Kai T. *Wayward Puritans: A Study in the Sociology of Deviance.* New York, 1966.

5 FEER, Robert A. "Imprisonment for Debt in Massachusetts before 1800." *Miss Val Hist Rev*, XLVIII (1961), 252–269.

6 FITZROY, Herbert W. K. "The Punishment of Crime in Provincial Pennsylvania." *Pa Mag Hist Biog*, LX (1936), 242–269.

7 GARD, Wayne. *Frontier Justice.* Norman, Okla., 1949.

8 GIPSON, Lawrence H. *Crime and Its Punishment in Provincial Pennsylvania: A Phase of the Social History of the Commonwealth.* Bethlehem, Pa., 1935.

9 GOEBEL, Julius, Jr., and T. Raymond NAUGHTON. *Law Enforcement in Colonial New York: A Study in Criminal Procedure (1664–1776).* New York, 1944.

10 HASKINS, George L. "Ecclesiastical Antecedents of Criminal Punishment in Early Massachusetts." *Proc Mass Hist Soc*, LXXII (1957–1960), 21–35.

11 HAYNES, Robert V. "Law Enforcement in Frontier Mississippi." *J Miss Hist*, XXII (1960), 27–42.

12 KARRAKER, Cyrus H. *The Seventeenth-Century Sheriff: A Comparative Study of the Sheriff in England and the Chesapeake Colonies 1607–1689.* Philadelphia, 1930.

13 LANE, Roger. "Crime and Criminal Statistics in Nineteenth-Century Massachusetts." *J Soc Hist*, II (1968), 156–163.

14 LUTZKER, Michael A. "Abolition of Imprisonment for Debt in New Jersey." *Proc N J Hist Soc*, LXXXIV (1966), 1–29.

15 PHILLIPS, Ulrich B. "Slave Crime in Virginia." See 40.2.

16 POST, Albert. "The Anti-Gallows Movement in Ohio." *Ohio State Arch Hist Q*, LIV (1945), 104–112.

17 POWERS, Edwin, ed. *Crime and Punishment in Early Massachusetts, 1620–1692.* Boston, 1966.

18 RANDALL, Edwin T. "Imprisonment for Debt in America: Fact and Fiction." *Miss Val Hist Rev*, XXXIX (1952), 89–102.

19 RANKIN, Hugh F. "Criminal Trial Proceedings in the General Court of Colonial Virginia." *Va Mag Hist Biog*, LXXII (1964), 50–74.

20 RYAN, Edward L. "Imprisonment for Debt—Its Origin and Repeal." *Va Mag Hist Biog*, XLII (1934), 53–58.

21 SCOTT, Arthur P. *Criminal Law in Colonial Virginia.* Chicago, 1930.

22 SEMMES, Raphael. *Crime and Punishment in Early Maryland.* Baltimore, 1938.

1 SHAIMAN, S. Lawrence. "The History of Imprisonment for Debt and Insolvency Laws in Pennsylvania as They Evolved from the Common Law." *Am J Leg Hist*, IV (1960), 205–225.

2 WILLIAMS, Jack K. "Crime and Punishment in Alabama, 1819–1840." *Ala Rev*, VI (1953), 14–31.

3 WILLIAMS, Jack K. *Vogues in Villainy: Crime and Retribution in Ante-Bellum South Carolina.* Columbia, S.C., 1959.

4 ZANGER, Jules. "Crime and Punishment in Early Massachusetts." *Wm Mar Q*, 3rd ser., XXII (1965), 471–477.

3. Prisons and Prison Reform

5 BARNES, Harry E. "The Evolution of American Penology as Illustrated by the Western Penitentiary of Pennsylvania." *W Pa Hist Mag*, IV (1921), 191–212.

6 BARNES, Harry E. *The Evolution of Penology in Pennsylvania: A Study in American Social History.* Indianapolis, Ind., 1927.

7 BARNES, Harry E. *A History of the Penal, Reformatory and Correctional Institutions of the State of New Jersey, Analytical and Documentary.* Trenton, N.J., 1918.

8 BARNES, Harry E. "Origins of Prison Reform in New York State." *Q J N Y Hist Assn*, XIX (1921), 89–99.

9 CARY, John H. "France Looks to Pennsylvania: The Eastern Penitentiary as a Symbol of Reform." *Pa Mag Hist Biog*, LXXXII (1958), 186–203.

10 CROWE, Jesse C. "The Origin and Development of Tennessee's Prison Problem, 1831–1871." *Tenn Hist Q*, XV (1956), 111–135.

11 DE PUY, Leroy B. "The Triumph of the 'Pennsylvania System' at the State's Penitentiaries." *Pa Hist*, XXI (1954), 128–144.

12 DOLL, Eugene E. "Trial and Error at Allegheny: The Western State Penitentiary, 1818–1838," *Pa Mag Hist Biog*, LXXXI (1957), 3–27.

13 GETTLEMAN, Marvin E. "The Maryland Penitentiary in the Age of Tocqueville, 1828–1842." *Md Hist Mag*, LVI (1961), 269–320.

14 KLEIN, Philip. *Prison Methods in New York State: A Contribution to the Study of the Theory and Practice of Correctional Institutions in New York State.* New York, 1920.

15 LEWIS, Orlando F. *The Development of American Prisons and Prison Customs, 1776–1845, with Special Reference to Early Institutions in the State of New York.* Albany, N.Y., 1922.

16 LEWIS, W. David. *From Newgate to Dannemora: The Rise of the Penitentiary in New York, 1796–1848.* Ithaca, N.Y., 1965.

17 MC KELVEY, Blake. *American Prisons: A Study in American Social History prior to 1915.* Chicago, 1936.

18 TEETERS, Negley K., and John D. SHEARER. *The Prison at Philadelphia, Cherry Hill: The Separate System of Penal Discipline, 1829–1913.* New York, 1957.

1 TEETERS, Negley K. *They Were in Prison: A History of the Pennsylvania Prison Society, 1787–1937, formerly The Philadelphia Society for Alleviating the Miseries of Public Prisons.* Philadelphia, 1937.

2 THOMPSON, E. Bruce. "Reforms in the Penal System of Mississippi, 1820–1850." *J Miss Hist*, VII (1945), 51–74.

3 THOMPSON, E. Bruce. "Reforms in the Penal System of Tennessee, 1820–1850." *Tenn Hist Q*, I (1942), 291–308.

XVI. Everyday Life

1. Recreation

4 AKERS, Dwight. *Drivers Up: The Story of American Harness Racing.* 2nd ed. New York, 1947.

5 DULLES, Foster Rhea. *America Learns to Play: A History of Popular Recreation, 1607–1940.* New York, 1940.†

6 DURANT, John, and Otto BETTMANN. *Pictorial History of American Sports: From Colonial Times to the Present.* New York, 1952.

7 EZELL, John S. *Fortune's Merry Wheel: The Lottery in America.* Cambridge, 1960.

8 GOODSPEED, Charles E. *Angling in America: Its Early History and Literature.* Boston, 1939.

9 HERVEY, John. *Racing in America: 1665–1865.* New York, 1944.

10 HOLLIMAN, Jennie. *American Sports (1785–1835).* Durham, N.C., 1931.

11 KROUT, John A. *Annals of American Sport.* New Haven, 1929.

12 MANCHESTER, Herbert. *Four Centuries of Sport in America, 1490–1890.* New York, 1931.

13 PARMER, Charles B. *For Gold and Glory: The Story of Thoroughbred Racing in America.* New York, 1939.

14 SEYMOUR, Harold. *Baseball: The Early Years.* New York, 1960.

2. Manners and Customs

15 BLAIR, Walter. *Native American Humor (1800–1900).* New York, 1931.†

16 BOATRIGHT, Mody C. *Folk Laughter on the American Frontier.* New York, 1949.†

17 BRIDENBAUGH, Carl. "Baths and Watering Places of Colonial America." *Wm Mar Q*, 3rd ser., III (1946), 151–181.

18 CARDWELL, Guy A. "The Duel in the Old South: Crux of a Concept." *S Atl Q*, LXVI (1967), 50–69.

19 CARSON, Gerald. *The Old Country Store.* New York, 1954.†

1 CARSON, Gerald. *The Polite Americans: A Wide-Angle View of Our More or Less Good Manners Over 300 Years.* New York, 1966.

2 CLARK, Thomas D. "The Country Store in American Social History." *Ohio State Arch Hist Q*, LX (1951), 126–144.

3 CLARK, Thomas D. *The Rampaging Frontier: Manners and Humors of Pioneer Days in the South and Middle West.* Indianapolis, Ind., 1939.†

4 CUMMINGS, Richard O. *The American and His Food: A History of Food Habits in the United States.* Rev. ed. Chicago, 1941.

5 DAVIS, Robert R., Jr. "Diplomatic Plumage: American Court Dress in the Early National Period." *Am Q*, XX (1968), 164–179.

6 DORSON, Richard M. *American Folklore.* Chicago, 1959.†

7 DOW, George F. *Every Day Life in the Massachusetts Bay Colony.* Boston, 1935.

8 EARLE, Alice M. *Colonial Days in Old New York.* New York, 1896.

9 EARLE, Alice M. *Costume of Colonial Times.* New York, 1894.

10 EARLE, Alice M. *The Sabbath in Puritan New England.* New York, 1891.

11 EARLE, Alice M. *Stage-Coach and Tavern Days.* New York, 1900.

12 EARLE, Alice M. *Two Centuries of Costume in America, MDCXX–MDCCCX.* 2 vols. New York, 1903.

13 EVANS, Meryle R. "Knickerbocker Hotels and Restaurants, 1800–1850." *N Y Hist Soc Q*, XXXVI (1952), 377–410.

14 FIELD, Edward. *The Colonial Tavern: A Glimpse of New England Town Life in the Seventeenth and Eighteenth Centuries.* Providence, R.I., 1897.

15 GARWOOD, Ellen. "Early Texas Inns: A Study in Social Relationships." *SW Hist Q*, LX (1956), 219–244.

16 GRAHAM, Robert E. "The Taverns of Colonial Philadelphia." *Trans Am Philos Soc*, XLIII (1953), 318–325.

17 HABENSTEIN, Robert W., and William M. LAMERS. *The History of American Funeral Directing.* Milwaukee, Wis., 1955.

18 HEDRICK, Ulysses P. *A History of Horticulture in America to 1860.* New York, 1950.

19 HUNT, Gaillard. *Life in America One Hundred Years Ago.* New York, 1914.

20 JOHNSON, Laurence A. *Over the Counter and on the Shelf: Country Store-keeping in America, 1620–1920.* Rutland, Vt., 1961.

21 JORDAN, Philip D. "Humor of the Backwoods, 1820–1840." *Miss Val Hist Rev*, XXV (1938), 25–38.

22 KIMBALL, Marie. "Some Genial Old Drinking Customs." *Wm Mar Q*, 3rd ser., VII (1945), 349–358.

23 KING, Doris E. "The First-Class Hotel and the Age of the Common Man." *J S Hist*, XXIII (1957), 173–188.

1 LATHROP, Elsie. *Early American Inns and Taverns*. New York, 1926.

2 LOVE, William D. *The Fast and Thanksgiving Days in New England*. Boston, 1895.

3 MURRELL, William. *A History of American Graphic Humor*. 2 vols. New York, 1933–1938.

4 NEUHOFF, Dorothy A. "Christmas in Colonial America." *Soc Stud*, XL (1949), 339–349.

5 PLUMMER, Wilbur C. "Consumer Credit in Colonial Philadelphia." *Pa Mag Hist Biog*, LXVI (1942), 385–409.

6 POSEY, Walter B. "The Public Manners of Ante-Bellum Southerners." *J Miss Hist*, XIX (1957), 219–233.

7 ROURKE, Constance M. *American Humor: A Study of the National Character*. New York, 1931.†

8 SCHLESINGER, Arthur M. "A Dietary Interpretation of American History." *Proc Mass Hist Soc*, LXVIII (1944–1947), 199–207.

9 SCHLESINGER, Arthur M. *Learning How to Behave: A Historical Study of American Etiquette Books*. New York, 1946.

10 STEVENS, William O. *Pistols at Ten Paces: The Story of the Code of Honor in America*. Cambridge, 1940.

11 STEWART, George R. *American Ways of Life*. Garden City, N.Y., 1954.

12 TANDY, Jennette R. *Crackerbox Philosophers in American Humor and Satire*. New York, 1925.

13 VAN ORMAN, Richard A. *A Room for the Night: Hotels of the Old West*. Bloomington, Ind., 1966.

14 WARWICK, Edward, Henry PITZ, and Alexander WYCKOFF. *Early American Dress: The Colonial and Revolutionary Periods*. New York, 1965.

15 WILLIAMS, Jack K. "The Code of Honor in Ante-Bellum South Carolina." *S C Hist Mag*, LIV (1953), 113–128.

16 WILLIAMSON, Jefferson. *The American Hotel: An Anecdotal History*. New York, 1930.

17 WRIGHT, Richardson. *Hawkers and Walkers in Early America*. Philadelphia, 1927.

18 YODER, Paton. "The American Inn, 1775–1850: Melting Pot or Stewing Kettle?" *Ind Mag Hist*, LIX (1963), 135–151.

19 YODER, Paton. "Private Hospitality in the South, 1775–1850." *Miss Val Hist Rev*, XLVII (1960), 419–433.

XVII. Journalism and Libraries

1. Newspapers and the Press

1 ANDERSEN, Arlow W. *The Immigrant Takes His Stand: The Norwegian-American Press and Public Affairs, 1847–1872*. Northfield, Minn., 1953.

2 BACKLUND, Jonas O. *A Century of the Swedish American Press*. Chicago, 1952.

3 BARTOW, Edith M. *News and These United States*. New York, 1952.

4 BAUMGARTNER, Apollinaris W. *Catholic Journalism*. See 61.19.

5 BRIGHAM, Clarence S. *History and Bibliography of American Newspapers, 1690–1820*. 2 vols. Worcester, Mass., 1947.

6 BRIGHAM, Clarence S. *Journals and Journeymen: A Contribution to the History of Early Newspapers*. Philadelphia, 1950.

7 CLARK, Thomas D. "The Country Newspaper as a Source of Social History." *Ind Mag Hist*, XLVIII (1952), 217–232.

8 CLARK, Thomas D. *The Southern Country Editor*. Indianapolis, Ind., 1948.

9 COHEN, Hennig. *The South Carolina Gazette, 1732–1775*. Columbia, S.C., 1953.

10 COOK, Elizabeth C. *Literary Influences in Colonial Newspapers, 1704–1750*. New York, 1912.

11 CROUTHAMEL, James L. "The Newspaper Revolution in New York, 1830–1860." *N Y Hist*, XLV (1964), 91–113.

12 DEMAREE, Albert L. *The American Agricultural Press, 1819–1860*. New York, 1941.

13 DICKERSON, Oliver M. "British Control of American Newspapers on the Eve of the Revolution." *N Eng Q*, XXIV (1951), 453–468.

14 ELLIOTT, Robert N., Jr. *The Raleigh Register, 1799–1863*. Chapel Hill, N.C., 1955.†

15 EMERY, Edwin, and Henry L. SMITH. *The Press and America*. New York, 1954.

16 FORD, Edwin H. *History of Journalism in the United States: A Bibliography of Books and Annotated Articles*. Minneapolis, Minn., 1938.

17 FORSYTH, David P. *The Business Press in America, 1750–1865*. Philadelphia, 1964.

18 HAGE, George S. *Newspapers on the Minnesota Frontier, 1849–1860*. St. Paul, Minn., 1967.

19 JONES, Robert W. *Journalism in the United States*. New York, 1947.

20 KOBRE, Sidney. *The Development of the Colonial Newspaper*. Pittsburgh, Pa., 1944.

21 KOBRE, Sidney. *Foundations of American Journalism*. Tallahassee, Fla., 1958.

22 LEDER, Lawrence H. "The Role of Newspapers in Early America: 'In Defense of Their Own Liberty.'" *Hunt Lib Q*, XXX (1966), 1–16.

1 LEE, Alfred M. *The Daily Newspaper in America: The Evolution of a Social Instrument.* New York, 1937.

2 LYON, William H. *The Pioneer Editor in Missouri, 1808–1860.* Columbia, Mo., 1965.

3 MERRITT, Richard L. "Public Opinion in Colonial America: Content-Analyzing the Colonial Press." *Pub Opin Q,* XXVII (1963), 356–371.

4 MILES, Edwin A. "The Mississippi Press in the Jackson Era, 1824–1841." *J Miss Hist,* XIX (1957), 1–20.

5 MOTT, Frank L. *American Journalism: A History of Newspapers in the United States Through 250 Years, 1690–1950.* Rev. ed. New York, 1950.

6 NEVINS, Allan. *The Evening Post: A Century of Journalism.* New York, 1922.

7 ROSEWATER, Victor. *History of Coöperative News-Gathering in the United States.* New York, 1930.

8 SCHLESINGER, Arthur M. *Prelude to Independence: The Newspaper War on Britain, 1764–1776.* New York, 1958.†

9 STROUPE, Henry S. *The Religious Press in the South Atlantic States, 1802–1865: An Annotated Bibliography with Historical Introduction and Notes.* Durham, N.C., 1956.

10 WEISBERGER, Bernard A. *The American Newspaperman.* Chicago, 1961.

11 WITTKE, Carl F. *The German-Language Press in America.* Lexington, Ky., 1957.

2. Freedom of the Press

12 DUNIWAY, Clyde A. *The Development of Freedom of the Press in Massachusetts.* New York, 1906.

13 LEVY, Leonard W. "Did the Zenger Case Really Matter?: Freedom of the Press in Colonial New York." *Wm Mar Q,* 3rd ser., XVII (1960), 35–50.

14 LEVY, Leonard W. *Legacy of Suppression: Freedom of Speech and Press in Early American History.* Cambridge, 1960.

15 MILLER, John C. *Crisis in Freedom: The Alien and Sedition Acts.* Boston, 1951.†

16 SCHUYLER, Livingston R. *The Liberty of the Press in the American Colonies before the Revolutionary War: With Particular Reference to Conditions in the Royal Colony of New York.* New York, 1905.

17 SMITH, James M. *Freedom's Fetters: The Alien and Sedition Laws and American Civil Liberties.* Ithaca, N.Y., 1956.†

3. *Magazines*

1 GOHDES, Clarence L. F. *The Periodicals of American Transcendentalism.* Durham, N.C., 1931.

2 LUXON, Norval N. *Niles' Weekly Register: News Magazine of the Nineteenth Century.* Baton Rouge, La., 1947.

3 MINOR, Benjamin B. *The Southern Literary Messenger, 1834–1864.* New York, 1905.

4 MOTT, Frank L. *A History of American Magazines.* 5 vols. Cambridge, 1938–1968.

5 RICHARDSON, Lyon N. *History of Early American Magazines, 1741–1789.* New York, 1931.

6 RILEY, Susan B. "The Hazards of Periodical Publishing in the South during the Nineteenth Century." *Tenn Hist Q*, XXI (1962), 365–376.

7 SKIPPER, Ottis C. *J. D. B. De Bow: Magazinist of the Old South.* Athens, Ga., 1958.

8 SMYTH, Albert H. *The Philadelphia Magazines and Their Contributors, 1741–1850.* Philadelphia, 1892.

9 STEARNS, Bertha M. "Early Western Magazines for Ladies." *Miss Val Hist Rev*, XVIII (1931), 319–330.

10 STEARNS, Bertha M. "Philadelphia Magazines for Ladies: 1830–1860." *Pa Mag Hist Biog*, LXIX (1945), 207–219.

11 WOOD, James P. *Magazines in the United States.* 2nd ed. New York, 1956.

4. *Libraries and American Culture*

12 BOLTON, Charles K. *American Library History.* Chicago, 1911.

13 BOLTON, Charles K. *Proprietary and Subscription Libraries.* Chicago, 1912.

14 DITZION, Sidney H. *Arsenals of a Democratic Culture: A Social History of the American Public Library Movement in New England and the Middle States from 1850 to 1900.* Chicago, 1947.

15 GRAY, Austin K. *The First American Library: A Short Account of the Library Company of Philadelphia 1731–1931.* Philadelphia, 1936.

16 GREEN, Samuel S. *The Public Library Movement in the United States 1853–1893.* Boston, 1913.

17 KEEP, Austin B. *History of the New York Society Library, with an Introductory Chapter on Libraries in Colonial New York, 1698–1776.* New York, 1908.

18 MEARNS, David C. *The Story up to Now: The Library of Congress, 1800–1946.* Washington, D.C., 1947.

19 SHERA, Jesse H. *Foundations of the Public Library: Origins of the Public Library Movement in New England, 1629–1855.* Chicago, 1949.

20 SHORES, Louis. *Origins of the American College Library 1638–1800.* Nashville, Tenn., 1934.

XVIII. Culture, Art, and Architecture

1. Cultural Life

1 BOWES, Frederick P. *The Culture of Early Charleston.* Chapel Hill, N.C., 1942.

2 CADY, Edwin H. *The Gentleman in America: A Literary Study in American Culture.* Syracuse, N.Y., 1949.

3 DALE, Edward E. "Culture on the American Frontier." *Neb Hist,* XXVI (1945), 75–90.

4 DAVENPORT, F. Garvin. *Cultural Life in Nashville on the Eve of the Civil War.* Chapel Hill, N.C., 1941.

5 DAVIS, David B. *Homicide in American Fiction, 1798–1860: A Study in Social Values.* Ithaca, N.Y., 1957.†

6 ESAREY, Logan. "Elements of Culture in the Old Northwest." *Ind Mag Hist,* LIII (1957), 257–264.

7 FOX, Dixon R., ed. *Sources of Culture in the Middle West: Backgrounds Versus Frontier.* New York, 1934.

8 JONES, Howard M. *O Strange New World.* See 7.6.

9 MILLER, James M. *The Genesis of Western Culture: The Upper Ohio Valley, 1800–1825.* Columbus, Ohio, 1938.

10 NYE, Russel B. *Cultural Life of the New Nation.* See 9.6.

11 SHANNON, Fred A. "Culture and Agriculture in America." *Miss Val Hist Rev,* XLI (1954), 3–20.

12 TOLLES, Frederick B. "The Culture of Early Pennsylvania." *Pa Mag Hist Biog,* LXXXI (1957), 119–137.

13 WECTER, Dixon. "Instruments of Culture on the Frontier." *Yale Rev,* XXXVI (1947), 242–256.

14 WERTENBAKER, Thomas J. *The Golden Age of Colonial Culture.* 2nd ed. New York, 1949.†

15 WRIGHT, Louis B. *Cultural Life of the American Colonies.* See 8.12.

16 WRIGHT, Louis B. *Culture on the Moving Frontier.* Bloomington, Ind., 1955.†

2. The Arts and Artists

17 BARKER, Virgil. *American Painting: History and Interpretation.* New York, 1950.

18 BORN, Wolfgang. *American Landscape Painting: An Interpretation.* New Haven, 1948.

1   BORN, Wolfgang. *Still-Life Painting in America.* New York, 1947.

2   BURROUGHS, Alan. *Limners and Likenesses: Three Centuries of American Painting.* Cambridge, 1936.

3   CAFFIN, Charles H. *The Story of American Painting: The Evolution of Painting in America from Colonial Times to the Present.* New York, 1907.

4   CALLOW, James T. *Kindred Spirits: Knickerbocker Writers and American Artists 1807–1855.* Chapel Hill, N.C., 1967.

5   CRAVEN, Wayne. *Sculpture in America: From the Colonial Period to the Present.* New York, 1968.

6   DICKSON, Harold E. *Arts of the Young Republic: The Age of William Dunlap.* Chapel Hill, N.C., 1968.

7   FLEXNER, James T. *America's Old Masters: First Artists of the New World.* New York, 1939.†

8   FLEXNER, James T. *First Flowers of Our Wilderness: American Painting.* Boston, 1947.

9   FLEXNER, James T. *The Light of Distant Skies, 1760–1835.* New York, 1954.

10 FLEXNER, James T. *That Wilder Image: The Painting of America's Native School from Thomas Cole to Winslow Homer.* Boston, 1962.

11 GARDNER, Albert Ten Eyck. *Yankee Stonecutters: The First American School of Sculpture, 1800–1850.* New York, 1945.

12 GOODRICH, Lloyd. "The Painting of American History: 1775–1900." *Am Q,* III (1951), 283–294.

13 GROCE, George C., and David H. WALLACE. *The New-York Historical Society's Dictionary of Artists in America 1564–1860.* New Haven, 1957.

14 HAGEN, Oskar. *The Birth of the American Tradition in Art.* New York, 1940.

15 HARRIS, Neil. *The Artist in American Society: The Formative Years, 1790–1860.* New York, 1966.

16 ISHAM, Samuel. *The History of American Painting.* New ed. with supplemental chaps. by Royal Cortissoz. New York, 1927.

17 LAFOLLETTE, Suzanne. *Art in America.* New York, 1929.

18 LARKIN, Oliver W. *Art and Life in America.* New York, 1949.

19 MC COUBREY, John W. *American Tradition in Painting.* New York, 1963.

20 MATHER, Frank J., *et al. The American Spirit in Art.* New Haven, 1927.

21 MENDELOWITZ, Daniel M. *A History of American Art.* New York, 1960.

22 MILLER, Lillian B. "Paintings, Sculpture, and the National Character, 1815–1860." *J Am Hist,* LIII (1967), 696–707.

1 MILLER, Lillian B. *Patrons and Patriotism: The Encouragement of the Fine Arts in the United States, 1790–1860.* Chicago, 1966.

2 RICHARDSON, Edgar P. *American Romantic Painting.* New York, 1944.

3 RICHARDSON, Edgar P. *Painting in America: The Story of 450 Years.* New York, 1956.

4 TAFT, Lorado. *The History of American Sculpture.* New ed. New York, 1930.

5 WEHLE, Harry B. *American Miniatures, 1730–1850.* Garden City, N.Y., 1927.

6 WEITENKAMPF, Frank. *American Graphic Art.* New ed. New York, 1924.

7 WHITEHILL, Walter M., *et al. The Arts in Early American History: Needs and Opportunities for Study.* Chapel Hill, N.C., 1965.

3. Theatre

8 BROWN, Thomas A. *A History of the New York Stage from the First Performance in 1732 to 1901.* 3 vols. New York, 1903.

9 CARSON, William G. B. *The Theatre on the Frontier: Early Years of the St. Louis Stage.* Chicago, 1932.

10 COAD, Oral S., and Edwin MIMS, Jr. *The American Stage.* New Haven, 1929.

11 CRAWFORD, Mary C. *The Romance of the American Theater.* New York, 1913.

12 DORMON, James H. *Theater in the Ante Bellum South 1815–1861.* Chapel Hill, N.C., 1967.

13 DORSON, Richard M. "The Yankee on the Stage—A Folk Hero of American Drama." *N Eng Q,* XIII (1940), 467–493.

14 DUNN, Esther C. *Shakespeare in America.* New York, 1939.

15 FOX, Dixon R. "The Development of the American Theater." *N Y Hist,* XVII (1936), 22–41.

16 GRAHAM, Philip. *Showboats: The History of an American Institution.* Austin, Tex., 1951.

17 GRIMSTED, David. *Melodrama Unveiled: American Theater and Culture, 1800–1850.* Chicago, 1968.

18 HORNBLOW, Arthur. *A History of the Theater in America from Its Beginnings to the Present Time.* 2 vols. Philadelphia, 1919.

19 HUGHES, Glenn. *A History of the American Theatre, 1700–1950.* New York, 1951.

20 JAMES, Reese D. *Cradle of Culture: The Philadelphia Stage, 1800–1810.* Philadelphia, 1957.

21 KENDALL, John S. *The Golden Age of the New Orleans Theatre.* Baton Rouge, La., 1952.

1   MC NAMARA, Brooks. *The American Playhouse in the Eighteenth Century.* Cambridge, 1969.

2   MAYORGA, Margaret G., ed. *A Short History of the American Drama.* New York, 1932.

3   ODELL, George C. D. *Annals of the New York Stage.* 15 vols. New York, 1927–1949.

4   POLLOCK, Thomas C. *The Philadelphia Theatre in the Eighteenth Century.* Philadelphia, 1933.

5   QUINN, Arthur H. *A History of the American Drama from the Beginning to the Civil War.* 2nd ed. New York, 1943.

6   RANKIN, Hugh F. *The Theater in Colonial America.* Chapel Hill, N.C., 1965.

7   SCHICK, Joseph S. *The Early Theater in Eastern Iowa: Cultural Beginnings and the Rise of the Theater in Davenport and Eastern Iowa, 1836–1863.* Chicago, 1939.

8   WILLIS, Eola. *The Charleston Stage in the XVIII Century, with Social Settings of the Time.* Columbia, S.C., 1924.

9   WITTKE, Carl F. "The Immigrant Theme on the American Stage." *Miss Val Hist Rev,* XXXIX (1952), 211–232.

10 WITTKE, Carl F. *Tambo and Bones: A History of the American Minstrel Stage.* Durham, N.C., 1930.

4. Architecture

11 ALEXANDER, Robert L. "Architecture and Aristocracy: The Cosmopolitan Style of Latrobe and Godefroy." *Md Hist Mag,* LVI (1961), 229–243.

12 ANDREWS, Wayne. *Architecture, Ambition and Americans: A History of American Architecture from the Beginning to the Present.* New York, 1955.†

13 BANKS, Charles E. *The English Ancestry and Homes of the Pilgrim Fathers.* New York, 1929.

14 BRIGGS, Martin S. *The Homes of the Pilgrim Fathers in England and America (1620–1685).* London, 1932.

15 BURCHARD, John, and Albert BUSH-BROWN. *The Architecture of America: A Social and Cultural History.* Boston, 1961.†

16 COFFIN, Lewis A., and Arthur C. HOLDEN. *Brick Architecture of the Colonial Period in Maryland & Virginia.* New York, 1919.

17 CONDIT, Carl W. *American Building Art: The Nineteenth Century.* New York, 1960.

18 CONDIT, Carl W. *American Building: Materials and Techniques from the Beginning of Colonial Settlements to the Present.* Chicago, 1968.

19 COOLIDGE, John P. *Mill and Mansion: A Study of Architecture and Society in Lowell, Massachusetts, 1820–1865.* New York, 1942.

20 COUSINS, Frank, and Phil M. RILEY. *The Colonial Architecture of Philadelphia.* Boston, 1920.

1 COUSINS, Frank and Phil M. RILEY. *The Colonial Architecture of Salem.* Boston, 1919.

2 DONNELLY, Marian C. *The New England Meeting Houses of the Seventeenth Century.* Middletown, Conn., 1968.

3 DOWNING, Antoinette F., and Vincent J. SCULLY, Jr. *The Architectural Heritage of Newport, Rhode Island, 1640–1915.* Cambridge, 1952.

4 EBERLEIN, Harold D., and Cortlandt Van Dyke HUBBARD. *American Georgian Architecture.* Bloomington, Ind., 1952.

5 EBERLEIN, Harold D. *The Architecture of Colonial America.* Boston, 1915.

6 FITCH, James M. *American Building: 1: The Historical Forces That Shaped It.* 2nd ed. Boston, 1966.

7 FORMAN, Henry C. *The Architecture of the Old South: The Medieval Style, 1585–1850.* Cambridge, 1948.

8 GARVAN, Anthony N. B. *Architecture and Town Planning in Colonial Connecticut.* New Haven, 1951.

9 GOWANS, Alan. *Architecture in New Jersey: A Record of American Civilization.* Princeton, 1964.

10 GOWANS, Alan. *Images of American Living: Four Centuries of Architecture and Furniture as Cultural Expression.* Philadelphia, 1964.

11 HAMLIN, Talbot F. *The American Spirit in Architecture.* New Haven, 1926.

12 HAMLIN, Talbot. F. *Benjamin Henry Latrobe.* New York, 1955.

13 HAMLIN, Talbot F. *Greek Revival Architecture in America.* New York, 1944.†

14 HANDLIN, David P. "New England Architects in New York, 1820–40." *Am Q*, XIX (1967), 681–695.

15 JACKSON, Joseph. *American Colonial Architecture: Its Origin and Development.* Philadelphia, 1924.

16 JACKSON, Joseph. *Development of American Architecture, 1783–1830.* Philadelphia, 1926.

17 JOHNSTON, Frances B., and Thomas T. WATERMAN. *The Early Architecture of North Carolina.* Chapel Hill, N.C., 1941.

18 KELLY, John F. *The Early Domestic Architecture of Connecticut.* New Haven, 1924.†

19 KIMBALL, Fiske. "Architecture in the History of the Colonies and of the Republic." *Am Hist Rev*, XXVII (1921), 47–57.

20 KIMBALL, Fiske. *Domestic Architecture of the American Colonies and of the Early Republic.* New York, 1922.†

21 KINGMAN, Ralph C. *New England Georgian Architecture.* New York, 1913.

22 KIRKER, Harold, and James KIRKER. *Bulfinch's Boston, 1787–1817.* New York, 1964.

1 MIXER, Knowlton. *Old Houses of New England.* New York, 1927.

2 MORRISON, Hugh S. *Early American Architecture from the First Colonial Settlements to the National Period.* New York, 1952.

3 MUMFORD, Lewis. *Sticks and Stones: A Study of American Architecture and Civilization.* 2nd ed. New York, 1955.†

4 NEWCOMB, Rexford. *Architecture of the Old Northwest Territory: A Study of Early Architecture in Ohio, Indiana, Illinois, Michigan, Wisconsin, & Part of Minnesota.* Chicago, 1950.

5 SALE, Edith T. *Manors of Virginia in Colonial Times.* Philadelphia, 1909.

6 SANFORD, Trent E. *The Architecture of the Southwest: Indian, Spanish, American.* New York, 1950.

7 SHURTLEFF, Harold R. *The Log Cabin Myth: A Study of the Early Dwellings of the English Colonists in North America.* Cambridge, 1939.

8 TALLMADGE, Thomas E. *The Story of Architecture in America.* Rev. ed. New York, 1936.

9 WATERMAN, Thomas T., and John A. BARROWS. *Domestic Colonial Architecture of Tidewater Virginia.* New York, 1932.

10 WATERMAN, Thomas T. *The Dwellings of Colonial America.* Chapel Hill, N.C., 1950.

11 WATERMAN, Thomas T. *The Mansions of Virginia, 1706–1776.* Chapel Hill, N.C., 1946.

5. *Decorative Arts and Interiors*

12 CHAMBERLAIN, Samuel. *Salem Interiors. Two Centuries of New England Taste and Decoration.* New York, 1950.

13 COMSTOCK, Helen. *American Furniture: Seventeenth, Eighteenth, and Nineteenth Century Styles.* New York, 1962.

14 CORNELIUS, Charles O. *Early American Furniture.* New York, 1936.

15 DREPPERD, Carl W. *Pioneer America: Its First Three Centuries.* Garden City, N.Y., 1949.

16 FLEMING, E. McClung. "Early American Decorative Arts as Social Documents." *Miss Val Hist Rev,* XLV (1958), 276–284.

17 KETTELL, Russell H., ed. *Early American Rooms: A Consideration of the Changes in Style between the Arrival of the Mayflower and the Civil War in the Regions Originally Settled by the English and the Dutch.* Portland, Me., 1936.†

18 KETTELL, Russell H. *The Pine Furniture of Early New England.* New York, 1929.

19 LANGDON, William C. *Everyday Things in American Life.* 2 vols. New York, 1937–1941.

20 LITTLE, Nina F. *American Decorative Wall Paintings, 1700–1850.* Sturbridge, Mass., 1952.

21 LOCKWOOD, Luke V. *Colonial Furniture in America.* 3rd ed. 2 vols. New York, 1926.

1 MC CLELLAND, Nancy V. *Furnishing the Colonial and Federal House.* Rev. ed. New York, 1947.

2 NAGEL, Charles. *American Furniture, 1650–1850: A Brief Background and an Illustrated History.* New York, 1949.

3 New York Museum of Modern Art. *American Folk Art: The Art of the Common Man, 1750–1900.* Ed. by Holger Cahill. New York, 1932.

4 ORMSBEE, Thomas H. *Early American Furniture Makers: A Social and Biographical Study.* New York, 1930.

5 PICKERING, Ernest. *The Homes of America, as They Have Expressed the Lives of Our People for Three Centuries.* New York, 1951.

6 ROGERS, Meyric R. *American Interior Design: The Traditions and Development of Domestic Design from Colonial Times to the Present.* New York, 1947.

7 SALE, Edith T. *Interiors of Virginia Houses of Colonial Times, from the Beginnings of Virginia to the Revolution.* Richmond, Va., 1927.

8 WHITE, Margaret E. *The Decorative Arts of Early New Jersey.* Princeton, 1964.

6. Music

9 AYARS, Christine M. *Contributions to the Art of Music in America by the Music Industries of Boston, 1640–1936.* New York, 1937.

10 CHASE, Gilbert. *America's Music: From the Pilgrims to the Present.* New York, 1955.

11 COVEY, Cyclone. "Puritanism and Music in Colonial America." *Wm Mar Q*, 3rd ser., VIII (1951), 355–377.

12 EBERLEIN, Harold D., and Cortlandt Van Dyke HUBBARD. "Music in the Early Federal Era." *Pa Mag Hist Biog*, LXIX (1945), 103–127.

13 ELLINWOOD, Leonard W. *The History of American Church Music.* New York, 1953.

14 ELSON, Louis C. *The History of American Music.* Rev. ed. New York, 1925.

15 EWEN, David. *Music Comes to America.* New York, 1947.

16 HATCH, Christopher. "Music for America: A Critical Controversy of the 1850s." *Am Q*, XIV (1962), 578–586.

17 HITCHCOCK, H. Wiley. *Music in the United States: A Historical Introduction.* Englewood Cliffs, N.J., 1969.†

18 HOWARD, John T. *Our American Music: Three Hundred Years of It.* 3rd ed. New York, 1946.

19 JOHNSON, H. Earle. *Musical Interludes in Boston, 1795–1830.* New York, 1943.

20 JORDAN, Philip D. *Singin' Yankees.* Minneapolis, Minn., 1946.

1 KMEN, Henry A. *Music in New Orleans: The Formative Years, 1791–1841*. Baton Rouge, La., 1967.

2 LAHEE, Henry C. *Annals of Music in America*. Boston, 1922.

3 MAC DOUGALL, Hamilton C. *Early New England Psalmody: An Historical Appreciation, 1620–1820*. Brattleboro, Vt., 1940.

4 MATES, Julian. *The American Musical Stage before 1800*. New Brunswick, N.J., 1962.

5 METCALF, Frank J. *American Writers and Compilers of Sacred Music*. New York, 1925.

6 National Society of the Colonial Dames of America, Pennsylvania. *Church Music and Musical Life in Pennsylvania in the Eighteenth Century*. 3 vols. in 4. Philadelphia, 1926–1947.

7 SABLOSKY, Irving L. *American Music*. Chicago, 1969.†

8 SCHOLES, Percy A. *The Puritans and Music in England and New England: A Contribution to the Cultural History of Two Nations*. London, 1934.

9 SEEGER, Charles. "Music and Class Structure in the United States." *Am Q*, IX (1957), 281–294.

10 SMITH, Carleton S. "America in 1801–1825: The Musicians and the Music." *Bull N Y Pub Lib*, LXVIII (1964), 483–492.

11 SONNECK, Oscar G. T. *Early Concert-Life in America (1731–1800)*. Leipzig, Germany, 1907.

12 SONNECK, Oscar G. T. *Early Opera in America*. New York, 1915.

13 SPAETH, Sigmund G. *A History of Popular Music in America*. New York, 1948.

NOTES

INDEX

Aaron, Daniel, 94.20
Abbott, Edith, 28.4, 5, 48.5, 85.15
Abbott, Grace, 49.14
Abbott, Richard H., 22.5
Abernethy, Thomas P., 14.3–8
Abrahams, Harold J., 89.18
Ackerknecht, Erwin H., 93.1
Adams, Alice D., 67.21
Adams, Charles F., 50.7
Adams, Evelyn C., 95.16
Adams, Henry, 8.13
Adams, Horace, 48.6
Adams, James T., 1.1, 6.13, 9.19, 10.1, 2
Adams, Percy G., 2.12
Adams, William F., 30.12
Addison, James T., 54.1
Adler, Selig, 63.2
Akagi, Roy H., 12.9
Akers, Dwight, 100.4
Albertson, Dean, 10.3
Albertson, Ralph, 71.16
Albion, Robert G., 10.4, 25.12
Albright, Raymond W., 54.2
Alden, John R., 14.9
Alexander, Robert L., 109.11
Allen, Phyllis, 88.13
Ambler, Charles H., 77.7, 86.21
Ambrose, Stephen E., 82.18
American Historical Association, 1.2, 3
American Jewish Archives, 63.3
American Psychiatric Association, 96.1
Ames, Susie M., 14.10
Ander, O. Fritiof, 28.6
Anderson, Arlow W., 103.1
Anderson, Fannie, 93.2
Anderson, Hattie M., 19.10
Anderson, Nels, 54.3
Andrews, Charles M., 6.14, 15
Andrews, Edward D., 71.17, 77.8
Andrews, Matthew P., 64.12
Andrews, Wayne, 109.12
Anthony, Susan B., 49.8, 73.5
Applewhite, Joseph D., 17.17
Aptheker, Herbert, 34.5, 6, 36.5, 44.9, 54.4, 67.22, 23
Arky, Louis H., 46.6
Arndt, Karl J. R., 71.18
Arnow, Harriette S., 19.11
Aronson, Sidney H., 8.14
Ash, Martha M., 25.13
Ashburn, Percy M., 88.14

Athearn, Robert G., 22.6
Atherton, Lewis E., 14.11, 19.12
Atkins, Gaius G., 54.5
Ayars, Christine M., 112.9
Ayer, Hugh M., 93.3

Babcock, Kendric C., 32.13
Backlund, Jonas O., 103.2
Bacot, D. Huger, 14.12
Bailyn, Bernard, 12.10, 75.11
Baird, Charles W., 32.7
Baisnée, J. A., 61.17
Baker, Paul, 2.15
Baker, William D., 8.15
Bald, F. Clever, 25.14
Baldwin, Alice M., 53.6
Baldwin, Leland D., 25.15
Ballagh, James C., 36.6, 47.13
Baltzell, E. Digby, 12.11
Bancroft, Frederic, 36.7
Banks, Charles E., 109.13
Barck, Oscar T., Jr., 24.14
Barclay, Wade C., 60.5
Bardolph, Richard, 34.7
Barker, Charles A., 17.18
Barker, Virgil, 106.17
Barnes, Gilbert H., 67.24
Barnes, Harry E., 99.5–8
Barnhart, John D., 19.13, 22.1, 7
Baron, Salo W., 63.4, 5
Barrett, John T., 91.6
Barrow, John G., 1.4
Barrows, John A., 111.9
Barry, Coleman J., 61.18, 74.2
Barth, Gunther, 34.4
Bartow, Edith M., 103.3
Bassett, John S., 36.8, 9, 68.1
Bassett, T. D. Seymour, 1.5, 10.5, 71.19
Bauer, Alice H., 36.10
Bauer, Raymond A., 36.10
Baumgartner, Apollinaris W., 61.19, 103.4
Baur, John E., 93.4
Baxter, William T., 12.12
Beale, Howard K., 75.12
Beale, Otho T., Jr., 88.15, 91.7
Bean, William G., 12.13
Beard, Augustus F., 60.6
Beard, Charles A., 4.10
Beard, Mary R., 4.10, 48.7
Beaver, R. Pierce, 60.7
Becker, Dorothy G., 86.22

INDEX

Beekman, Fenwick, 91.8
Beers, Henry P., 1.6
Behnke, Helen D., 91.9
Beinfield, Malcolm S., 91.10
Bell, Howard H., 34.8–12, 66.9
Bell, Sadie, 77.9
Bell, Whitfield J., Jr., 10.6, 91.11, 12
Belok, Michael V., 82.7
Bennett, Charles A., 75.13
Benson, Adolph B., 32.14, 15
Benson, Mary S., 48.8
Benton, Elbert J., 25.16
Benton, Josiah H., 87.1
Berger, Max, 4.1, 74.3
Berkhofer, Robert F., Jr., 60.8
Berman, Alex, 93.5, 6
Bernstein, Leonard, 46.7
Berthoff, Rowland T., 4.11, 12.14, 29.16
Berwanger, Eugene H., 44.10
Best, Harry, 85.16, 17
Bestor, Arthur E., Jr., 66.10, 71.20
Bettmann, Otto, 100.6
Bidwell, Charles E., 77.10
Biehl, Katherine L., 47.14
Billias, George A., 97.1
Billington, Ray A., 19.14–17, 74.4
Binger, Carl, 91.13
Bingham, Robert W., 25.17
Birdsall, Richard D., 10.7
Bittinger, Lucy F., 31.2
Black, George F., 29.17
Blackwell, Alice S., 72.14
Blair, Walter, 100.15
Blake, John B., 23.13, 48.9, 88.16, 91.14–16, 93.7, 95.4, 5
Blake, Nelson M., 23.14, 50.8
Blanton, Wyndham B., 91.17, 18, 93.8
Blau, Joseph L., 63.5
Blegen, Theodore C., 28.7, 32.16
Bloch, Herman D., 42.1
Blumenthal, Walter H., 48.10
Boase, Paul H., 54.6, 7, 68.2
Boatright, Mody C., 100.16
Bode, Carl, 75.14
Bodo, John R., 53.7
Bogue, Allan G., 19.18
Bolton, Charles K., 29.18, 105.12, 13
Boman, Martha, 25.18
Bond, Beverley W., 6.16, 20.1, 2
Bond, Earl D., 96.2
Bone, Robert G., 77.11
Bonner, James C., 14.13, 17.19

Boone, Richard G., 77.12
Boorstin, Daniel J., 6.17, 8.16
Born, Wolfgang, 106.18, 107.1
Botkin, Benjamin A., 36.11
Bourdin, Henri L., 2.14
Bousfield, M. O., 34.13, 88.17
Bowers, David F., 1.7, 4.12
Bowes, Frederick P., 106.1
Boyd, Minnie C., 14.14
Brackett, Jeffrey R., 36.12
Bradford, S. Sydney, 36.13
Bradley, Phillips, 3.17
Branch, E. Douglas, 66.11
Brand, Carl F., 74.5
Brauer, Jerald C., 51.10
Breckinridge, Sophonisba P., 50.9, 87.3, 88.9
Bremner, Robert H., 5.19, 85.18, 86.1
Brewer, Clifton H., 60.9
Brewer, James H., 42.2
Brewster, Robert W., 68.3
Bridenbaugh, Carl, 3.2, 12.15, 17.20, 24.15–17, 28.8, 46.8, 51.11, 64.13, 100.17
Bridenbaugh, Jessica, 24.17
Bridges, William E., 50.10
Brigham, Clarence S., 103.5, 6
Brigham, R. I., 44.4
Briggs, Martin S., 109.14
Brinton, Howard H., 54.8, 82.19
Britton, Margaret, 51.2
Brock, Henry I., 54.9
Brock, Peter, 73.17
Broderick, Francis L., 83.1
Brodie, Fawn M., 54.10
Bronner, Edwin B., 54.11
Bronson, Walter C., 83.2
Brooks, Elaine, 68.4
Brooks, John G., 4.2
Brown, A. Theodore, 23.17, 25.19
Brown, B. Katherine, 12.16–18, 18.1
Brown, Elmer E., 77.13
Brown, Ira V., 66.12, 72.15
Brown, James H., 54.12
Brown, Robert E., 6.18, 12.19, 18.1
Brown, Robert M., 58.16
Brown, Roy M., 87.2
Brown, Samuel W., 75.15
Brown, Thomas A., 108.8
Browne, Henry J., 77.14
Browning, Charles H., 29.19
Browning, James B., 42.3
Brubacher, John S., 83.3
Bruce, Isabel C., 87.3

INDEX

Bruce, Kathleen, 36.14
Bruce, Philip A., 14.15–17, 83.4
Brydon, George M., 54.13
Brynestad, Lawrence E., 58.17
Buchler, Joseph, 63.6
Buck, Elizabeth H., 10.8
Buck, Paul H., 18.2
Buck, Solon J., 10.8, 20.3
Buley, R. Carlyle, 20.4, 94.13
Bullock, Henry A., 44.5, 75.16
Burchard, John, 24.1, 109.15
Burlingame, Roger, 4.13
Burns, James A., 61.20, 62.1, 2, 77.15–17
Burr, George L., 65.17, 18
Burr, Nelson R., 1.8, 54.14, 77.18
Burrage, Walter L., 89.19
Burritt, Elihu, 73.18
Burroughs, Alan, 107.2
Bush-Brown, Albert, 109.15
Bushman, Richard L., 12.20
Butcher, Margaret J., 34.14
Butler, James D., 28.9
Butler, Vera M., 75.17
Butts, R. Freeman, 75.18, 76.1
Byrne, Frank L., 73.9

Cabaniss, Frances A., 54.15
Cabaniss, James A., 54.15
Cady, Edwin H., 106.2
Caffin, Charles H., 107.3
Cahill, Holger, 112.3
Caley, Percy B., 49.15
Calhoun, Arthur W., 50.11
Calhoun, Daniel H., 27.17, 18
Calligaro, Lee, 42.4
Callow, James T., 107.4
Calvert, Monte A., 27.19, 68.5
Calverton, Victor F., 71.21
Canby, Henry S., 6.6
Cannon, M. Hamlin, 54.16
Cantor, Milton, 34.15
Capen, Edward W., 87.4
Capers, Gerald M., 25.20
Carden, Maren L., 72.22
Cardwell, Guy A., 100.18
Carlson, Eric T., 96.5
Carlton, Frank T., 76.2
Carpenter, Charles, 82.8
Carrell, William D., 83.5
Carrigan, Jo Ann, 93.9–11
Carroll, Joseph C., 36.15

Carroll, Kenneth L., 44.11, 54.17–19, 68.6
Carson, Gerald, 100.19, 101.1
Carson, William G. B., 108.9
Carter, Harvey L., 20.5
Caruso, John A., 20.6
Cary, John, 12.21, 99.9
Cash, Wilber J., 14.18
Cassidy, Francis P., 62.3, 83.6
Catterall, Helen T., 36.16
Caulfield, Ernest, 91.19, 92.1
Cavins, Harold M., 95.6
Chamberlain, Samuel, 111.12
Chambers, John S., 88.18
Chase, Gilbert, 112.10
Chase, Wayland J., 58.18, 83.7
Chastellux, Francois Jean, Marquis de, 2.8
Chenault, William W., 22.8
Cherrington, Ernest H., 73.10
Chevalier, Michel, 2.9
Cheyney, Edward P., 83.8
Childs, Frances S., 32.8
Childs, St. Julian R., 92.2
Chitwood, Oliver P., 97.14
Chroust, Anton-Hermann, 27.20, 97.2
Chumbley, George L., 97.15
Chyet, Stanley F., 63.7
Clark, Blanche H., 18.3
Clark, Ernest J., Jr., 36.17
Clark, Joseph B., 60.10
Clark, Thomas D., 14.19, 20.7, 36.18, 101.2, 3, 103.7, 8
Clebsch, William A., 51.12
Cleveland, Catherine C., 58.19
Clews, Elsie W., 76.3
Coad, Oral S., 108.10
Cobb, Sanford H., 64.14
Cobbett, William, 2.10
Cochran, Thomas C., 4.14, 15, 27.21
Cochrane, Hortense S., 96.3
Coffin, Lewis A., 109.16
Cohen, Hennig, 103.9
Cole, Arthur C., 4.16, 8.17, 20.8, 74.6, 83.9
Cole, Charles C., 53.8, 58.20
Cole, Donald B., 25.21
Cole, Margaret, 72.1
Coleman, J. Winston, Jr., 14.20, 36.19
Coleman, Kenneth, 15.1
Coleman, Peter J., 97.16
Coleman, Sydney H., 86.2

INDEX

Coll, Blanche D., 86.3, 4
Collins, Winfred H., 36.20
Come, Donald R., 83.10
Cometti, Elizabeth, 48.11
Commager, Henry S., 2.11, 28.10, 66.13, 14
Commons, John R., 4.17, 46.9
Comstock, Helen, 111.13
Conant, H. J., 97.17
Condit, Carl W., 109.17, 18
Conkin, Paul, 54.20
Connolly, Thomas E., 63.2
Conrad, Alfred H., 36.22, 23
Conway, Alan, 29.20
Cook, Elizabeth C., 103.10
Cooke, George W., 54.21
Cooley, Henry S., 36.21
Coolidge, John P., 109.19
Coon, Charles L., 77.19
Corbett, Doris S., 12.8
Cornelius, Charles O., 111.14
Corry, John P., 78.1
Cortissoz, Royal, 107.16
Cotterill, Robert S., 15.2
Coulter, Edith M., 1.9
Coulter, E. Merton, 83.11
Cousins, Frank, 109.20, 110.1
Covey, Cyclone, 112.11
Cowan, Helen I., 29.21
Cowen, David L., 89.20
Cowie, Alexander, 83.12
Cowing, Cedric B., 58.21
Cowley, Malcolm, 39.5
Cox, John, Jr., 54.22
Crandall, John C., 66.15
Crane, Verner W., 15.3
Crary, Catherine S., 28.11
Craven, Avery O., 15.4, 18.4, 36.24
Craven, Wayne, 107.5
Craven, Wesley F., 15.5
Crawford, Mary C., 10.9, 108.11
Creech, Margaret, 87.5, 6, 7
Cremin, Lawrence A., 76.1, 78.2
Crèvecoeur, Michel G. St. Jean de, 2.12–14
Crockett, Bernice N., 93.12
Cromwell, Otelia, 72.16
Cross, Arthur L., 53.9
Cross, Whitney R., 59.1, 66.16
Crouthamel, James L., 103.11
Crowe, Jesse C., 99.10
Crowl, Philip A., 18.5
Crum, Mason, 34.16
Cubberley, Ellwood P., 76.4, 5

Culver, Raymond B., 78.3
Cummings, Richard O., 101.4
Cunz, Dieter, 31.3
Curran, Francis X., 51.13, 14, 78.4
Curti, Merle E., 4.18, 5.1, 8.18, 22.2, 73.18, 19, 76.6, 86.5–7
Cushing, John D., 68.7
Cutler, James E., 98.1

D'Agostino, Lorenzo, 87.8
Dain, Floyd R., 25.22
Dain, Norman, 96.4, 5
Daitsman, George, 46.10
Dale, Edward E., 93.13, 106.3
Dalzell, George W., 51.15
D'Arusmont, Frances, 2.15
Danhof, Clarence H., 22.9, 10
Daniels, George H., 27.22
Davenport, F. Garvin, 15.6, 7, 106.4
Davidson, Elizabeth H., 54.23
Davidson, Marshall, 5.2
Davies, John D., 66.17
Davis, Charles S., 15.8
Davis, David B., 37.1, 55.1, 68.8, 74.7, 8, 98.2, 106.5
Davis, Richard B., 2.17, 65.19
Davis, Robert R., Jr., 101.5
Davison, Sol, 22.14, 15
Dawes, Norman H., 13.1
Degler, Carl N., 5.3, 22.11, 37.2, 44.12
De Groot, Alfred T., 55.16
Demaree, Albert L., 103.12
Demarest, William H. S., 83.13
Demos, John, 10.10, 50.12, 68.9
De Pillis, Mario S., 55.2
DePuy, Leroy B., 99.11
Des Champs, Margaret B., 55.3, 60.11
Deutsch, Albert, 87.9, 92.3, 96.6, 7
Dexter, Elizabeth W., 48.12
Diamond, Sigmund, 6.19, 18.6
Dick, Everett N., 15.9, 20.9, 10
Dickerson, Oliver M., 103.13
Dickins, Charles, 2.16
Dickson, Harold E., 107.6
Dickson, R. J., 29.22
Diffenderffer, Frank R., 31.4
Dillon, Merton L., 68.10, 11
Ditzion, Sidney H., 48.13, 50.13, 105.14
Dodd, William E., 15.10, 11, 18.7
Doherty, Robert W., 55.4, 5

INDEX

Doll, Eugene E., 99.12
Donald, David, 68.12
Donnan, Elizabeth, 37.3–5
Donnelly, Marian C., 110.2
Donovan, George F., 30.13
Dormon, James H., 108.12
Dorson, Richard M., 101.6, 108.13
Douglass, Harlan P., 55.6
Dow, George F., 101.7
Dowd, Douglas, 36.23
Dowie, J. Iverne, 32.17
Downes, Randolph C., 20.11
Downing, Antoinette F., 110.3
Doyle, Bertram W., 44.13
Drake, Frederick C., 65.20
Drake, Samuel G., 65.21
Drake, Thomas E., 44.14, 55.7, 68.13
Drepperd, Carl W., 111.15
Drewry, William S., 37.6
Drews, Robert S., 87.10, 93.14
Drummond, Andrew L., 51.16
Drury, Clifford M., 60.12
Duberman, Martin, 68.14
Du Bois, W. E. Burghardt, 35.1, 37.7, 43.9
Duffy, John, 23.15, 89.5, 90.1, 92.4–6, 93.15–20, 95.7
Duker, Abraham G., 63.8
Dulles, Foster Rhea, 100.5
Dumond, Dwight L., 68.15
Dunaway, Wayland F., 10.11, 29.23
Dunbar, Seymour, 4.3
Dunbar-Nelson, Alice, 37.8
Duniway, Clyde A., 104.12
Dunlap, William C., 78.5
Dunn, Esther C., 108.14
Dunn, Richard S., 13.2
Dunn, William K., 78.6
Durant, John, 100.6
Dykstra, Robert R., 5.4

Earle, Alice M., 48.14, 49.16, 50.14, 98.3, 101.8–12
Earnest, Ernest P., 83.14
Earnest, Joseph B., 43.10
Eaton, Clement, 15.12–14, 18.8, 37.9, 59.2
Eaton, Leonard K., 93.21
Eberlein, Harold D., 110.4, 5, 112.12
Eckenrode, Hamilton J., 64.15
Eddy, George S., 51.17
Eddy, Richard, 55.8
Edwards, George W., 24.18

Edwards, Newton, 76.7
Egbert, Donald D., 1.5, 5.5, 72.2
Eggleston, Edward, 6.20, 92.7
Eickhoff, Edith, 87.3
Eide, Richard B., 20.12
Elkins, Stanley M., 5.14, 37.10–12
Ellinwood, Leonard W., 112.13
Elliott, Robert N., Jr., 103.14
Ellis, David M., 10.12, 13.3, 22.12
Ellis, John T., 1.10, 62.4, 5
Elsbree, Oliver W., 60.13
Elson, Louis C., 112.14
Elson, Ruth M., 82.9
Emery, Edwin, 103.15
Emmanuel, I. S., 63.9
Engerman, Stanley, 36.23
England, J. Merton, 42.5, 82.10
English, William F., 97.3
Erbacher, Sebastian A., 62.6, 83.15
Erikson, Kai T., 98.4
Ernst, Robert, 25.23, 28.12, 74.9
Ervin, Spencer, 55.9, 10
Esarey, Logan, 22.3, 106.6
Espelie, Ernest M., 32.17
Evans, Meryle R., 101.13
Evans, W. A., 42.6
Everett, Donald E., 42.7, 8, 93.22
Ewen, David, 112.15
Ezell, John S., 100.7

Fagley, Frederick L., 54.5
Farmer, Harold E., 35.2, 88.19
Faulk, Odie B., 15.15
Faust, Albert B., 31.5
Feer, Robert A., 98.5
Fell, Sister Marie Léonore, 74.10
Field, Edward. 101.14
Filler, Louis, 68.16
Fish, Carl R., 8.19
Fishbein, Morris, 90.2, 96.15
Fisher, Bernice M., 76.8
Fisher, Miles M., 37.13
Fisher, Sydney G., 10.13
Fisher, Walter, 37.14, 94.1
Fitch, James M., 110.6
Fitzroy, Herbert W. K., 98.6
Fladeland, Betty L., 68.17, 18
Flaherty, David H., 97.4
Flanders, Ralph B., 37.15, 42.9
Flanders, Robert B., 55.11
Fleming, E. McClung, 111.16
Fleming, Sanford, 49.17
Fletcher, John G., 15.16

Fletcher, Robert S., 83.16
Fletcher, Stevenson W., 10.14
Flexner, Eleanor, 72.17
Flexner, James T., 89.1, 107.7–10
Flick, Alexander C., 10.15
Flom, George T., 32.18
Fogel, Edwin M., 31.6
Folks, Homer, 87.11
Foner, Philip, 46.11, 63.10
Forbes, Allan W., 46.12
Ford, David B., 64.16
Ford, Edwin H., 103.16
Ford, Henry J., 30.1
Foreman, Grant, 15.17
Forman, Henry C., 110.7
Forsyth, David P., 103.17
Fortenbaugh, Robert, 44.15, 55.12, 68.19
Fosdick, Lucian J., 32.9
Fossier, A. E., 94.2
Foster, Charles I., 35.3, 60.14
Foster, Margery S., 83.17
Foster, Sir Augustus John, bart., 2.17
Fox, Dixon R., 5.6, 6.6, 9.1, 10.16, 13.4, 106.7, 108.15
Fox, Early L., 68.20
Fox, Sanford J., 66.1
Francis, Russell E., 59.3
Franklin, John Hope, 15.18, 35.4, 37.16, 17, 42.10, 43.11
Frazier, E. Franklin, 35.5, 42.11, 43.12, 50.15, 16
Fredrickson, George M., 37.18
French, Joseph L., 20.13
Friedman, Lee M., 63.11
Frost, James A., 20.14
Fuller, George N., 20.15
Furniss, Norman F., 55.13
Fussell, Clyde G., 78.7

Gabriel, Ralph H., 2.14, 83.18
Gage, Matilda J., 49.8, 73.5
Gaines, Francis P., 15.19, 37.19
Galdston, Iago, 94.19
Galpin, W. Freeman, 73.20
Gambrall, Theodore C., 55.14
Gambrell, Mary L., 53.10
Gara, Larry, 68.21
Gard, Wayne, 98.7
Gardiner, John H., Jr., 55.15
Gardner, Albert Ten Eyck, 107.11
Garfinkle, Norton, 82.11
Garis, Roy L., 28.13

Garrison, Winfred E., 55.16
Garvan, Anthony N. B., 110.8
Garvin, Russell, 42.12
Garwood, Ellen, 101.15
Gatell, Frank O., 66.18
Gates, Paul W., 22.13
Gaustad, Edwin S., 51.18, 59.4
Geffen, Elizabeth M., 60.15
Gehrke, William H., 37.20
Geiser, Karl F., 68.22
Genovese, Eugene D., 18.9, 19, 37.21, 22
Gerstenfeld, Melanie, 1.9
Gettleman, Marvin E., 99.13
Gewehr, Wesley M., 59.5
Gilchrist, David T., 26.1
Gillin, John L., 87.12
Gilpin, Lawrence H., 10.17
Ginger, Ray, 46.13
Ginzberg, Eli, 36.23
Gipson, Lawrence H., 6.21, 98.8
Gitelman, Howard M., 30.14, 46.14
Glaab, Charles N., 23.16, 17
Glasgow, Maude, 30.2
Glazer, Nathan, 63.12
Gobbel, Luther L., 64.17, 78.8
Godbold, Albea, 83.19
Goebel, Edmund J., 62.7, 78.9
Goebel, Julius, Jr., 98.9
Goen, C. C., 59.6
Gohdes, Clarence L. F., 105.1
Gohmann, Sister Mary de Lourdes, 74.11
Goldstein, Naomi F., 44.16
Gollin, Gillian L., 55.17
Goodman, Abram, 63.13
Goodman, Nathan G., 92.8
Goodman, Paul, 7.1, 13.5
Goodrich, Carter, 22.14, 15
Goodrich, Lloyd, 107.12
Goodsell, Willystine, 50.17, 18
Goodspeed, Charles E., 100.8
Goodwin, Edward L., 55.18
Goodwin, Mary F., 43.13
Goodwin, Maud W., 30.3
Goodykoontz, Colin B., 60.16
Gordon, Maurice B., 92.9
Gordy, John P., 78.10
Gossett, Thomas F., 44.17
Govan, Gilbert E., 15.20
Govan, Thomas P., 15.21
Gowans, Alan, 110.9, 10
Graham, Ian C. C., 30.4
Graham, John J., 64.18

Graham, Philip, 108.16
Graham, Robert E., 101.16
Grant, A. Cameron, 37.23
Grant, Charles S., 13.6
Grant, Elliott M., 3.9
Gray, Austin K., 105.15
Green, Constance M., 23.18, 19, 26.2–5, 44.18
Green, E. R. R., 30.5
Green, Fletcher M., 15.22, 60.17
Green, Samuel S., 105.16
Greene, Evarts B., 7.2, 3, 55.19, 64.19, 76.9
Greene, John C., 44.19
Greene, Lorenzo J., 35.6
Greene, M. Louise, 64.20
Greenwald, William I., 8.20
Greer, Thomas H., 20.16
Greven, Philip J., Jr., 7.4, 50.19
Griffin, Clifford S., 60.18, 66.19, 20, 68.23, 74.12
Griffin, Richard W., 46.15
Grimes, Alan P., 48.15, 72.18
Grimshaw, Allen D., 45.1
Grimsted, David, 108.17
Grinstein, Hyman B., 63.14
Grizzell, Emit D., 78.11
Grob, Gerald N., 96.8
Groce, George C., 107.13
Gross, Bella, 35.7
Grund, Francis J., 3.1
Guerrieri, Dora, 62.8
Gusfield, Joseph R., 73.11
Guttmann, Allen, 5.7

Haar, Charles M., 47.15
Habenstein, Robert W., 101.17
Hacker, Louis M., 5.8
Haddow, Anna, 83.20
Hage, George S., 103.18
Hagen, Oskar, 107.14
Haggard, J. Villasana, 94.3
Hale, William H., 66.21
Hall, Clifton L., 76.14
Hall, J. K., 96.1
Haller, Mabel, 83.21
Haller, William, Jr., 10.18
Hamer, Philip M., 90.3
Hamilton, Alexander, 3.2
Hamilton, William B., 15.23
Hamlin, Talbot F., 110.11–13
Handlin, David P., 110.14

Handlin, Mary F., 10.19, 16.1, 38.1, 46.16
Handlin, Oscar, 1.11, 3.3, 10.19, 16.1, 24.1, 26.6, 28.14–16, 30.15, 38.1, 46.16, 63.15
Hanley, Thomas O., 52.1, 64.21
Hanna, Charles A., 30.6
Hansen, Allen O., 76.10, 78.12
Hansen, Chadwick, 66.2
Hansen, Klaus J., 55.20
Hansen, Marcus L., 28.17–19, 30.16
Hardon, John A., 52.2
Hardy, C. De Witt, 84.3
Hardy, James D., Jr., 28.20
Harlow, Ralph V., 66.22
Harrell, David E., Jr., 55.21
Harrington, Virginia D., 7.2, 13.7
Harris, N. Dwight, 38.2
Harris, Neil, 107.15
Harstad, Peter T., 94.4, 5
Hart, Albert B., 10.20
Hartmann, Edward G., 30.7
Hartz, Louis, 5.9, 10.21
Haskins, George L., 97.5, 6, 98.10
Hatch, Christopher, 112.16
Hathway, Marion, 96.9
Hawgood, John A., 31.7
Hayes, Cecil B., 76.11
Haynes, Leonard L., Jr., 43.14
Haynes, Robert V., 98.11
Hays, Elinor R., 72.19
Haywood, C. Robert, 16.2, 38.3
Heale, M. J., 67.1
Heath, Milton S., 16.3
Heaton, Claude E., 92.10, 11
Heaton, Herbert, 29.1
Heaton, Oliver S., 89.2
Hedin, Naboth, 32.14, 15
Hedrick, Ulysses P., 10.22, 101.18
Heffner, William C., 87.13
Heimert, Alan, 52.3
Hendrick, Irving G., 78.13
Henretta, James A., 13.8
Henry, Howell M., 38.4
Herrick, Cheesman A., 47.16
Herskovits, Melville, 35.8
Hervey, John, 100.9
Higgins, Ruth L., 22.16
High, James, 18.10
Higham, John, 1.12, 13, 63.16, 74.13
Hill, Leslie G., 20.17
Hillquit, Morris, 5.10
Hinckley, Ted C., 74.14
Hinds, William A., 72.3

INDEX

Hinsdale, Burke A., 78.14
Hirsch, Arthur H., 32.10
Hitchcock, H. Wiley, 112.17
Hobson, Elsie G., 78.15
Hofstadter, Richard, 5.11, 84.1–3
Hogan, William R., 16.4
Holbrook, Stewart H., 22.17
Holden, Arthur C., 109.16
Holliday, Carl, 48.16
Holliman, Jennie, 100.10
Hollon, William E., 16.5
Holloway, Mark, 72.4
Holmes, Chris, 92.12
Holt, Bryce R., 38.5
Holtz, Adrian A., 78.16
Homan, Walter J., 49.18, 56.1
Hoogenboom, Ari, 8.2
Hoover, Dwight W., 24.2
Hoover, Thomas N., 84.4
Hopkins, Charles H., 60.19
Horine, Emmet F., 94.6
Hornberger, Theodore, 84.5
Hornblow, Arthur, 108.18
Howard, George E., 50.20
Howard, John T., 112.18
Howard, Warren S., 38.6
Howard, William T., 95.8
Hubbard, Cortlandt Van Dyke, 110.4, 112.12
Hubbart, Henry C., 20.18
Hudson, Arthur P., 16.6
Hudson, Winthrop S., 52.4–6
Hughes, Glenn, 108.19
Hull, William I., 33.10
Humphrey, Edward F., 52.7
Hunt, Gaillard, 101.19
Hunter, Frances L., 38.7
Hunter, Robert J., 92.13
Hurd, Henry M., 96.10
Hurst, James W., 97.7–9

Imes, William L., 38.8
Indiana Historical Commission, 3.4
Inglis, Alexander J., 78.17
Isham, Samuel, 107.16
Ireland, Ralph R., 38.9
Ives, Joseph M., 62.9, 65.1

Jackson, George L., 78.18
Jackson, James C., 43.15
Jackson, Joseph, 110.15, 16
Jackson, Luther P., 42.13, 43.16, 17

Jackson, Sidney L., 78.19
Jacoby, George P., 49.19, 62.10, 86.8
James, D. Clayton, 16.7, 26.7
James, Reese D., 108.20
James, Sydney V., 61.1, 86.9
Jameson, J. Franklin, 7.5
Jamison, A. Leland, 1.8, 52.21
Jamison, Wallace N., 52.8
Janson, Florence E., 32.19
Jenkins, William S., 45.2
Jernegan, Marcus W., 38.10, 46.17, 47.17, 76.12, 78.20, 87.14
Johnson, Allen, 1.14
Johnson, Amandus, 33.1
Johnson, Charles A., 59.7
Johnson, Guion G., 16.8, 9, 51.1, 59.8, 9
Johnson, H. Earle, 112.19
Johnson, James E., 59.10
Johnson, Laurence A., 101.20
Johnson, Roy H., 56.3
Johnston, Frances B., 110.17
Johnston, James H., 16.10
Johnston, Ruby F., 43.18
Johnston, William D., 38.11
Jones, Billy M., 94.7
Jones, Gordon W., 92.14
Jones, Howard M., 7.6, 11.1, 106.8
Jones, Jerome W., 45.3, 61.2
Jones, Maldwyn A., 29.2
Jones, Mary J. A., 11.2
Jones, Matt B., 11.3
Jones, Robert W., 103.19
Jones, Rufus M., 56.4
Jordan, Philip D., 101.21, 112.20
Jordan, Weymouth T., 16.11
Jordan, Winthrop D., 38.12, 45.4
Jorgenson, Lloyd P., 79.1
Judd, Jacob, 26.8, 9, 95.9

Kaganoff, Nathan M., 63.17
Kaiser, Laurina, 62.11, 79.2
Kandel, Isaac L., 79.3
Kane, Murray, 22.18
Kaplan, Sidney, 13.9
Karraker, Cyrus H., 98.12
Kates, Don B., 69.1
Katz, Michael, 79.4, 5
Keefer, Mary W., 88.9
Keep, Austin B., 105.17
Keim, C. Ray, 18.11
Keller, Charles R., 59.11, 67.2
Kelly, John F., 110.18

INDEX

Kelly, Robert L., 84.6
Kelly, Sister Mary G., 29.3
Kelso, Charles, 36.23
Kelso, Robert W., 87.15
Kemble, Frances A., 3.5
Kemp, William W., 61.3
Kendall, John S., 38.13, 108.21
Kendrick, B. B., 16.12
Kennedy, Aileen E., 87.16
Kennedy, Charles J., 26.10
Kenney, Alice P., 13.10
Kett, Joseph F., 28.1, 90.4
Kettell, Russell H., 111.17, 18
Kiefer, Monica M., 49.20
Kilpatrick, William H., 79.6, 7
Kilson, Marion D. de B., 38.14
King, Doris E., 101.23
Kimball, Fiske, 110.19, 20
Kimball, Marie, 101.22
Kingman, Ralph C., 110.21
Kinney, Charles B., Jr., 65.2
Kirker, Harold, 110.22
Kirker, James, 110.22
Kirkland, Edward C., 11.4
Kirkpatrick, R. L., 26.11
Kirwan, Albert D., 15.12
Kittredge, George L., 11.5, 66.3
Klebaner, Benjamin J., 29.4, 5, 38.15,
    87.17–21, 88.1, 2
Klees, Fredric, 31.8
Klein, Herbert S., 38.16
Klein, Milton M., 13.11, 79.10
Klein, Philip, 99.14
Klement, Frank, 69.2
Klett, Guy S., 56.5
Kline, Priscilla C., 11.6
Klingberg, Frank J., 35.9, 38.17,
    43.19, 56.2, 61.4–6
Kmen, Henry A., 113.1
Knauss, James O., Jr., 31.9
Knight, Edgar W., 76.13, 14, 79.8, 9
Knittle, Walter A., 31.10
Kobre, Sidney, 103.20, 21
Koch, G. Adolf, 52.9
Kohlbrenner, Bernard J., 62.2, 77.17
Kommers, Donald P., 97.10
Konold, Donald E., 90.5
Koos, Leonard V., 79.11
Korn, Bertram W., 45.5, 63.18–21
Korngold, Ralph, 69.3
Kraditor, Aileen S., 48.17, 69.4, 5,
    76.20
Krafka, Joseph, Jr., 92.15
Kramer, Howard D., 95.10

Kraus, Michael, 1.15, 7.7, 8
Krout, John A., 9.1, 73.12, 100.11
Krueger, Lillian, 20.19
Kuehl, Warren F., 1.16
Kuhn, Anne L., 50.1
Kuhns, Oscar, 31.11

Labaree, Benjamin W., 13.12
Labaree, Leonard W., 7.9, 59.12
Lader, Lawrence, 69.6
LaFollette, Suzanne, 107.17
Lahee, Henry C., 113.2
Lamers, William M., 101.17
Land, Aubrey C., 18.12
Lander, Ernest M., Jr., 38.18
Lane, Roger, 26.12, 98.13
Langdon, George D., 11.7
Langdon, William C., 111.19
Langley, Harold D., 67.3
Lankard, Frank G., 61.7
Lannie, Vincent P., 62.12, 65.3, 79.12
Lantz, Herman R., 51.2
Larkin, Oliver W., 107.18
Lasch, Christopher, 37.18
Lathrop, Elsie, 102.1
Lauber, Almon W., 47.18
Laux, James B., 32.11
Lawrence, George, 3.16
Leach, Richard H., 29.6
Lebeson, Anite L., 63.22
Leder, Lawrence H., 103.22
Lee, Alfred M., 104.1
Lefler, Hugh T., 16.13
Leiby, Adrian C., 33.2, 11
Leiby, James, 86.10
Lemon, James T., 13.13, 24.19
Leopold, Richard W., 67.4
Lerner, Gerda, 69.7
Lerski, Jerzy Jan, 34.2
Leslie, William R., 38.19
Levy, Babette M., 56.6
Levy, Leonard W., 69.8, 104.13, 14
Lewis, Orlando F., 99.15
Lewis, W. David, 99.16
Lewit, Robert T., 61.8
Leyburn, James G., 20.20, 30.8
Library of Congress, 1.17
Lindley, Harlow, 3.4, 56.7
Lingelbach, William E., 5.12
Lippincott, Horace M., 24.20
Lipset, Seymour M., 3.6, 5.13
Little, Nina F., 111.20
Littlefield, George E., 79.13

INDEX

Littlefield, Henry M., 22.19
Litwack, Leon F., 42.14, 69.9
Livingood, Frederick G., 61.9
Livingood, James W., 15.20
Lloyd, Arthur Y., 69.10
Lockard, E. Kidd, 84.7
Locke, Alain, 34.14
Locke, Mary S., 69.11
Lockwood, George B., 72.5
Lockwood, Luke V., 111.21
Loetscher, Lefferts A., 52.10
Lofton, John, 38.20
Lofton, William H., 69.12
Long, Esmond R., 89.3
Louhi, Evert A., 33.3
Love, William D., 102.2
Loveland, Anne C., 69.13
Low, W. A., 18.13
Lubove, Roy, 86.11
Lucas, Henry S., 33.12
Ludlum, David M., 67.5
Luke, Myron H., 13.14
Lutz, Alma, 48.18, 69.14, 72.21, 22
Lutzker, Michael A., 98.14
Luxon, Norval N., 105.2
Lynch, William O., 16.14, 20.21, 23.1, 59.13
Lyon, William H., 104.2

Mabee, Carleton, 44.6
McAnear, Beverly, 84.8–10
McAvoy, Thomas T., 62.13
McBee, Alice E., 72.6
MacBride, Thomas H., 20.22
McCadden, Joseph J., 79.14
McCamic, Charles, 88.3
McCaul, Robert L., 79.15, 16
McClelland, Clarence P., 48.19
McClelland, Nancy V., 112.1
McCluskey, Neil G., 79.18
McColley, Robert, 38.21
McConnell, Roland C., 42.15
McConville, Sister Mary St. Patrick, 74.15
McCormac, Eugene I., 47.19
McCoubrey, John W., 107.19
McCrady, Edward, 38.22
McCulloch, Margaret C., 96.11
McCulloch, Samuel C., 61.10
McDonald, Sister M. Justille, 30.17
MacDougall, Hamilton C., 113.3
McDougle, Ivan E., 39.1
McGann, Sister Agnes G., 74.16

McGiffert, Michael, 1.18
McGrath, Sister Paul of the Cross, 74.17
McKee, Samuel, Jr., 46.18
McKeehan, Louis W., 84.11
McKelvey, Blake, 24.3, 26.13, 14, 99.17
Mackey, Howard, 88.4, 5
McKibben, Davidson B., 39.2
McKitrick, Eric L., 5.14, 37.12
McLaughlin, Andrew C., 6.6
MacLear, Anne B., 24.21
MacLear, Martha, 79.17
McLoughlin, William G., Jr., 59.14
McManis, Douglas R., 1.19
McManus, Edgar J., 39.3
McMaster, John B., 5.15, 16
McNamara, Brooks, 109.1
McNamara, Robert F., 62.14
McNiff, William J., 56.8
McPherson, Robert G., 39.4
Madsen, David, 84.12
Main, Jackson T., 7.10–13, 18.14
Manchester, Herbert, 100.12
Mandel, Bernard, 69.15
Mangum, Vernon L., 79.19
Mann, Mary T., 79.20
Mannix, Daniel P., 39.5
Manross, William W., 56.9
Marcus, Jacob R., 2.1, 64.1, 2
Mark, Irving, 13.15
Marraro, Howard R., 33.17–20
Marshall, Helen E., 96.12
Marshall, Leon S., 24.4
Marti-Ibanez, Felix, 89.4
Martin, Asa E., 69.16
Martin, Edgar W., 9.2
Martin, George H., 79.21
Martin, William J., 79.22
Martineau, Harriet, 3.6
Matas, Rudolph, 89.5
Mates, Julian, 113.4
Mather, Frank J., 107.20
Mathews, Donald G., 45.6, 56.10, 59.15, 69.17, 18
Mathews (Rosenberry), Lois K., 23.2
Matthews, William, 2.2
Maxson, Charles H., 59.16
Mayer, J. P., 3.16
Maynard, Douglas H., 69.19
Maynard, Theodore, 62.15
Mayorga, Margaret G., 109.2
Mead, David, 76.15
Mead, Frank S., 52.11

INDEX

Mead, Nelson P., 65.4
Mead, Sidney E., 52.12–14, 65.5
Mearns, David C., 105.18
Mecklin, John M., 39.6
Meier, August, 35.10, 11
Melcher, Marguerite F., 72.7
Melder, Keith, 49.1, 86.12
Mendelowitz, Daniel M., 107.21
Menn, Joseph K., 18.15
Mereness, Newton D., 3.7
Meriwether, Colyer, 80.1
Merrill, Walter M., 69.20
Merritt, Richard L., 104.3
Merritt, Webster, 94.8
Mesick, Jane L., 4.4
Messerli, Jonathan, 76.16, 80.2
Metcalf, Frank J., 113.5
Metzger, Walter P., 84.2
Meyer, Duane, 30.9
Meyer, Jacob C., 65.6
Meyer, John R., 36.22, 23
Meyers, Mary A., 80.3
Middlekauff, Robert, 80.4
Middleton, Arthur P., 47.1, 84.13
Miles, Edwin A., 39.7, 104.4
Miller, Douglas T., 13.16, 17, 29.7
Miller, Edward A., 80.5
Miller, Elizabeth W., 2.3
Miller, Genevieve, 92.16
Miller, George F., 80.6
Miller, Howard S., 86.13
Miller, James M., 106.9
Miller, John C., 104.15
Miller, Lillian B., 107.22, 108.1
Miller, Perry, 16.15, 16, 56.11
Miller, William, 4.14, 47.20
Miller, William D., 11.8
Miller, William M., 39.8
Mims, Edwin, Jr., 108.10
Minnich, Harvey C., 82.12
Minnigerode, Meade, 9.3
Minor, Benjamin B., 105.3
Mitchell, Broadus, 16.17
Mitchell, Martha C., 94.9
Mitchell, Mary H., 39.9, 59.17
Mixer, Knowlton, 111.1
Miyakawa, T. Scott, 56.12
Moats, Francis I., 56.13
Mode, Peter G., 52.15
Moller, Herbert, 7.14
Monaghan, Jay, 21.1
Money, Charles H., 69.21
Monroe, Paul, 76.17
Monroe, Will S., 80.7, 8

Montgomery, David, 24.5, 47.2
Moody, V. Alton, 39.10, 56.14
Mooney, Chase C., 39.11
Moore, Albert B., 16.18
Moore, Arthur K., 21.2
Moore, Gay M., 26.15
Moore, George H., 39.12
Moore, John H., 16.19
Moore, Thomas E., Jr., 90.6
Moore, Wilbert E., 39.13
Morais, Herbert M., 52.16
Moran, Denis M., 74.18, 19
Moreau de Saint-Méry, Médéric
    Louis Elie, 3.8
Morehouse, Frances, 30.18
Morgan, David T., Jr., 59.18
Morgan, Edmund S., 51.3, 4
Morison, Samuel E., 13.18, 84.14, 15
Morize, André, 3.9
Morris, Richard B., 2.4, 7.15, 39.14,
    15, 47.3, 4, 47.21, 64.3, 97.11
Morrison, Hugh S., 111.2
Morse, Jarvis M., 11.9
Morton, Richard L., 16.20
Moses, Mary S., 49.2
Mosier, Richard D., 82.13
Moss, Simeon F., 39.16
Mott, Frank L., 104.5, 105.4
Meulder, Herman R., 70.1
Mulder, Arnold, 33.13
Mulhern, James, 80.9
Mumford, Lewis, 111.2
Muncy, William L., 59.19
Munford, Beverley B., 39.17
Murray, Andrew E., 45.7, 56.15
Murray, David, 80.10
Murrell, William, 102.3
Mussey, June B., 3.10
Myer, Jesse S., 94.10
Myers, Albert C., 30.19, 56.16
Myers, Gustavus, 5.17
Myers, Jacob W., 31.12
Myers, John L., 70.2–4
Myrdal, Gunnar, 35.12

Nagel, Charles, 112.2
Nash, Gary B., 13.13, 25.1
National Research Council, 2.5
National Society of the Colonial
    Dames of America, Pennsylvania,
    113.6
Naughton, T. Raymond, 98.9
Nelson, William H., 7.16

INDEX

Neu, Irene D., 30.20
Neufeld, Maurice, 2.6
Neuhoff, Dorothy A., 102.4
Nevins, Allan, 3.11, 7.17, 9.4, 5, 104.6
Newcomb, Rexford, 111.4
Newcomer, Lee N., 11.10
Newsome, Albert R., 16.13
Newton, Earle, 11.11
New York Museum of Modern Art, 112.3
Nichols, Charles H., Jr., 39.18
Nichols, Roy F., 21.3, 52.17
Niebuhr, H. Richard, 52.18, 19
Niehaus, Earl F., 30.21
Nietz, John A., 82.14
Noble, Stuart G., 80.11
Noel-Hume, Ivor, 16.21
Noonan, Carroll J., 75.1
Nordhoff, Charles, 72.8
Nordroff, Ellen von, 23.3
Norman, E. R., 65.7
Norwood, John N., 45.8, 56.17, 70.5
Norwood, William F., 90.7
Nottingham, Elizabeth K., 56.18
Noyes, John H., 72.9
Nuermberger, Ruth K., 45.9, 56.19, 70.6
Nuhrah, Arthur G., 80.11
Nye, Russel B., 9.6, 70.7, 8, 106.10

Oberholzer, Emil, Jr., 56.20
O'Brien, Edward J., 50.2, 86.14
O'Brien, William J., 70.9
O'Conner, Stella, 94.11
O'Connor, Lillian, 72.23
O'Dea, Thomas F., 56.21
Odell, George C. D., 109.3
Oldham, Ellen M., 30.22, 70.10
Olmsted, Frederick L., 3.12, 13
Olson, Edwin, 39.19
O'Neill, Charles E., 65.8
Onis, José de, 4.5
Ormsbee, Thomas H., 112.4
Orr, Dorothy, 80.12
Osgood, Herbert L., 7.18, 19
Osofsky, Gilbert, 45.10
Osterweis, Rollin G., 16.22, 26.16
Ostrander, Gilman M., 5.18, 73.13
Overdyke, W. Darrell, 75.2
Oviatt, Edwin, 84.16
Owsley, Frank L., 18.16–18, 23.4
Owsley, Harriet C., 18.16, 17

Packard, Francis R., 89.6
Page, Evelyn, 33.4, 14
Palmer, Paul C., 39.20
Pankhurst, Jessie W., 39.21
Park, Charles E., 56.22
Parke, Francis N., 66.4
Parker, Robert A., 72.10
Parkes, Henry B., 11.12, 13
Parkhurst, Eleanor, 88.6
Parmer, Charles B., 100.13
Pascoe, Charles F., 61.11
Pattee, Fred L., 9.7
Patton, James W., 16.23
Pease, Jane H., 70.11
Pease, Theodore C., 21.4
Pease, William H., 70.11
Pelling, Henry, 47.5
Pendleton, O. A., 88.7
Pennington, Edgar L., 56.23, 24
Perkins, Haven P., 43.20
Perry, Lewis, 70.12
Persons, Stow, 1.5, 5.5, 19, 72.2
Pessen, Edward, 9.8, 47.6, 7
Peters, John L., 57.1
Petersen, William J., 94.12
Peterson, Arthur E., 25.2
Peterson, Charles E., 25.3
Phelps, Christina, 74.1
Philips, Edith, 57.2
Phillips, James D., 25.4–6
Phillips, Ulrich B., 16.24, 18.19, 39.22, 40.1, 2, 98.15
Pickard, Madge E., 94.13
Pickering, Ernest, 112.5
Pickett, Robert S., 50.3, 86.15
Pierce, Bessie L., 26.17, 18
Pierson, George W., 4.6, 5.20–22, 6.1
Pinchbeck, Ivy, 49.3
Pitz, Henry, 102.14
Plummer, Wilbur C., 102.5
Pole, J. R., 7.20
Pollock, Thomas C., 109.4
Pomerantz, Sidney I., 25.7
Pomeroy, Earl, 21.5
Pomfret, John E., 11.14
Pool, David de Sola, 64.4
Pope-Hennessy, James, 40.3
Porter, Kenneth W., 35.13
Posey, Walter B., 45.11, 12, 52.20, 57.3–7, 102.6
Post, Albert, 98.16
Postell, William D., 40.4, 90.8, 94.14
Potter, David, 84.17

INDEX

Potter, David M., 6.2
Potter, David M., Jr., 40.5
Powell, Chilton L., 51.5
Powell, John H., 92.17
Powell, Lyman P., 80.13
Powell, Sumner C., 13.19
Power, Edward J., 62.16, 84.18
Power, Richard L., 21.6, 23.5, 67.6
Powers, Edwin, 98.17
Pratt, John W., 65.9, 80.14
Preyer, Norris W., 40.6
Price, Martin S., 45.19, 64.11
Primm, James N., 21.7
Prince, Walter F., 11.15
Proctor, Samuel, 64.5
Proctor, William G., Jr., 40.7
Proper, David R., 66.5
Pryde, George S., 30.10
Pulliam, John, 80.15
Pumphrey, Muriel W., 86.16
Pumphrey, Ralph E., 86.16
Purcell, Richard J., 11.16, 30.23

Qualey, Carlton C., 33.5
Quarles, Benjamin, 35.14, 15, 70.13, 14
Quinn, Arthur H., 109.5

Raesly, Ellis L., 11.17
Randall, Edwin T., 98.18
Rankin, Hugh F., 98.19, 109.6
Ransom, John E., 89.7
Ratner, Lorman, 67.7, 70.15, 16
Ray, Mary A., 62.17
Rayback, Joseph G., 47.8, 70.17
Reavis, William A., 18.20
Reddick, L. D., 45.13
Redding, J. Saunders, 35.16
Redekop, Calvin W., 31.13
Reed, Susan M., 65.10
Reeves, Dorothea D., 96.16
Reinders, Robert C., 22.8, 26.19, 40.8, 42.16, 45.14, 57.8
Reinsch, Paul S., 97.12
Reps, John W., 24.6, 25.8
Rezneck, Samuel, 9.9, 10
Rice, Edwin W., 61.12
Rice, Howard C., Jr., 2.8
Rice, Madeleine H., 62.18
Richardson, Edgar P., 108.2, 3
Richardson, James F., 26.20, 21
Richardson, Leon B., 84.19

Richardson, Lyon N., 105.5
Richardson, Rupert N., 17.1
Richey, Herman G., 76.7
Richman, Irwin, 90.9
Riegel, Robert E., 9.11, 49.4, 51.6, 73.1, 2
Rightmyer, Nelson W., 53.11, 57.9, 10
Riley, Arthur J., 62.19
Riley, Martin L., 80.16
Riley, Phil M., 109.20, 110.1
Riley, Susan B., 105.6
Risch, Erna, 29.8
Rister, Carl C., 17.1
Riznik, Barnes, 90.10
Roach, Hannah B., 25.9
Roberson, Nancy C., 18.21
Robert, Joseph C., 17.2, 45.15
Roberts, Anna M., 3.8
Roberts, Kenneth, 3.8
Roberts, L. E., 80.17
Robertson, Archibald T., 59.20
Robinson, G. Canby, 94.15
Rodabaugh, James H., 89.8
Rodabaugh, Mary J., 89.8
Rogers, Fred B., 90.11
Rogers, Meyric R., 112.6
Roll, Charles, 21.8, 57.11
Roseboom, Eugene H., 21.9, 10
Rosen, George, 90.12, 92.18, 94.16, 95.11
Rosenbach, Abraham S. W., 50.4, 82.15
Rosenberg, Carroll S., 95.12
Rosenberg, Charles E., 26.22, 28.2, 90.13, 94.17, 95.12
Rosenberry, Lois K. M. See Mathews (Rosenberry), Lois K.
Rosenbloom, Joseph R., 64.6
Rosewater, Victor, 104.7
Ross, Ishbel, 86.17
Rossiter, Clinton, 7.21
Rothan, Emmet H., 31.14, 62.20
Rothermund, Dietmar, 31.15, 59.21
Rothman, David J., 51.7
Rottenberg, Simon, 40.9
Rourke, Constance M., 102.7
Ruchames, Louis, 45.16–18, 64.7, 70.18, 19
Rudolph, Frederick, 76.18, 84.20, 21
Rudolph, Lloyd L., 8.1
Rudwick, Elliott M., 35.11
Rudy, Willis, 83.3
Russel, Robert R., 17.3

INDEX

Russell, C. Allyn, 72.11
Russell, John H., 42.17
Russell, Marion J., 40.10
Russell, William L., 96.13
Rutman, Darrett B., 13.20, 25.10
Ryan, Edward L., 98.20
Ryan, Lee W., 4.7

Sablosky, Irving L., 113.7
Sachs, William S., 8.2
Sachse, Julius F., 31.16
Sack, Saul, 80.18, 85.1
St. Henry, Sister M., 75.3
Sale, Edith T., 111.5, 112.7
Sandler, Philip, 64.8
Sanford, Trent E., 111.6
Savage, William S., 70.20
Saveth, Edward N., 6.3
Saye, Albert B., 17.4
Sayre, A. Reasoner, 90.11
Scarborough, Ruth, 40.11
Scarborough, William K., 40.12
Schafer, Joseph, 6.4, 21.11, 22.4,
    23.6– 8, 80.19
Schantz, Franklin J. F., 31.17
Schappes, Morris U., 64.9, 10
Scheiber, Harry N., 36.23
Schiavo, Giovanni, 34.1
Schick, Joseph S., 109.7
Schlesinger, Arthur M., 3.12, 6.5,
    8.3–5, 24.7, 67.8, 102.8, 9, 104.8
Schlesinger, Arthur M., Jr., 9.12,
    67.9
Schmeckebier, Lawrence F., 75.4
Schmidt, Albert J., 17.5
Schmidt, George P., 85.2–4
Schmitt, Raymond, 51.2
Schneider, David M., 88.8
Schnell, Kempes, 40.13
Schoen, Harold, 42.18
Scholes, Percy A., 113.8
Schrott, Lambert, 31.18, 62.21
Schuricht, Hermann, 31.19
Schuyler, Livingston R., 104.16
Schwartz, Harold, 67.10, 70.21
Scisco, Louis D., 75.5
Scott, Arthur P., 98.21
Scott, John A., 3.5
Scott, Kenneth, 40.14
Scriven, George R., 92.19
Scroggs, William O., 21.12
Scully, Vincent J., Jr., 110.3
Sears, Clara, 57.12, 67.12

Seeger, Charles, 113.9
Seidman, Aaron B., 65.11
Seifman, Eli, 70.22
Seiler, William H., 57.13
Sellers, James B., 40.15, 73.14
Semmes, Raphael, 26.23, 98.22
Senese, Donald J., 42.19
Senning, John P., 75.6
Sessler, Jacob J., 31.20
Settle, E. Ophelia, 40.16
Sewell, Richard H., 70.23
Seybolt, Robert F., 80.20–22, 81.1–4
Seymour, Harold, 100.14
Shafer, Henry B., 28.3, 90.14
Shaffer, Alice, 88.9
Shaiman, S. Lawrence, 99.1
Shannon, Fred A., 23.9, 106.11
Shaughnessy, Gerald, 29.9, 62.22
Shea, John D. G., 62.23
Shearer, John D., 99.18
Shera, Jesse H., 105.19
Sherer, Robert G., Jr., 44.1
Sherrill, Charles H., 3.14
Sherwin, Oscar, 67.11, 71.1
Sherwood, Henry N., 35.17
Shipton, Clifford K., 11.18, 53.12,
    81.5, 6
Shira, Donald D., 90.15
Shlakman, Vera, 26.24
Shoemaker, Ervin C., 76.19
Shores, Louis, 105.20
Shryock, Richard H., 17.6, 32.1, 89.9–
    13, 90.16, 17, 91.7, 92.20, 94.18–
    20, 95.13, 96.17, 18
Shugg, Roger W., 19.1
Shurter, Robert L., 59.22
Shurtleff, Harold R., 111.7
Sibley, Marilyn M., 4.8
Sidwell, Robert T., 81.7
Siebert, Wilbur H., 40.17, 71.2
Sigerist, Henry E., 94.21
Silveus, Marian, 61.13
Simkins, Francis B., 17.7
Simler, Norman J., 23.10
Simmons, Richard C., 13.21
Simms, Henry H., 71.3
Sinclair, Andrew, 49.5, 73.3
Singleton, Esther, 11.19, 20
Sio, Arnold A., 40.18
Sirmans, M. Eugene, 40.19
Sizer, Theodore, 6.6
Skaggs, David C., 19.2
Skipper, Ottis C., 105.7
Sloane, William, 50.5, 82.16

134

INDEX

Slosser, Gaius J., 57.14
Slosson, Edwin E., 76.20
Small, Walter H., 81.8
Smalley, Donald, 3.18
Smillie, Wilson G., 95.1, 14
Smith, Abbot E., 29.10, 47.22, 48.1, 2
Smith, Carlton S., 113.10
Smith, Charles H., 32.2
Smith, Elwyn A., 57.15
Smith, Henry L., 103.15
Smith, James M., 8.6, 104.17
Smith, James W., 1.8, 52.21
Smith, Sherman M., 65.12, 81.9
Smith, Thelma M., 49.6, 73.4
Smith, Timothy L., 52.22, 59.23,
  61.14, 67.13, 76.21
Smith, W. Wayne, 19.3
Smith, Warren B., 48.3
Smith, William A., 81.10
Smith, Wilson, 81.11, 84.1
Smyth, Albert H., 105.8
Smythe, Hugh H., 45.19, 64.11
Snyder, Eloise C., 51.2
Sonne, Niels H., 67.14
Sonneck, Oscar G. T., 113.11, 12
Sosin, Jack M., 8.7
Spaeth, Sigmund G., 113.13
Spalletta, Matteo, 51.8
Spaulding, E. Wilder, 11.21
Spear, Allan H., 29.11
Spector, Robert M., 40.20
Spruill, Julia C., 49.7
Sprunger, Keith L., 73.15
Stahl, Annie L. W., 42.20
Staiger, C. Bruce, 57.16, 71.4
Stampp, Kenneth M., 40.21
Stanard, Mary N., 17.8
Stanton, Elizabeth C., 49.8, 73.5
Stanton, William R., 45.20
Starkey, Marion L., 66.6
Starobin, Robert, 40.22
Staudenraus, Philip J., 71.5
Stavisky, Leonard P., 35.18, 19
Stearn, Allen E., 89.14
Stearn, E. Wagner, 89.14
Stearns, Bertha M., 73.6, 105.9, 10
Steely, Will F., 45.21, 57.17
Steiner, Bernard C., 40.23, 81.12, 13
Stephenson, George M., 29.12, 33.6,
  57.18, 75.7
Stevens, Raymond B., 85.5
Stevens, William O., 102.10
Stewart, George, 61.15
Stewart, George R., 102.11

Still, Bayard, 24.8, 26.25, 26, 27.1
Stilwell, Lewis D., 23.11
Stokes, Anson P., 65.13
Stokes, I. N. Phelps, 24.9
Stookey, Byron, 90.18
Stopak, Aaron, 71.6
Storr, Richard J., 85.6
Strickland, Arvarh E., 35.20
Strickland, Reba C., 65.14
Stritch, Alfred G., 62.24
Stroupe, Henry S., 104.9
Struble, George G., 32.12
Suarez, Raleigh A., 57.19
Sullivan, William A., 47.9
Summersell, Charles G., 27.2
Sutch, Richard, 36.23
Sutherland, Stella H., 8.8
Sutton, Robert P., 19.4
Swadoes, Felice, 41.1, 95.2
Swanson, Joseph A., 27.14
Sweet, William W., 53.1–5, 57.20, 21,
  60.1
Sydnor, Charles S., 17.9, 10, 41.2,
  43.1
Szasz, Ferenc M., 41.3

Taft, Lorado, 108.4
Talpalar, Morris, 17.11
Tallmadge, Thomas E., 111.8
Tandy, Jeannette R., 102.12
Tate, Thad W., Jr., 35.21
Taylor, Alrutheus A., 35.22
Taylor, George R., 9.13, 24.10
Taylor, James M., 49.9, 85.7
Taylor, Joe G., 41.4
Taylor, John M., 66.7
Taylor, Orville W., 41.5, 51.9
Taylor, Paul S., 41.6
Taylor, Rosser H., 17.12, 19.5, 41.7
Taylor, William R., 17.13, 81.14
Teeters, Negley K., 88.10, 99.18,
  100.1
Tewksbury, Donald G., 85.8
Thacker, Joseph A., Jr., 57.22
Tharp, Louise H., 81.15
Theobold, Stephen L., 46.1, 63.1
Thernstrom, Stephen, 13.22, 27.3
Thistlethwaite, Frank, 9.14
Thom, William T., 65.15
Thomas, Allen C., 58.1
Thomas, Benjamin P., 71.7
Thomas, John L., 67.15, 71.8
Thomas, Sister M. Evangeline, 75.8

INDEX

Thompson, E. Bruce, 96.14, 100.2, 3
Thompson, Warren S., 6.7
Thoms, Herbert, 90.19
Thornbrough, Emma Lou, 43.2, 71.9
Thursfield, Richard E., 81.16
Thwaites, Reuben G., 3.15
Thwing, Charles F., 77.1, 85.9
Tilghman, Tench F., 85.10
Tocqueville, Alexis de, 3.16, 17
Todd, Willie G., 46.2, 58.2
Tolles, Frederick B., 8.9, 13.23, 58.3,
    4, 60.2, 106.12
Tolman, William H., 85.11
Top, Franklin H., 89.15
Tope, Melancthon, 82.17
Torbet, Robert G., 58.5
Towner, Lawrence W., 48.4
Tregle, Joseph G., Jr., 27.4
Tremain, Mary, 41.8
Treudley, Mary B., 49.10, 86.18
Trexler, Harrison A., 41.9
Trinterud, Leonard J., 58.6
Trollope, Frances M., 3.18
Tryon, Warren S., 3.19
Tucker, Rufus S., 23.12
Tuckerman, Henry T., 4.9
Turner, Edward R., 41.10, 43.3
Turner, Frederick J., 6.8, 9.15
Turner, Gordon, 65.16
Turner, Lorenzo D., 71.10
Turner, Wallace B., 41.11, 67.16,
    75.9
Tyler, Alice F., 67.17

U.S. Bureau of the Census, 2.7, 35.23
Updegraff, Harlan, 81.17
Upham, Charles W., 66.8
Upton, Richard F., 11.22
Utter, William T., 21.13

Vail, Robert W. G., 21.14
Van Deusen,Glyndon G., 9.16, 67.18,
    19, 81.18
Van Orman, Richard A., 102.13
Van Tyne, Claude H., 53.13
Ver Steeg, Clarence L., 8.10
Viets, Henry R., 89.16
Violette, Augusta G., 73.7
Vogel, William F., 21.15
Voight, Gilbert P., 32.3
Vorphal, Ben M., 58.7

Wabeke, Bertus H., 33.16
Wade, Richard C., 27.5, 6, 41.12, 13,
    43.4
Waite, Frederick C., 90.20, 91.1–5
Wall, Robert E., Jr., 14.1
Wallace, David D., 17.14
Wallace, David H., 107.13
Walls, Otto F., 88.11
Walsh, James J., 85.12, 89.17
Walsh, Richard, 47.10
Ward, Christopher, 33.7, 15
Ward, John W., 2.9
Ware, Norman J., 47.11
Warfel, Harry R., 77.2
Waring, Joseph I., 92.21, 95.3
Warner, Robert A., 43.5
Warner, Sam B., Jr., 24.11, 25.11,
    27.7
Warren, Charles, 97.13
Warwick, Edward, 102.14
Waterman, Thomas T., 110.17,
    111.9–11
Watson, Frank D., 86.19
Wax, Darold D., 36.1, 41.14, 15,
    46.3, 58.8
Weatherford, Willis D., 46.4, 58.9
Weathersby, William H., 81.19
Weaver, Herbert, 19.6, 29.13, 14
Webber, Everett, 72.12
Weber, Adna F., 24.12
Weber, Samuel E., 81.20
Wecter, Dixon, 6.9, 10, 106.13
Weeden, William B., 11.23, 12.1
Weeks, Stephen B., 46.5, 58.10, 71.11,
    81.21, 22
Wehle, Harry B., 108.5
Weis, Frederick L., 53.14–18
Weisberger, Bernard A., 60.3, 104.10
Weisenburger, Francis P., 21.10, 16,
    27.8
Weiss, Harry B., 12.2
Weitenkampf, Frank, 108.6
Weld, Ralph F., 27.9, 10
Wells, Guy F., 61.16
Welter, Barbara, 49.11, 12, 73.8
Welter, Rush, 21.17, 18, 77.3
Wentz, Abdel R., 58.11
Wertenbaker, Thomas J., 8.11, 12.3,
    4, 17.15, 19.7, 8, 21.19, 27.11,
    85.13, 106.14
Wesley, Charles H., 36.2, 3, 47.12
West, Roscoe L., 81.23
Westin, Gunnar, 33.8
Wharton, Anne, 9.17

INDEX

Wheeler, Kenneth W., 27.12
Whelpton, Pascal K., 6.7
Whitaker, A. P., 82.1
White, Margaret E., 112.8
Whitehill, Walter M., 27.13, 108.7
Whitener, Daniel J., 73.16
Whitfield, Theodore M., 41.16
Wickersham, James P., 77.4
Wiebe, Robert H., 77.5
Wilbur, Earl M., 58.12, 13
Williams, Edward I. F., 82.2
Williams, Edwin L., Jr., 41.17
Williams, Helen D., 21.20
Williams, Jack K., 99.2, 3, 102.15
Williams, Ralph C., 95.15
Williams, Samuel C., 3.20
Williams, Stanley T., 2.14
Williamson, Chilton, 9.18
Williamson, Jefferson, 102.16
Williamson, Jeffrey G., 24.13, 27.14
Willis, Eola, 109.8
Willison, George F., 12.5
Wilson, Charles J., 43.6
Wilson, Gold F., 44.2
Wilson, Harold F., 12.6
Wilson, James G., 27.15
Wilson, William E., 72.13
Windell, Marie G., 60.4, 67.20
Winslow, Ola E., 12.7
Winsor, Justin, 27.16
Winther, Oscar O., 21.21
Wish, Harvey, 3.13, 6.11, 41.18, 19
Wishy, Bernard, 50.6
Wisner, Elizabeth, 88.12
Wittke, Carl F., 29.15, 31.1, 32.4, 104.11, 109.9, 10
Wolf, Hazel C., 71.12

Wood, James P., 105.11
Wood, Ralph, 32.5
Woodman, Harold D., 41.20
Woodson, Carter G., 36.4, 43.7, 44.3, 7, 77.6
Woodward, C. Vann, 71.13
Woody, Thomas, 49.13, 82.3–5
Woolfolk, George R., 41.21
Wright, Conrad, 58.14
Wright, James M., 43.8
Wright, John E., 12.8
Wright, Louis B., 8.12, 19.9, 106.15, 16
Wright, Marian, 44.8, 82.6
Wright, Richardson, 102.17
Wuorin, John H., 33.9
Wust, Klaus G., 75.10
Wyckoff, Alexander, 102.14
Wyllie, Irvin G., 6.12, 86.20
Wytrwal, Joseph A., 34.3

Yakeley, Leon, 85.14
Yearley, Clifton K., 30.11
Yoder, Paton, 102.18, 19
Yoshpe, Harry J., 41.22
Young, Chester R., 17.16
Young, James H., 96.19
Younger, Richard D., 41.23

Zanger, Jules, 99.4
Zilversmit, Arthur, 41.24, 71.14
Zorn, Roman J., 71.15
Zucker, Adolf E., 32.6
Zuckerman, Michael, 14.2
Zwierlein, Frederick J., 58.15